SCOTLAND
AND THE LOWLAND
TONGUE

David D Murison
photograph by Andrew Fenton

SCOTLAND AND THE LOWLAND TONGUE

Studies in the language and literature
of Lowland Scotland

in honour of
DAVID D MURISON

edited by
J DERRICK McCLURE

with a Foreword by
A J AITKEN

ABERDEEN UNIVERSITY PRESS

First published 1983
Aberdeen University Press
A member of the Pergamon Group

© Aberdeen University Press 1983

The publisher acknowledges subsidy from the
Scottish Arts Council towards the publication
of this volume

British Library Cataloguing in Publication Data

Scotland and the Lowland tongue
   1. English language—Dialect—Scotland
   I. McClure, J Derrick
   427′.941   PE1771

ISBN 0-08-028482-5

PRINTED IN GREAT BRITAIN
THE UNIVERSITY PRESS
ABERDEEN

CONTENTS

FOREWORD

Will I write in 'Scots' or in 'English', and if in Scots, what sort of Scots and how Scots? Questions like these have engaged all writers hailing from the Lowlands of Scotland since before Gavin Douglas first made them overt in the Prologue to his Virgil in 1513. For the early poets, perhaps, doubts were mostly resolved by the rules or norms which I have tried to describe in the essay which follows. The questions were more open for writers of polemic prose from the time of the Reformation, as Mairi Robinson shows in her contribution to this volume.

That these issues were fully alive, albeit for a time somewhat muted, in the seventeenth century, is evidenced, *inter alia*, by that curious work *The Pockmanty Preaching* (1638), which I have called 'the only Scottish sermon ever to achieve something like best-seller status' and 'exceptionally informal and vernacular in its style, both informal and very Scots': its exceptional popularity was doubtless in part a consequence of its Scottish vernacular language. This implies awareness by seventeenth-century preachers, publishers and reading public of a difference in literary appropriateness between their normal Standard English printed sermon language and the oral Scottish vernacular manner adopted by John Row for his *Red-Shankes Sermon,* as *The Pockmanty Preaching* was originally called.

The language question sounded out openly and stridently in the following century, from many authors (such as Allan Ramsay, Robert Burns, Alexander Ross) and critics (such as James Beattie, Henry Mackenzie, etc.), and has been more or less loudly audible since then, not least from Scottish Renaissance makars like Hugh MacDiarmid and Douglas Young. Often, and especially of late, the question has been held to transcend literature and seen as one for the whole life of the Scot; one consequence of this has been a serious attempt, the first ever to be at all sustained, to revive an expository prose in Scots, notably in the shape of the Scots Language Society's journal *Lallans.*

From the beginning, more than one kind of Scots has been on offer. Since the seventeenth century, alongside the 'mainstream' or 'Standard' Scots, such as that of the writers just mentioned, an increasing number of regional standards have been created and developed, most persistently and successfully those of Buchan and of Shetland. Since that time, too, the choice of any of these kinds of Scots, for verse or for dialogue or monologue or other 'oral-referenced' prose, has carried with it some implications as to social attitudes and degree of solemnity intended by the author and for the reader. A regional-cum-social identification has been an especially prominent feature of some recent manifestations of literary Scots, notably those discussed by Professor Morgan below. Another recent development has been to exploit the attitudinal effects of deviance from orthographic norms—from the normal orthographies both of Standard English and of dignified Mainstream Literary Scots.

In such ways as these some form of vernacular Scots diction has existed as an optional or an essential component of much of the best of Lowland Scottish literature throughout its history. This book was conceived as a first sustained examination of its nature and the contribution it has provided, over a range of periods and aspects, by a group of knowledgeable scholars.

David Murison

That was one purpose of this book. Its germinal purpose, however, was to bring together a series of essays by a group of his friends for presentation to the scholar who has done most to further the philological study of Scots, both along the lines of the theme of this book and in all other ways.

Our modest act of homage is of course no monument, since no Scot is less in need of that than is David Donald Murison. In institutional and private libraries in every land, and in many schools and homes in Scotland, the ten majestic volumes of *The Scottish National Dictionary* (or SND) commemorate the vision, enthusiasm and learning of William Grant, the Dictionary's creator and first editor, and the erudition, lexicographical flair and unremitting toil of Murison.

It may come as a surprise to those unfamiliar with the histories of large academic dictionaries that in comparison with other dictionaries of its kind and of comparable scale, SND was completed with unusual speed—a mere forty-five years separating A and Z. This triumph of expedition was most of all due to Murison's drive and dedication. Between 1946 and 1976 he personally edited seven-and-a-half of SND's ten volumes, from the latter part of C to the end of the alphabet, along with a Supplement which is in effect a revision of the earlier volumes. Since the scale of the later volumes is much larger than that of the earlier ones, this amounts to seven-eighths of the whole work.

Though of course he had able and energetic assistants, and financial and other support from many well-wishers and, especially, the office-bearers of the Scottish National Dictionary Association and of the Scottish Dictionaries Joint Council, in a real sense this was more than usually one man's accomplishment. Not only did he oversee every single entry, revising and sometimes re-shaping those which he did not edit entirely himself, but also the essays on the treatment of each alphabetic letter as a Scottish speech-sound and spelling, the essays on prefixes and suffixes, and the erudite and perceptive etymological notes to each word, all of which together enshrine so much of the philological history of Scots, are almost exclusively Murison's own. So too the Miscellanea included in the final volume—inventories of Scottish personal names, of the popular forms of Scottish place-names, of fairs and markets, of weights and measures, and of scientific terms with Scottish connections—these also were compiled by Murison himself after the final disbandment of his staff: I do not believe there is any other person, living or dead, who could have executed so well these fascinating cameos of lexicography. In a tribute of his own to his predecessor, Murison quotes as the latter's watchwords *nil desperandum* and *never deval*. No-one has ever better lived up to these principles than himself.

As well as editing the Dictionary, Murison was also in effect its publisher and one of its most successful publicists. Since the Dictionary was published by the Scottish National Dictionary Association, it fell to Murison to oversee from his own office all the publication arrangements and records. He it was who drafted most of the Scottish National Dictionary Association's publicity material— which helped both to sell the Dictionary and to attract donations to fund the editing. He was in constant demand as a speaker about the work of the Dictionary. The very healthy financial state of the Association on his retirement following the completion of the Dictionary, which has enabled the Association to launch a new project for a one-volume Scots dictionary based on the SND and the *Dictionary of the Older Scottish Tongue* (DOST), was to a significant extent thanks to David Murison's efforts in these ways.

No doubt the Dictionary is Murison's major legacy to scholarship and to his country. It is far from being the only one. With one or two others he helped to found and to develop the study of Lowland Scots as an academic subject in Scotland. Before the 1950s Scots language barely existed as a taught subject in any Scottish university, and only in the form of philological *explications de textes* of some Middle Scots poems. Today the scope of this subject is very much wider, and the subject itself is firmly established in the Universities of Glasgow, Aberdeen and Edinburgh. A significant part of the credit for this is due to Murison. Throughout his career he has been unremitting, both in public and behind the scenes, as a propagandist for the study of Scottish language and Scottish literature. He has served quietly and effectively on many committees for the furtherance of these and other Scottish studies, and has contributed more or less anonymously to several bibliographies and surveys of Scotland.

As part of the arrangement for conferring University status on the Editors of the two Scottish Dictionaries, in 1954 Murison was given the rank of Lecturer and from 1965 Senior Lecturer in St Andrews and Aberdeen Universities. Through the 1960s he travelled once each week for ten weeks from Edinburgh (where the Dictionary was located from 1954) to Aberdeen to lecture on Scots language in the English Department of Aberdeen University, at the invitation of the head of that Department; rather to his disappointment, he never received a similar invitation from St Andrews. Once Aberdeen had in 1972 appointed a full-time lecturer with special responsibility for Scots (in the person of the editor of this volume), Murison contributed to the teaching of Scots in the University of Edinburgh. Between 1975 and 1978 he served (in his own right rather than as Editor of the Dictionary) as Senior Lecturer then Reader in Scottish Language in the University of Glasgow, again travelling regularly from Edinburgh to meet his students and carry out his duties as a member of the Departments of English Language and of Scottish Literature.

In 1971, Murison and I were jointly responsible, with Dr H H Speitel, for the first ever conference on Scottish language, which all three of us addressed; and this led to the formation of a Language Committee of the then fairly fledgeling Association for Scottish Literary Studies, and to a succession of conferences and other activities and a spate of publications on Scottish language such as had never previously been seen. To all of this Murison himself very substantially contributed, in lectures and articles covering the whole chronological span of the history of Scots from the early Middle Ages to the present. In 1977 he also produced the only overall survey since James A H Murray's *The Dialect of the Southern Countries of Scotland*, published in 1873, in the shape of *The Guid Scots Tongue*, a small popular handbook, at once highly readable and of impeccable authority. Several of his writings explore the topics in which I think may lie his greatest enthusiasm and of which his knowledge is unmatched, the language of Burns, of Scott and of the ballads. Between them his writings on these subjects splendidly complement the contents of the present book.

While he was engaged on the Dictionary Murison was known as a man who never took holidays. (In this he differs from some other distinguished lexico-graphers; even such a prodigiously eident worker as Sir James Murray enjoyed a respite now and again from his toil.) And he resisted the calls which he sometimes received to attend conferences or to lecture abroad, being content to leave such jaunts to others. Such was his unswerving determination to 'get to Z'. Only in the few last years before he retired did he begin taking a few days off each year. Since his return to Fraserburgh in 1979 he and his wife Hilda have had one very short visit to Edinburgh. To my knowledge he has visited London once, and only very briefly. Otherwise I am not aware that since his graduation in Cambridge in the late 1930s he has ever left the Scottish mainland except once to attend the Viking Congress in Lerwick in 1950. This last expedition certainly was one that the Murisons greatly enjoyed. They were evidently in their element among these scholars of a congenial interest and as guests of the Shetland people, northern rural folk of mixed Scandinavian and Scottish background.

But if David Murison did not seek out the world, the world beat a path to his door. To his offices and his homes in Aberdeen and in Edinburgh scholars and students of Scottish language, Scottish literature and Scottish history were constant and welcome visitors, genially received and with no indication of hurry. I have myself enjoyed many hours of cheerful counsel, and careful scrutiny of the memoranda or manifestoes, as he called them, on concerns of the two Dictionaries, to the composition of which I was, according to him, over-addicted. Naturally, both of us had visits from historical and other lexico-graphers and linguists from many countries, and there must be many makers of dictionaries around the world who continue to be influenced by his suggestions, counsel and example.

Murison supervised several important research degrees by others, and his suggestions and advice are acknowledged by a host of authors of books and articles on innumerable topics within his favoured fields of study.

His erudition over a broad sweep of Scottish linguistic, literary and historical studies, not to mention also European and classical philology, is immense, though this emerges only incidentally: he has always been much too reticent of his own accomplishments and achievements. For the same reason, the list of publications that follows is certainly incomplete; he is not at all good at distributing copies of his writings. Any action tending towards self-congratulation has always been anathema to him.

Apart from the professional scholars in his own field Murison seems to have known personally virtually everyone who was anyone in Scottish life and letters, from his old friend C M Grieve downwards, and many of the stalwarts of Scottish Nationalism from the 'thirties onwards. He held in particular affection and respect the late R E Muirhead, the veteran Scottish nationalist of Murison's earlier years. And he was a close lifelong friend and admirer of the late Douglas Young, 'poet and polymath', ever since they were both assistants together to the Professor of Greek in Aberdeen in the late 1930s. It is hard to imagine two men more superficially unlike than these friends, the ebullient, passionate, outspoken and much-travelled giant that was Douglas Young, and the restrained, stay-at-home, physically compact Murison. But of course they shared the same devotion to their native land and its Lowland tongue, and were alike in certain personal traits, such as courtesy, consideration and immense capacity for work.

Another scholar whom Murison specially admired and liked, and whom perhaps he most of all regards as his mentor, is the great Scottish philologist and lexicographer, Sir William Craigie, editor of, *inter alia,* the *Oxford English Dictionary* and the *Dictionary of the Older Scottish Tongue,* who died in 1957. Murison resembles Craigie in many ways (including small physical stature and other similarities in outward appearance, recalling, as Craigie liked to claim, that of the ancient Picts who earlier occupied the North-East Scottish districts native to both himself and Murison). Both were of relatively humble origins—Craigie as the son of a jobbing gardener, Murison of a joiner; both began their brilliant academic careers as classicists, and went on to become the leading philologists and lexicographers of Scots of their time. More significantly, perhaps, both had an abiding love for Scotland, both regretted the failure of the Scots to maintain their national tongue, and both had a strong fellow-feeling for other small northern nations with cultural problems analogous to those of the Scots. As performers in lexicography, both possessed immense stamina and acuteness in rapid problem-solving.

Another notable group of close friends of the Murisons are people of about their own age from the North-East, among them a number of distinguished academics and poets, whom one or other of the Murisons had known at school or at Aberdeen or Cambridge Universities. One of these was the late John Low, who contributed to this volume and whom I further mention below.

At first sight it is puzzling that a man who has chosen to spend most of his life firmly bound to his desk (or rather the large table at which he preferred to work) should have so much minutely detailed knowledge of the local history and the topography of, seemingly, every corner of Scotland. In part this results merely from book-learning and an excellent memory, in part from constant study of detailed maps; I have also been told that he was given to browsing in railway time-tables so that he knew how to get around Scotland, even if he only occasionally did so. His native North-East Scotland he knows of course from his childhood and youth. David Murison was born in Fraserburgh in 1913. When he was seven his father moved to Aberdeen, and David attended Aberdeen Grammar School and Aberdeen University, where he took a First-class Honours MA in Classics in 1933. A year later he proceeded to Cambridge University to take there a First-class Honours BA in Classics in 1936. After further study of Celtic and Anglo-Saxon at Cambridge, he returned to King's College, Aberdeen, as assistant to the Professor of Greek (alongside Douglas Young). During the War he worked on a small-holding in the neighbourhood of Stirling, and so came to know that region. In 1946 he was invited to apply for the post of deputy editor to William Grant on *The Scottish National Dictionary*, then in Aberdeen, and succeeded Grant on the latter's death in the same year. From 1946 to 1954 he edited the Dictionary in Aberdeen and from 1954 till their retirement back to Fraserburgh in 1979 the Murisons occupied their weel-kent and much-visited household in Comiston Drive, Edinburgh.

From Edinburgh Murison made occasional brief trips back to the North-East on some of his innumerable speaking engagements. He was in great demand as a Burns orator and has proposed the Immortal Memory or given other entertaining and instructive Burns orations in Fraserburgh, Peterhead and other north-eastern localities on a fair number of successive years. But of course he has entertained and stimulated audiences on many other days and evenings than during the Burns season, and on other themes central to his interests—the work of the Dictionary, the history of the Scots tongue, the techniques of Scots writers other than Burns, such as Walter Scott and Lewis Grassic Gibbon—and these engagements have taken him to airts far removed from the North-East. For example, he has made several visits to Dumfries to address the Dumfriesshire and Galloway Natural History and Antiquarian Society. He evidently made the most of all of these opportunities to learn about the localities he was visiting.

From early in his career David Murison has commanded gratitude for his unique service to the scholarship of his country and admiration for his erudition. He is also someone whom people enjoy being with for his un-assumingness and geniality and his fund of germane anecdote and gentle repartee. The same qualities, and his gift of uncomplex, lucid and succinct presentation, supported by an abundance of apt and interesting information or example, have secured his popularity as a lecturer and a writer. But there is

another side to this welcoming and genial and at the same time modest and un-
assuming man. He has been known to refuse stubbornly to act a part (as he saw
it) when he thought this might compromise his principles or his personal
integrity. Pawky he always is, proud and dour on occasion he can also be. This
led him on several occasions to refuse offers of academic honours. On the other
hand, his unwillingness to occupy certain more or less honorific offices, which
have also been offered to him, results from nothing more than a simple desire
to keep out of the limelight, combined with a wish to remain free of activities
distracting from his principal goals.

Needless, perhaps, to say, Murison has never been a trendy person. He is
sceptical of the usefulness of modern technological aids in dictionary-making;
in his view simpler traditional methods are usually more cost-effective; and he
would hold that most effective of all towards completing a dictionary is steady
application by its human staff. Like some other great lexicographers, he has
remained unimpressed by the various trends and fashions in linguistic theory
which he has seen succeed one another or compete with one another during his
lifetime; and privately he pokes fun at some of their jargon.

Certain modern trends in education he regards as misguided. He believes
that children are no longer being adequately grounded in the 'three Rs' and he
regrets the virtual disappearance of traditional grammar from the curriculum of
many schools. He is concerned at what he sees as abandonment by younger
people of traditional modes of speech; and of the prolonged survival of the
copious, distinctive and grammatically consistent Scots speech of which he
approves he is mostly pessimistic. He modestly sums up his own cultural credo
by ranging himself with those of mankind 'who realise that they are the heirs of
the ages and should hand on their inheritance a little richer than they found it
and to do this should first try to learn what it is'. He has also been known to
express the fear that too few of his countrymen may share and act upon these
ideals even to maintain their inheritance.

At times David Murison's patriotism for Scotland has been subordinated to
his local patriotism for the Scottish North-East, which, like other north-
easterners, he is given to presenting as the true centre of Scottish civilisation,
sometimes jocularly, often with undertones of earnest. Whereas his great
predecessors, Murray and Craigie, were happy to settle finally in or near
Oxford, even Edinburgh was too southerly (and anglified) for Murison. It is in
Fraserburgh in the heart of the North-East where he was born and grew up that
he believes his roots are, and thither he has now returned after a lifetime of
service to the whole Scottish nation. In his retirement he has taken up the study
of the history of this fifth University town of Scotland (as he likes reminding
people) and of the dialect of the region, and is still busy compiling the kinds of
book for which he is so well equipped. While he knows more Scots speech of all
districts than does any other single person, he has always favoured the north-
easternisms of his childhood and has, I understand and can well imagine,

reverted easily into the local ways of speaking (as Craigie and he believe most people do in their senior years).

He has enjoyed robust physical health and for many years walked four times most days the more than two miles between his office and his home, and he has always taken pleasure in the work of his garden.

It would be wrong to leave the impression that David Murison's achievements were solely his. All who know them well think of him as part of the partnership of David and Hilda. As his devoted companion, as the gently persuasive advocate of all the causes which mattered to her husband and especially of the Dictionary, as the warm and sympathetic friend of his friends and the generous and welcoming hostess of close friends, of colleagues and of visitors from many lands, Hilda has constantly supported David in all possible ways and so promoted all his achievements.

John Low

David and Hilda will share the sadness of the other authors of this book that their old friend, Dr John T Low, will not be present to enjoy its submission to them. John was enthusiastic for the making of the book as a tribute to David. Of all the essays his was the first to be completed. Nor will his own large and various service to Scottish language and literature soon be forgotten.

While Murison and others were developing the teaching of Scots in the universities, much of the drive towards an awakened attention to the native literature and speech in colleges of education and in schools was being provided by John Low.

To this end, he helped to found in 1967 the Committee for the Advancement of Scottish Literature in Schools, and thereafter energetically promoted its work; he was active in suggestion and in administrative work on several other committees with aims allied to those of CASLS; engagingly and forcefully he spoke up on the need to remedy the long neglect of Scottish language and literature in education from the rostrum and from the floor of many a conference; he published a number of these lectures, as well as many other writings, reports and reviews for the educational press, inspired by the same causes; he carried his great gift of enthusiasm also into his work as a teacher of teachers of English and Scottish literature; and he has provided for us an excellent edition of Gibbon's *Sunset Song*, a valuable book on Bridie, and, with his colleague Robert Millar, several collections of Scots stories and plays for use by schools. His friends will not easily forget the energy, cheerfulness and generosity of John Low's personality, and his love of literature, as critic, teacher and practitioner.

A J AITKEN

March 1983

DAVID D MURISON: PUBLICATIONS

BOOKS

The Scottish National Dictionary, ten volumes, 1931-76. Eds William Grant, 1929-46, and David D Murison, 1946-76. Edinburgh: The Scottish National Dictionary Association Limited. (Murison edited vols. III-X, and the Miscellanea and Supplement contained in vol. X.)

(With Clara Young.) *A clear voice: Douglas Young, poet and polymath; a Selection from his Writings, with a Memoir.* Loanhead: Macdonald, 1977.

The Guid Scots Tongue. Edinburgh: Blackwood, 1977.

Scots Saws. Edinburgh: The Mercat Press, 1981.

The Scottish Year. Edinburgh: The Mercat Press, 1982.

EDITION

Selections from the Poems of Robert Henryson. (Edinburgh: Oliver and Boyd for the Saltire Society, 1952).

ARTICLES

'Studies in Scots since 1918,' in *Anglia* **69,** (1949), pp. 388-97.

'The Language of Burns,' in *Robert Burns Chronicle,* (1950), pp. 39-47.

'Scots Speech in Shetland,' in *The Viking Congress,* ed. W D Simpson. (Edinburgh: Oliver and Boyd, 1954), pp. 255-60.

'The Speech of Ayrshire in the time of Burns,' in *Trans. Ayrshire and Galloway Nat. Hist. Assoc.,* (1959), pp. 222-31.

'Scotland's Debt to John Jamieson,' in *The Scotsman,* (4 March 1959), p. 6.

'Shetland Speech Today,' in *Fróðskaparrit* **13,** (1964), pp. 122-9.

'The Scots Tongue—the Folk-Speech,' in *Folklore* **75,** (1964), pp. 37-47.

'Scottish Variants of the English Language,' in *Books,* (July-August 1965), pp. 124-8.

'A Survey of Scottish Language Studies,' in *Forum for Modern Language Studies* **3,** (1967), pp. 276-85.

'MacDiarmid and Lallans,' in *New North* **1,** (1967), pp. 8-11.

'Scottish Language,' in *Reader's Guide to Scotland,* National Book League, (1968), pp. 52-3.

'Nationalism as expressed in Scottish Literature,' in *Government and Nationalism in Scotland,* ed. J N Wolfe. (Edinburgh: University Press, 1969), pp. 189-99.

'The Two Languages in Scott,' in *Scott's Mind and Art,* ed. A N Jeffares. (Edinburgh: Oliver and Boyd, 1970), pp. 206-29.

'The Future of Scots,' in *Whither Scotland,* ed. D Glen. (London: Gollancz, 1971), pp. 159-77.

'The Dutch Element in the Vocabulary of Scots,' in *Edinburgh Studies in English and Scots,* eds A J Aitken *et al.* (London: Longman, 1971), pp. 159-77.

'The Scottish National Dictionary,' in *University of Edinburgh Journal* **25,** (1972), pp. 305-9.

'The trade in words,' in *The Scotsman,* 14 February 1973, p. 8.

'Linguistic relationships in medieval Scotland,' in *The Scottish Tradition: Essays in Honour of R. G. Cant,* ed. G W S Barrow. (Edinburgh: Scottish Academic Press, 1974), pp. 71-83.
'The vocabulary of the Kirk (Part 1),' in *Liturgical Review* 4, (1974), 2: pp. 45-9.
'The vocabulary of the Kirk (Part 2),' in *Liturgical Review* 5, (1975), 1: pp. 53-5.
'The language of Sydney Goodsir Smith,' in *For Sydney Goodsir Smith.* (Edinburgh: M Macdonald, 1975), pp. 23-9.
'The language of Burns,' in *Critical Essays on Robert Burns,* ed. Donald A Low. (London: Routledge and Kegan Paul, 1975), pp. 54-69.
'Knox the writer,' in *John Knox: a Quatercentenary Reappraisal,* ed. Duncan Shaw. (Edinburgh: St Andrew Press, 1975), pp. 33-50. (Later separately re-issued as a pamphlet, St Andrew Press, 1980.)
'The speech of Moray,' in *The Moray Book,* ed. Donald Omand. (Edinburgh: Paul Harris, 1976), pp. 275-82.
'The language of the ballads,' in *Scottish Literary Journal* Supplement No. 6, (1978), pp. 54-64.
'Some thoughts on the man and his work,' (on Hugh MacDiarmid), in *Lines,* No. 67, (Dec. 1978), pp. 12-15.
'The Buchan Tongue,' in *Trans. Buchan Field Club* 18, (1979), pp. 28-39.
'The future of Scots,' in *Chapman* 23-4, (1979), pp. 58-62.
'Norse influence on Scots,' in *Lallans* No. 13 (Martinmas, 1979), pp. 31-4.
'The language problem in Hugh MacDiarmid's work' in *The Age of MacDiarmid,* eds P H Scott and A C Davis. (Edinburgh: Mainstream, 1980), pp. 83-99.
'Sixty Years Since: Return to Fraserburgh,' in *The Scottish Review* 20, (1980), pp. 4-8.
'Northeast Scots as a Literary Language,' in *Grampian Hairst,* eds William Donaldson and Douglas Young. (Aberdeen: University Press, 1981), pp. 187-95.
'George Buchanan,' in *The Scottish Review* 27, (1982), pp. 30-5.

REVIEW ARTICLES

'Mapping the language of Scotland,' Review of *The Linguistic Atlas of Scotland. Scots Section.* Vol. I, eds. J Y Mather and H H Speitel, in *The Scotsman,* (Saturday, 22 March 1975), Weekend Scotsman, p. 2.
'Oil Rigs and Barley Rigs: *Poetry of Northeast Scotland,* ed. James N Alison; *Two North-East Makars: Alexander Scott and Alastair Mackie,* by Leonard Mason,' in *The Scottish Review,* 3, (1976), pp. 31-4.

REVIEWS

Introduction to a Study of Scottish Dialects, by A McIntosh. *Sc. Hist. Rev.* 33, (1954), pp. 82-3.
The Poems of James VI of Scotland, ed. James Craigie, vol. I, *Anglia* 75, (1957), pp. 110-13.
The James Carmichaell Collection of Proverbs in Scots, by M L Anderson. *Sc. Hist. Rev.* 38, (1959), pp. 145-7.
The Poems of James VI of Scotland, ed. James Craigie, vol. II, *Anglia* 78, (1960), 89-91.
Robert Henryson: Poems. Selected and edited by Charles Elliott. *Archiv für das Studium der Neueren Sprachen und Literaturen* 202, (1965), pp. 291-2.

Erik Frykman: *W. E. Aytoun. Archiv für das Studium der Neueren Sprachen und Literaturen* 202, (1966), pp. 470-1.
Virgil's Aeneid, translated by Gavin Douglas, ed. David F C Coldwell. *Sc. Hist. Rev.* 46, (1967), pp. 66-8.
The Oxford Book of Scottish Verse, eds J MacQueen and T Scott. *Library Review* 21, (1967), pp. 37-8.
The Origin of English Surnames, by P H Reaney. *Library Review* 21, (1967), pp. 157-8.
Leslie Mitchell: Lewis Grassic Gibbon, by I S Munro. *Scottish Studies* 11, (1967), pp. 109-13.
Charles Mackay: *Mackay's Dictionary. Studies in Scottish Literature* 8, (1971), pp. 206-8.
Mark A Weinstein: *William Edmonstoune Aytoun and the Spasmodic Controversy. Archiv für das Studium der Neueren Sprachen und Literaturen* 207, (1971), pp. 467-8.
A Henderson, *Scottish Proverbs. J. Engl. Linguistics* 6, (1972), pp. 54-8.
The ballad and the folk, by David Buchan. *Library Review* 23, (1972-3), pp. 355-6.
A Scottish ballad book, ed. David Buchan. *Library Review* 24, (1973-4), p. 178.
The ballad and the folk, by David Buchan, and *A Scottish ballad book*, ed. David Buchan. *Scottish Studies* 18, (1974), pp. 139-43.
Andrew Crawford's collection of ballads and songs, ed. E B Lyle. *Scottish Studies* 19, (1975), pp. 87-9.
Beyond the sunset, by Douglas F Young, and *Neil M Gunn: the man and the writer*, eds. A Scott and D Gifford. *Scottish Studies* 19, (1975), pp. 89-91.
A dictionary of Scottish history, by G Donaldson and R S Morpeth. *University of Edinburgh Journal* 28, (1978), pp. 217-8.
A history of the public library movement in Scotland to 1955, by W R Aitken. *Bibliothek* 6, (1972), pp. 86-7.
The Linguistic Atlas of Scotland. Scots Section. Vol. II, eds J Y Mather and H H Speitel. *The Scottish Review*, 9, (1978), pp. 45-8.

CONTRIBUTORS

ADAM J AITKEN, MA, D LITT, Editor, *Dictionary of the Older Scottish Tongue*

KENNETH BUTHLAY, MA, Senior Lecturer, Department of Scottish Literature, Glasgow University

THOMAS CRAWFORD, MA, Reader, Department of English, Aberdeen University

HAMISH HENDERSON, MA, Hon LL D, Hon D (Univ), Senior Lecturer, School of Scottish Studies, Edinburgh University

†JOHN THOMAS LOW, BA, M LITT, Ph D, Part-time Tutor, Department of Extra-Mural Studies, Edinburgh University

J DERRICK McCLURE, MA, M LITT, Lecturer, Department of English, Aberdeen University

MATTHEW P McDIARMID, MA, B LITT, Reader, Department of English, Aberdeen University

JOHN MacQUEEN, MA, Professor, School of Scottish Studies, Edinburgh University

EDWIN MORGAN, OBE, MA, Emeritus Professor, Department of English, Glasgow University

WILHELM F H NICOLAISEN, Dr PHIL, M LITT, Professor of English and Folklore, State University of New York at Binghamton

MAIRI ROBINSON, MA, Editor-in-Chief, *Concise Scots Dictionary*

ONE

The *Gododdin* and Other Heroic
Poems of Scotland

M P Mcdiarmid

The literature of the land now known as Scotland has been composed in diverse
tongues, and in each of them heroic poetry has been recited and written. In the
Brythonic speech now represented only by Welsh but once spoken in both
Highlands and Lowlands, and around Glasgow as late as the twelfth century,[1]
was made the late sixth century *Gododdin*. In Gaeldom, the successor to
Brythonic Scotland, there circulated Ulster-derived legends of Finn mac
Cumhail and his strife with Goll mac Morna and with the sons of Uisnach ('The
Sorrows of Deirdre'), that were later not unknown to the differently languaged
but kindred *makars*,[2] and in the eighteenth century were to suggest the latest
and not the least influential of Europe's national epics, James Macpherson's
Fingal.[3] In Lowland Scots of the twelfth century was made a saga of the deeds of
Macbeth and Malcolm Canmore, of which fragments survive, mixing fantasy
with fact but generally not unlike the heroic lays of the Independence wars;[4]
and in the fourteenth, fifteenth and sixteenth centuries were composed John
Barbour's *Bruce* (1376-8), Hary's *Wallace* (*c.*1476) and Gavin Douglas's
Eneados (1511). In Latin Bruce's great chancellor Bernard of Linton wrote not
only the immortal Declaration of Arbroath but also Annals in verse that
celebrated his master's achievements, spirited enough in the chronicler's
selections;[5] and in the seventeenth century Patrick Panter and James Philip
laboured at their not so inspiring epics on Wallace and Graham of Claverhouse
('Bonnie Dundee'). English, of course, was the medium of *Fingal* and Walter
Scott's *Marmion*, best remembered today for its description of Flodden field,
'Where shivered was fair Scotland's spear/And broken was her shield'. The
many national histories, in verse or prose, seem to be written by men who feel
themselves to be recording an epic action renewed from age to age. Why they
should see history in this way needs no explanation, or why there should be so
long continued a tradition of heroic composition.[6] (Grassic Gibbon's trilogy, *A
Scots Quair,* may be said to have an epic concept.) The list might be

[1] Notes at end of essays

1

lengthened to include poems of lesser scope but kindred matter such as the great ballad of *Otterburne*, Burns's *The Vision*, and in this century Hugh MacDiarmid's *The Wreck of The Swan*.

The concern of this study is to demonstrate the kinship of Aneirin's *Gododdin*, the earliest extant poem of Scotland, and Europe's earliest extant heroic poem in a vernacular tongue, with later Scottish works in the same kind. Space does not allow appreciation of related but shorter poems in Gaelic—it would seem that the Irish inheritance was felt to be unsurpassable. And the Latin Muse must be neglected because it found no George Buchanan to loose its heroes from the direction of fact or tradition and let them assume life. Comparison of the *Gododdin*, however, with corresponding works in Lowland Scots, and with some reference to the English ones, should suffice to reveal one recognisably charactered tradition, with individual spirit and individual imaginative treatment.

Regrettably the proposed comparison must be preceded by a factual introduction to the too little known *Gododdin* which involves argumentation, the present writer finding himself in disagreement on points of substance with the authors of previous commentaries.[7]

The Book of Aneirin is in a manuscript of about 1250 and comprises two versions, A the later one preserving much more of the original content but B, as its archaic spelling shows, deriving from a copy probably made in the ninth century. The two versions, neither complete but sharing matter and linguistic features intruded in the process of bardic recitation, represent a form of the poem that was popular in Strathclyde some two generations after Aneirin's death. The dating of that form, however, is best affirmed after a consideration of the historical references provided in both the original poem and its not greatly altered successor. Not all these references have been noted by students of the poem.

About Aneirin himself a little is known and something more can be surmised. In the early ninth century *Historia Brittonum* Nennius places him in the second half of the sixth century, mentioning him along with Taliesin in the context of wars waged by the northern kings against the Angles of Bernicia and Deira.[8] His poem suggests to me that he was a Pict; he speaks of a 'cousin', 'kinsman', called Llifiau coming from 'beyond Bannog', that is, from beyond the range of hills that survey the Bannock burn, so very likely from Liff, a district near Dundee. It is at least conformable to this suggestion that he mentions and praises the Picts who sailed to Din Eidyn's defence from Din Dywid, which must have been near Dundee if not Dundee itself. Then there is the prefatory report of a Strathclyde bard that he was 'the son of Dywai', a name that should have some connection with the above-mentioned Din Dywid. To the same bard we owe the pleasant picture of the poet keeping a warm hearth and open house for the benighted traveller. His poem is more likely to have been composed in his dwelling beside Dundee than in the hall at

Edinburgh, though it was there that he came to know the men who fell at Catraeth.

The period of his poem's composition can be reckoned within fairly narrow limits. Taliesin sang the praises of the Border king Urien and lamented the death of his son Ywain, an event that occurred about 590 or so.[9] Taliesin's death cannot have come much later, so that one takes note when he is spoken of as if still alive (A45), though this may be rhetorical. The collapse of Urien's Carlisle-centred kingdom of Rheged before an Anglian counter-attack that seems to have been launched at this time, and with it the loss of his lordship of Catraeth, must surely be closely connected with the battle that occasioned the making of the *Gododdin*. The poem therefore belongs to the 590s, and most probably the first half of the decade. Two references in it support this dating, especially when one considers the generally youthful impression made by Aneirin's descriptions of his heroes. One is to 'the famous son of Ceidio', who has to be a younger brother of the chieftain Gwendoleu killed at Arthuret in 574; the other is to the especially praised Cynon, son of Clydno Eidyn and apparently now lord of Aeron (Ayrshire), which had been Urien's land. Clydno, presumably deceased since he has no part in the action, is said in The Book of Chirk to have led a northern band to Arfon in Welsh Gwynedd a little after 547 to avenge the slaying of a relative who had disputed the succession;[10] and the tradition seems to be remembered in a slip of the scribe or bard (noticed by Jackson but not explained), who calls Cynon 'the avenger of Arfon', where Aneirin must have intended Aeron. Both references imply that their subjects are men of advanced years, and therefore unlikely about 600 to have shone so 'surpassingly' in the warrior's role as they are said to have done. The military situation as known points the same way. One cannot imagine the garrison of Din Eidyn making an attempt on Rheged's Catraeth, with whatever advantage of surprise, at a date much later than 590, when the Anglian occupation was new and unsettled. The thorough rout of the much stronger Dalriadan host at Degsastan (?Dawstone in Liddisdale, not far from where I would put Catraeth) in 603 enforces the point. The probable dating of Aneirin's battle and its celebration is therefore between 590 and 595.

In this context the period at which the interpolations were made has its importance. The Strathclyde interpolator was at Strathcarron when his king Ywain defeated and slew Domhnall Brecc of Dalriada in 642 (B1, A78), and it should be the poem as he recited it then or a few years later that has survived in manuscript. Certainly, whatever linguistic tampering duly occurred, we have no detectable reason for considering, as Charles-Edwards does in his 'Historian's View', the possibility that substantial changes were subsequently made. Even the insertions made about 642—about four in B and eight in A (not counting two cases of bardic repetition)—are only such relatively insubstantial changes as might be made by a bard who respected his author.

None the less, at least three additions not noticed by Jackson were made, additions that stress further the Strathclyde element in the text.

The long-since-made identification of the victorious 'grandson of Nwython' with Ywain should have alerted scholars to other mentions of the House of Dumbarton, one or two of these being made by Aneirin himself. Nwython would appear to have succeeded Rhydderch the Generous about the year of St Kentigern's death, according to the *Annales Cambriae* 612 but more probably 603 as indicated in the Aberdeen Breviary.[11] 'Nai son of Nwython' (B26), who came to Catraeth with a hundred men and before he died 'slew a hundred princes bearing gold torques so that he might be celebrated', is surely the uncle of Ywain and brother of Nwython's successor Beli, who is said in A39 to have raided the Anglian East with the support of the grey-haired Cadfannan. Unfortunately the reign-lengths of these three kings can only be given as reasonable guesses: Nwython ruling *c*.603–*c*.620, Beli *c*.620–*c*.640 (his youngest son Brude ruled Pictland 672–93), and Ywain dying not many years after his victory of 642, only succeeded by his young son Dyfnwal when the latter's uncle Gwriad died in 658.

For Nai son of Nwython to have died as a young man at Catraeth when his father was not yet king is chronologically possible. The mention of Beli raiding with the help of Cadfannan 'of the red herd of horses' suggests, however, that he was then king, and if that is the case the eulogies of Cadfannan in A3, 39, 61, do not belong to Aneirin. Notably neither Beli nor Cadfannan is named in connection with Catraeth. There are two other references that involve Strathclyde but need not be denied to Aneirin: one is to the defence of the ford Penclwyd by Gwair who died at Catraeth (A88), the other to 'the wicked sons of Godebog' (A15). The ford Penclwyd (Welsh for 'head of the Clyde') must be the 'Cunclut' mentioned in Prince David's 1124 Inquisition of the lands of the diocese of Glasgow. The Welsh name has been Gaelicised (Ken Clut) and pertains to a part of the modern Glasgow Green.[12] Gwair's horses had been foremost when he defended the crossing that would have led the enemy to Dumbarton. The 'sons of Godebog' are the descendants of the 'Coel Hen Guotepauc' who figures in the Genealogies as the ancestor of Urien. The rulers of Strathclyde, and of Manau Gododdin it would appear from the poem, were members of the rival House of Dyfnwal Hen.[13] So also, according to the early Harleian Genealogies, was the father of Aneirin's hero, Cynon. This mentioned enmity is important because we learn from Taliesin that Urien had raided Manau[14]—doubtless also Strathclyde—and we may guess that he did so from Catraeth on his northern frontier. Previous raids from there would make the place a specially attractive target for attack in the confusion that followed the disintegration of Rheged.

As will have been seen, it has been worthwhile to pursue the Strathclyde connections in the verses of both Aneirin and his fellow bard. They are consonant with the times of composition allowed to each poet; they throw light on the political situation that Aneirin and his unlucky friends would have known; they remind us that it was for the royal family at Dumbarton that the substantially final form of the poem was shaped.

Much has been written about the fighting celebrated by Aneirin, but always with a single-minded concentration on the heroism at Catraeth that ignores both its context and its timing as represented by the poet. Thus scholars have without exception written as if the poem noticed only the above-mentioned action, and without exception have accepted the identification of Catraeth with Yorkshire's Catterick, at best a philologist's guess.[15]

Kenneth Jackson remarks on intermittent allusions to a 'previous' action at Din Eidyn and does not recognise in this the setting of the poem's main event. Edinburgh 'of the many goldsmiths' has been beleaguered, and its lord Mynydogg—a mysterious figure who has no part in the ultimate battle and possibly keeps to his strength at Stirling—duly orders the counter-attack which produces the disaster at Catraeth. Heroes of Catraeth who are also named as heroes of the defence are these—Morien who fought 'looking at Eidyn' (B6), Tudfwlch who won fame 'defending the woods and mead of Eidyn' (B17), Urfai 'that lord of Eidyn' (B28), Edar whose prowess was such that the enemy 'fled before Eidyn' (B34), and the anonymous warrior who 'did not retreat in front of Eidyn' (A76). Jackson is plainly correct in his identification of Eidyn with Din Eidyn (the fort Edinburgh), as the praise of Tudfwlch in the same passage as the one cited above makes clear, putting the Anglian foe 'to flight from the stronghold of Eidyn'. The defence of a fortress only less tactically important than that of Stirling was a much more likely occasion for the support of men from Pictland and Strathclyde than a suicidal expedition into the distant Northumbrian heartland. The lesson of what had happened to Rheged after Urien's leading of a federated northern army, it is said as far as Lindisfarne, would have deterred any such venture by little Manau Gododdin, for there is no hint in the poem, contrary to the assumptions of many scholars, of any such federated power.

The episode of Catraeth, whether connected with the defence of Din Eidyn or immediately subsequent to that defence, was admittedly the source of Aneirin's inspiration, so that it is of some, not paramount, importance that we should know where to look for it. The usual identification is impossible. A first point, additional to those already made, is that nothing in the poem, in record or later tradition, allows us to equate Gododdin with the great territory of the Votadini as it was known to the Romans, stretching from the Forth to the Weir. Jackson speaks of the 'kingdom of the Gododdin', and assuming it to have the ancient extent makes it reach almost, if not quite, to Catterick, yet we have no knowledge of such an extensive kingdom in Aneirin's day or for long before. We find Nennius mentioning Manau, which is the same name as the Manann of the Irish chroniclers, remembered today in place-names like Clackmannan, Slamannan, perhaps Kilmeny and Dalmeny, all pertaining to areas around the

inner reaches of the Forth. The same chroniclers mention 'Fotudan', which is
Gododdin, with reference to the same areas, and the Harleian Genealogies
gloss the northern homeland of Gwynedd's founder, Cunedda, as 'Manau
Guotodin'. In all these cases, in respect of place at least, no distinction is made
between Manau and Gododdin. When we examine the poem the land of
Gododdin is seen always to refer to the country about Din Eidyn. Thus in A3
'Before the army of Gododdin' and 'before the land of Manawyd'—surely this
has to do with Manau—have the same reference. When it is said that 'The men
went to Gododdin' (A67) their arrival at Din Eidyn is meant, and when such
heroes as Cynon son of Clydno Eidyn, Urfai 'a lord of Eidyn', Gwlyged who
ordered the feasting in the great hall, are said to be 'of Gododdin', again the
land that Din Eidyn defends is meant. It is plain, therefore, that when the men
'went to Catraeth' and died 'before (outside) the borderland of Gododdin' all
that is said is that they travelled some distance, but no great distance, beyond
the well understood bounds of Manau Gododdin. Ifor Williams notes that they
were cut down in 'Lloegr' (A41) and takes this to mean in England, but on this
reading Rachel Brompton comments that 'Lloegr' could have been applied to
any Angle-held territory;[16] and, of course, South-East Scotland to the Forth had
long been in Germanic hands, and much of the Borders had become Anglian
land. Only the recently overthrown Rheged in the west, a kingdom that had
extended widely about the Solway Firth, could have been thought vulnerable
to a surprise attack from Din Eidyn.

What space of time the journey of mounted men and footmen took is a
useful question to which the poem actually supplies an answer, at least the only
one available to us. The rhetorical diary in B29, A68, of the week that ended
with the battle may be summarised as follows: on Monday the enterprise was
noisily acclaimed in the great hall; on Tuesday armour was readied and
donned; on Wednesday lime-white shields were brought out; on Thursday
'envoys were pledged' (?oaths were taken); on Friday men boasted what
numbers they would slay; on Saturday the little army was free to set out ('their
united deeds were unrestricted'); on Sunday their swords were red; on Monday
'streams of blood were seen up to the knees'. Jackson understands this account
to mean that the battle began on Sunday and was finished on Monday; but he
does not make the relevant point that the men of Din Eidyn reached their
objective in at most a day and a night's journey. In precisely that space of time,
marvels Jean le Bel who took part in a fruitless campaign of Edward III, one of
Bruce's raiding parties could cover the astonishing distance of twenty leagues,
which amounts to less than sixty miles.[17] Cynon may have been as good a war-
captain as Sir James Douglas but he is not likely to have done much better; and
unlike Sir James he had footmen to slow his progress. The diary and Jean's
computation rule Catterick out of consideration as the place of combat; it
should be at the indicated distance or less, and for above-mentioned reasons in
a South-West or middle-Border direction from Din Eidyn.

Catraeth had been a lordship of Urien, a centre from which he raided his neighbours, and I have suggested that it was from there that he raided Manau. Very probably it was on the frontier of his Scottish lands, which included Ayrshire, Dumfriesshire, parts of Ettrick Forest, and possibly the southwest corner of Lanarkshire to which the Nithsdale track laid down by the Romans conveniently led. Aneirin attaches one or two place-names to Catraeth that have no parallel around Catterick. Apparently it was in 'the land of Gwanannon', and this may well be the district that contains the mountain Gana, and several names in *Wan-* though this may derive from Welsh *Gwen*. An alternative location in the same direction is Loch Macatterick (Welsh *ma*: plain, *cader*: fort, suffix *awc*) in Carrick beside the fortified Loch Doon and the Hooden hills (?the hill *Hyddwn* in the poem). Another is Fanna Hill at the watershed of Teviotdale and Liddisdale, just north of the Redesdale landmarks, Carter Fell and Catcleugh.

Much has been made of the notion of a year's preparation for a great enterprise, simply because the heroes are said in A6 to have had 'a year of peace undisturbed', and among them were men of diverse regions, at least one from 'the South', a group from North Wales, warriors from Pictland and Strathclyde. But we have seen that they had fought in the defence of Din Eidyn, and if they came from many parts this need not mean that they made up a great force. Aneirin alludes once or twice to footmen but his stress is on a body of three hundred horsemen. The strangers may have been like Heilyn who 'assaulted every borderland', that is, they were roving warriors who went wherever there was fighting and hospitable treatment, receiving and earning their 'mead'. And the short year of peace can only be a phrase that contrasts their prosperous service and entertainment in Din Eidyn's hall with its abrupt and violent ending at Catraeth. What happened, I suggest, was that in a spell of respite from attack a raid in force, nothing more ambitious, was attempted against the Anglian enemy in another quarter but ran into an overwhelming ambush. The ambush is implied in everything Aneirin says, for example, in B19 'As they strove with the mongrel hosts of England there were nine score around each one', and in the several places where warriors are praised because they did not flee 'when the ranks were broken'. The poet seeks effect by exaggerating the disparity of numbers and the roll of death; only one man, he repeatedly says, escaped—though in the later version, indicative perhaps of the location, three Ayrshiremen are said to have won away. Discounting these devices the clear impression is given that the force found itself in a hopeless position; the horsemen of Din Eidyn could do little, fighting with a slope before them and a river or stream behind them, the one in which young Ywain fell as he died (A69-71).

With this reconsideration and restatement of the temporal and local circumstances of the story of Catraeth out of the way, one can proceed to the promised comparison with other, and much later, works in Scotland's long tradition of heroic poetry. What will be attempted here is a review of the interpretative mode in the *Gododdin* and its poetical descendants, and a statement of what appears to be its continuing character.

But first one must appreciate the surprising excellencies of treatment in Aneirin's poem, so much superior in sensibility to those later and better known Germanic and Romance narratives, *Beowulf, Le Chanson de Roland, El Cid*. It is a pertinent comment on the Anglo-Saxon hero that he is less memorable than his exploits or the society to which he belongs; he is eminently forgettable. For the two other heroes it can be said that they have a comprehensible cause and an appealing code of behaviour, even if they impress more as admirable attitudes than as persons. The appealing essence of Roland is in certain famous lines on his lonely plight at Roncesvalles and the themes that his mind turns to with such noble simplicity. I venture to translate them.

> Under a pine-tree the count Roland lay
> And as a victor turned his face to Spain.
> There he began his last remembering:
> The many lands and battles he had won,
> His love for France, the good men of his kin,
> And Charlemagne his lord's great care for him.

And I venture this rendering of the Cid's vision of Gabriel as a sufficient introduction to the hero:

> 'Ride forth, my Cid, good fighter that you are,
> For never so well fortuned rode a man,
> Until death's day it will go well with you.'
> Waking he made the sign before his face.

If something is missing here it is the poet, who distances himself throughout from his impressive matter. It is the *idea* of Roland, the *idea* of the Cid, that concerns him.

Everything is different with Aneirin; one might say of him, as of so many modern writers, the poet is the poem. It is a conspicuous merit of the *Gododdin*, owing much to its form, a series of eulogies that are also elegies, that while it never allows us to forget the action or virtues it celebrates it concentrates attention on what was individual in its heroes and on what the poet felt for them. Admiration and pity go together in a universally meaningful way. Jackson's translation is in concise, sensitive prose, a medium that has the advantage over verse of not diverting attention from the matter. His rendering of A1 makes my claims for the poet brilliantly clear: 'A man in vigour, a boy in years, boisterous in courage; there were thick-maned horses under the thigh of the handsome youth, with light broad shield on the crupper of his slender speedy horse; bright blue swords and fringes of worked gold. There shall be no hatred between you and me, I shall do better with you— praise you in song. He would sooner have gone to the battlefield than to a wedding, he would sooner have been food for the ravens than get due burial. A beloved friend was Ywain, it is a shame that he is under a cairn. I marvel in what land the slaying of the only son of Marro could come to pass.'

Everything is personal with Aneirin, it is his feelings that he sees in his subjects. They were, after all, his friends; thus of Tudfwlch and 'Cyfwlch the tall', 'though we drank bright mead by the light of tapers, though its taste was good its bitterness was long-lasting' (A15). And of the related Llifiau, 'My kinsman, my very gentle one, does not cause us anxiety, unless it were because of the feast of the harsh dragon' (A22), the dragon being the lord who sent Llifiau to his death. At times a sequence of brilliantly vivid phrases seems about to leave the reality of things, when it is restored to it by plain statements and natural images that bring in the pathos of the event, the bright spirit quenched, as in this description of Buddfan 'under the hill of Eleirch'—'The warrior of the protective shield . . . and with the gallop of a colt, he was an uproar on the battle slope, he was a fire, his spears were impetuous, were flashing; he was the food of ravens, he was prey for ravens; and before the eagle of the graceful swoop was left at the fords with the falling of the dew, and by the spray of the wave beside the hill, the bards of the world judged him to be of manly heart' (A24).

Aneirin abounds in brief, bright strokes that make a picture: 'he slew . . . as when a reaping party strikes in unsettled weather' (A26), 'when Cynon sped forth with the green dawn' (A36), 'the pine-logs blazing from dusk to dusk, the lit-up doorway open for the purple-clad traveller' (A52), 'there was a red herd of horses, the horseman fierce in the morning' (A61).

Admittedly, to the present-day reader the convention of the ferocious combatant can seem primitive and come to be wearisome, and he may even think that Aneirin too often approaches emotionalism; yet it is part of the hero's code that his ferocity is reserved for battle, and it is just such very personal responses that humanise the narrative. Such a response is the simple statement, 'I have lost too many of my true kinsmen', where it would seem that all the men that died are considered as his kin; and another is the unrestrained description of how their loss affects him: 'When there comes upon me a host of anxieties . . . my breath fails as if with strenuous running, and straightway I weep' (A84).

Perhaps these citations stress too much the elegiac element, for the affirmation of the dead men's achievement in giving their lives for a loyalty, in so dearly earning their 'mead', is everywhere. The poem is above all celebratory.

In respect of the kinds of authorial intervention the sixth-century *Gododdin* is a more modern poem than the medieval *Bruce*. Yet, though John Barbour may speak less directly about himself, his feelings about both cause, action and persons, are made equally plain and in their more deliberative fashion are equally intense, more intense than was recognised by Walter Scott when so misleadingly he compared him to that connoisseur of feats of arms, Froissart. His involvement with the persons of his narrative is what he most shares with Aneirin. Thus it is characteristic of him that he should record how at Bannock-burn, in the moment of victory that he had done so much to secure, that fierce fighter Edward Bruce should stoop over the body of a dead friend and wish 'That journey wer/Undone than he sua ded had bene' (XIII. 484-5), or that in their fugitive existence comrades should meet with tears of joy. Warriors weep about their dying king as he orders that the heart in which was conceived the intent of pilgrimage should be casketed and carried to Jerusalem after his death. We know life by its 'contraries', says Barbour,[18] and illustrates the point in the same way as does Aneirin, doing justice to the gentleness in the warrior —the 'ful gret courtesy', as he calls it, in Bruce when he halts his army at Limerick to give protection to a laundress having her baby.

What is patently different in Barbour's poem is the concept of leadership; it includes the idea of a *communitas* and not merely a *comitatus*, of a responsible and caring government or governor, and in the business that directly concerns both poets, warfare, of the careful tactician as against the simple fighting-man. Again, Barbour's heroic world is not exclusively aristocratic but has a place in it for the achievements of ordinary men, a William Binning or a John Thomasson, who can act effectively without orders from a superior. None the less, the comparative modernity of the later poet in these respects, if not in others, does not derive altogether from the difference in times: Barbour's ideal of a 'popular' leadership would have seemed even more foreign to his contemporaries Chaucer and Froissart than to Aneirin. It derives in part from the imaginative response of educated men in a nation with an unsettled crown to the precedents of republican Rome, but much more from a shared Celtic tradition—most of the country was still Gaelic-speaking, as was the greater part of Barbour's diocese, and he himself may have come from the Gaelic South-West. The two writers share more than the same 'auld enemy'. The absolute concernment of their heroes—not, of course, the necessarily prudent king—with their personal reputations as loyal and daring fighting-men is carried a passionate degree beyond the normally sober acceptance of debts owing and to be paid according to Germanic conventions or the terms of a feudal society. 'Quha dars de for his lord?', cries Niel Fleming at Carrickfergus when the odds are impossible, and has the savage tears of Edward Bruce, who later leads his men at Dundalk against odds that all know to be equally impossible. Paradoxically it may have been from just those extreme and seemingly archaic notions of a loyalty *between* lord and man that Scotland's historically precocious sentiment of democracy—serfdom had been done away with by the time the *Bruce* was written—was born. Shared loyalties, shared griefs, knowing and expressing them, the primitive and the medieval poet live for us in the same very human world. Both exult in what men can dare, and both know the *lacrimae rerum.*

The most original and the greatest of Scottish heroic poems, though the one that least accommodates itself to liberal modes of feeling, or to the political attitudes of those whom Hary damns as mere 'thrifty men'—the main reason why it is so neglected in *British* criticism—is unquestionably the *Wallace*. Of course, it owes much of its quality and appeal to its subject, a figure even more admirable in history than in the legend that he naturally became. It is not Hary's fault that his fiction falls short of the facts. If not historical knowledge— he had the conventional reading of the day, Latin and vernacular, the latter inclusive of French—he brought to his storytelling something of his hero's own daemonic energy, and he knew how to direct it. The *Wallace* is the best constructed of Scotland's longer narrative poems. Its thrice repeated pattern of suffering, success and failure, with final martyrdom interpreted as the greatest of successes, is vividly and movingly, if sometimes shockingly, developed. It is understandable that the poem should stir the imagination of generations of ·Scotsmen, Burns among them, and even a member of the eighteenth-century *literati* like Lord Hailes, whatever he might say about Hary's handling of history;[19] understandable that its effects should move the English poet William Wordsworth searching for an epic theme to think of Wallace as the type 'Of independence and stern liberty', and that he should realise that his talent and way of thinking led another way.[20]

Unlike the *Bruce* but like the *Gododdin* the story is heroi-tragic. The hero strives and suffers with such alternations of triumph and defeat that 'he seis the warld so full of fantasie' (X. 853), much as Aneirin felt when he marvelled at a world in which the only son of Marro could die. As with Aneirin too the sense of loss marches with exultation over the desperate but decided courage, as in the account of the rearguard action at Falkirk (XI. 327–44):

> Mekill he trows in god, and his awn weid,
> Till sayff his men he did full douchty deid . . .
> Sic a flear befor was nevir seyn
> Nocht at Gadders of Gawdyfer the keyn
> Quhen Alexander reskewed the forryours
> Mycht till him be comparit in tha hours.

> *trows*: trusts   *weid*: sword
> *forryours*: forragers   *tha*: those

And the contraries of which Barbour speaks are illustrated in the 'fers Wallace' who vengefully watches the Barns of Ayr blaze, 'Quhill the rede fyr had that fals blude ourgane' (VII. 470); yet can say of an English commander, 'Plesand it is to se a chyftane ga/Sa chyftanlik', and unburden himself of his grief for a murdered wife to an English queen (VIII. 382–84):

> 'Madem', he said, 'as god giff me gud grace,
> Intill hir tym scho was as der to me,
> Prynsace or queyn, in quhat stait so thai be.'

This development of the hero in terms more emotive than Barbour, if not
Aneirin, normally uses, shows equally in a briefly appearing Bruce, here
represented as taking the English side at Falkirk and afterwards, from an inter-
view, learning from Wallace where his loyalty must lie: 'This blud is myn. That
hurtis maist my thocht.' It is by such feeling concentration on his subject that
Hary succeeds in creating a figure on the scale of the heroes of Elizabethan
tragedy. He is at the same time, and without contradiction, very much what
Wordsworth (in a pejorative sense that is not justified here) was to call Scott, a
'physical' poet; and I repeat what I have written elsewhere: 'There is, perhaps,
no parallel in poetry to the power of suggesting the sensations of strenuous
movement, the emotions of violent and desperate action, that is exhibited in
the man-hunt (of which the hero is the prey) of Book V.'[21] Yet we have seen
something of this faculty in the cited description by Aneirin of Buddfan's
uphill assault on the foe, and it shows in Barbour's realistic conveyance of the
heat and sweat suffered by Randolph's defending schiltrom (spear circle) at
Bannockburn. It must be said once more, however, that notable as such
physical effects are it is the man of feeling who knows the cost of battle that
most impresses in each one of these poets. Aneirin and Barbour would have
responded to Hary's picture of Wallace and his friends revisiting the late scene
of strife at Falkirk (XI. 559–61):

> Full weyll arrayt intill thar armour clen
> Past to the feild quhair that the chas had ben,
> Amang the ded men sekand the worthiast.

One curious consequence, perhaps advantageous, of concentrating on the
almost solitary role of the hero as 'resistance leader' is that the fact of the few
faithful comrades not having a place in a national structure of king and king's
commanders, such as Douglas and Randolph enjoy in the *Bruce*, has the effect
of a reversion to the primitive *comitatus* with a mainly personal loyalty that is
found in Aneirin's poem. These lesser figures, however, do not stand out with
the individual brilliance that Aneirin's sketches allow.

From the two later heroic poems Gavin Douglas caught the impulse to write
his *Eneados*. It must have occurred to him that if Wallace and Bruce had not, as
pius Aeneas had done, founded a kingdom, they had at least, and with as great
pains, re-established one; and that they had felt the compulsion of duty or
destiny no less than the Trojan hero. When Douglas asserts as a true Humanist
and educationist that his work will be recited by Scottish boys he may have the
schools in mind, but he must also be remembering himself 'as a page' listening
to favourite passages in the popular national epics. Certainly the best moments
in his creative translation owe something to the heroic ethos as Barbour and
Hary interpreted it. For, fortunately, the *Eneados* is not 'classical' in anything
but its content; style and stress, to adapt his own idiom, come from a very
Scottish wine-press (in his day Scotland cultivated its own vines). Such

descriptive lines as this for the serpents leaving the sea to seek out the priest Laocoon, 'With tongis quhislying in thar mouthis rede', or this for the heedless Trojan youth rejoicing about the fatal horse, 'Syngand karrells and dansand in a ryng', do not convey Virgil, they improve on him.

Naturally, though the translator is interested in the leadership of service, a theme very congenial to the tradition—witness Lindsay's question and answer in *The Thrie Estaitis*, 'Quhat is a king, nocht bot ane officer'—it is the scenes of action where the visual imagination is dramatically engaged, or the affections of family are involved, that Douglas develops with most effect. In these the manner and impression made is the most Scottish, the poet is most himself and least Virgilian; it may even be claimed that here he is more affective than the Roman poet. Space does not allow more than these two instances.[22]

The first describes a moment in Aeneas's escape from burning Troy, his aged father on his back, wife and son at his side.

> Lytil Iulus gripps me by the hand,
> With onmeit pays his fader fast followand;
> Neir at our bak Creuse my spous ensews;
> We pass by secret wents and quyet rews.
> And me, quham laitly na wapyn nor dartis kast,
> Nor press of Grekis rowtis maid agast,
> Ilk swowch of wynd and every quhispir now
> And alkyn sterage affrayt and causit grow,
> Baith for my birdyng and my litill mait.
> Quhen we war cummyn almaist to the yet
> And al danger we thocht eschapit neyr,
> A fellon dyn belyve of feyt we heir;
> My fader than lukand furth throw the sky
> Crys on me, 'Fle, son! Fle son in hy,
> Thai cum at hand.' Behynd me I gat a sycht
> Of lemand armour and schynand scheildis brycht.[23]

onmeit: unequal	*wents*: ways
rews: streets	*rowtis*: blows
swowch: breath	*sterage*: movement
grow: fear	*birdyng*: burden
yet: gate	*fellon*: great
belyve: suddenly	*hy*: haste
lemand: gleaming	

We have here the driving and moving simplicity of style that Hary taught Douglas. The 'litill mait' makes a homely and un-Virgilian effect, rhythm and words are dense with dramatic implication. Aneirin does not leave his heroic action long enough to develop the domestic theme in this way, but his recurrent mention of the fact that this or that doomed hero is his father's only son, and that the warrior's blow makes mothers weep, is in the same line of imaginative understanding. He would have responded to the mother's lament for young Eurialus, which has such unrestrained, almost wake-like, force of feeling in Douglas's version.

> 'O thou, the lattyr quyet of myne age,
> Quhow mycht thou be sa cruell in thy rage
> As me to leif alyve, thus myne allane?
> O my maist tendir hart, quhar art thou gane?
> Na licens grantit was, nor tyme ne space,
> To me thy wrachit moder, allace, allace,
> Quhen thou thy self onto sik perrels set
> That I with the mycht samekill laser get
> As for to tak my leif for ever and ay,
> Thy last regrait and quething words to say.
> Ochane, allace, intill ane oncouth land
> Nakyt and bair thy fair body on sand
> To fowls of reif and savage doggis wild
> Sall ly as pray, myne awne deir only child!
> Nor I thy moder layd not thy corps on beir,
> Nor with my hands lowkit thyne eyn so cleir,
> Nor wysche thy wondis to reduce thy spreit,
> Nor drest the in thy lattir clathis meyt,
> The quhilkis I wrocht, God wayt, to mak the gay,
> Full bissely spynnand baith nycht and day,
> And with sic wobbs and wark for the, my page,
> I comfort me in myne onweldy age,
> And irkyt not to laubour for thy sake. .
> Quhar sall I seik the now, allake, allake?'

ne: nor	*quething*: parting
oncouth: strange	*lowkit*: closed
wysche: washed	*reduce*: bring back
wobbs: webbs	*page*: boy
comfort: comforted	*onweldy*: cumbrous

Emotionalism is too strong a term for the sentiment indicated by it in the more affective parts of these four poems, but certainly the human meaning of a heroic action or end is conveyed with less matter-of-factness and restraint than is normally shown in classical, Germanic or Romance poetry in this kind. The abandonment and degree of intensity with which the *lacrimae rerum* are given expression appears to be characteristic of the Celtic tradition as it is illustrated in Scotland. And it is inexperience or a foolish modern convention that objects, in these poems and their heroes, to the response of tears. Yet the point should not be made so forcibly as to suggest that heroism is not the supreme value that it is for the poets, or that their prevailing manner is not celebratory. The courage is itself a triumph, and it is true for the heroic poets, as in a special sense it is for the author of *The Battle of Otterburne* (who celebrates an ancestor of Gavin Douglas), that dead men can win battles:

'Last night I dreamed a dreary dream
Beyond the Isle of Sky,
I dreamed that a dead man wan a fight
And I dreamed that that man was I.'

Aneirin says of the men at Catraeth, 'in close ranks and stubbornly the bloodhounds fought' (A9), and the adverb recalls at once Scott's lines on the doomed but unyielding men at Flodden:

The stubborn spearmen still made good
The dark impenetrable wood,
Each stepping where his comrade stood,
The instant that he fell.

Even for the diffuse and pervasively melancholy 'Ossian', melancholy in a Romantic mode quite untypical of Celtic composition, it should be claimed that one memorable statement does catch the essence of the heroic tradition as Scotland has mostly known it: 'They went forth to the war but they always fell.'[24] It is life itself that Macpherson describes, despite experience still ready to gird on 'the sword what will not save'.

The *Gododdin* does belong, not only by locale but also by spirit, with the several heroic poems that follow it at an interval of centuries and in different languages. Perhaps the term 'heroic' has been too often used in this essay; each of these works is above all a human record, and if a celebration one that moves to pity.

NOTES

1 W J Watson, *The History Of The Celtic Place-Names Of Scotland* (1926), p. 132. Watson adds that in 1305 Edward I ordered the disuse of the customs of 'the Scots (Gaels) and the Brets'. Jocelyn's twelfth-century Life of St Kentigern used an anonymous Life that drew from traditions of a Welsh-speaking community in and about Glasgow cathedral (R Cunliffe Shaw, *The Men of the North* (1973), p. 162).

2 Lowland writers who knew Celtic traditions and tales are Barbour and Fordun (both of whom seem to have known some Gaelic), Wyntoun, John Mair, probably Dunbar, certainly Kennedy, Douglas, Boece, the Gaelic-speaking Buchanan. Of course, Highland noblemen such as the earls, later Dukes, of Argyle both spoke and wrote in Gaelic, some in verse (The Book Of The Dean Of Lismore). It is remarkable how knowledge of the 'Brett-speaking' Highlands and Lowlands came to be effaced in Scottish history and was recovered only in the last century.

3 M P McDiarmid, 'Ossian As Scottish Epic', *Scottish Literary News*, Ossian Number, vol. 3, no. 3 (November 1973).

4 The fragments of heroic lays on both these themes are in the fourteenth-century chronicle of John of Fordun and the early fifteenth century one of Andrew of Wyntoun; Barbour and Hary make notable use of such lays. Menendez y Pelayo observes that early Spanish chronicles Latinised the *romances* and this was probably the case in Fordun's *Historia* and Walter Bower's *Scotichronicon*. See n. 5.

5 Bernard's verses can be seen in Walter Bower's brief selections. See particularly
   Bruce's speech at Bannockburn, XII. cap. XXI; the same chapter disguises Bernard
   in prose.
6 One illustration of the epic conception, imitative of the *Aeneid* and the Old
   Testament, is a racial derivation from a Greek prince and his Egyptian wife Scota,
   still maintained in 1520 by Gavin Douglas against the criticism of John Mair and
   Polydore Vergil.
7 The main commentaries are these—Ifor Williams, *Canu Aneirin* (1938); his
   Lectures on Early Welsh Poetry, ed. Rachel Bromwich, (1980); Kenneth Jackson,
   The Gododdin (1969); T M Charles-Edwards, 'The Authenticity of *The Gododdin*:
   An Historian's View', in *Astaedtaethau Ar Yr Hengerdd*, eds. Rachel Bromwich,
   R. Brinley Jones, (1978). Jackson's translation with preface and running comment is
   the most convenient reference, and only for that reason has my criticism been
   directed against him rather than against other writers whose views do not differ
   notably from his. His version is more impressive than the poetical one of Joseph P
   Clancy in *The Earliest Welsh Poetry* (1970).
8 See the prefaced translation by A W Wade-Evans (1938), pp. 80, 81.
9 For my references to Taliesin and his information about Urien see *The Poems of
   Taliesin* ed. Ifor Williams, English Version by J E Caerwyn Williams, (1968).
10 Rachel Bromwich, *Troiedd Ynys Prydein The Welsh Triads* (1961), p. 501
11 A O Anderson, *Early Sources of Scottish History*, vol. 1 (1922), p. 139, hesitantly
   prefers the date 612; Cunliffe Shaw simply states 603. Anderson is invaluable for
   his quoted references to the kings of Strathclyde.
12 A C Lawrie, *Early Scottish Charters* (1905), pp. 406, 301: 'a croft now part of
   Glasgow Green, situate near the Clyde.' Penclwyd equates with Ken Clut; the
   description was natural enough in its time if not to the modern geographer.
13 See the Genealogies in the *Nennius* of Wade-Evans, pp. 104–6. Rachel Bromwich,
   op. cit., publishes the much later *Bonhed* descents which assign Clydno Eidyn,
   most improbably, to the Coel Hen branch. In the *Gododdin* A15 makes clear the
   connection of Manau, and with it Clydno's son Cynon, with the Dyfnwal Hen
   family.
14 Taliesin's mention of the attack on Manau is in J Clancy's translation, op. cit., 'The
   War-Band's Return', which shows Urien 'set to raid Manaw'.
15 The derivation of Catterick from a hypothesised *Cadracht* has required argument.
   The Roman Cataractorium, Old English Cetreht, were surely adapted from the
   native name of the river, which passed a hill-fort. The name was possibly the one
   represented in three Scottish rivers adjoining forts, Catter (Welsh *cader*, fort). Of
   course, there is no record of Catterick ever being called Catraeth. The location of
   Catraeth can only be generally indicated and by such practical arguments as I have
   used.
16 Ifor Williams, *Lectures on Early Welsh Poetry*, ed. Rachel Bromwich, (1980), p. 68,
   n. 82, 'Lloegr' may have spread to become 'a more general term for the English, as
   it is in the poems of Aneirin and Taliesin'.
17 *Les Chroniques de Sire Jean Froissart*, livre I, partie 1, ch. xxiv. Froissart
   incorporates the narrative of Jean le Bel.
18 'Thus contrar thingis evirmar/Discoveryngis off the tothir ar' (I. 241–2)
19 Sir David Dalrymple, later Lord Hailes, in his Annals of Scotland (1776), p. 281,

mentions 'Blind Harry [assuredly not blind when he wrote his poem!] whom every historian copies, yet whom no historian but Sir Robert Sibbald ventures to quote'. Hailes may not quote Hary but unconsciously he fetches details and interpretations from him.

20 *The Prelude,* lines 214-20
21 Hary's *Wallace*, ed. M P McDiarmid, vol. 1 (Scottish Text Society, 1968), p. xc.
22 The two citations are from D C Caldwell's edition, 4 vols (Scottish Text Society, 1957-64). See n. 23. For the convenience of some readers unsounded i/y in endings has been omitted, though unsounded *is* in *quhilkis*, plur., is retained.
23 Caldwell's punctuation follows Virgil's sense but Douglas's shift to the past tense, 'I gat a sicht', suggests to me that he attributes *cerno* to Aeneas and not to his father. My punctuation certainly fits better with the dramatic effect Douglas aimed at.
24 The sentence is quoted by Matthew Arnold in *The Study of Celtic Literature*, ed. Alfred Nutt, (1910), p. 90 in a passage contrasting Celtic sensibility and failure with English practicality and success. But in the *Study* it is not the interesting critic but the uninteresting Englishman who speaks; and it is the latter who impatiently dismisses the *Gododdin* as a work 'in which the art of *not* furnishing definite information is carried to extreme lengths'.

TWO

The Language of Older Scots Poetry

A J Aitken

1 *Introduction*

This essay sets out some ideas which I have long held about the ways in which Older Scots poets deployed their linguistic and stylistic options. To some readers the gist of what I say, and some of the details, will be familiar. I have expounded the generality and some of the particulars that follow in lectures and hand-outs since the early 1950s. These have included a public lecture with the same title as the present essay which I gave in 1972, and which has since then been accessible in xeroxed form. I am especially grateful to Dr Suzanne Romaine for publishing recently a neat and very fair summary of this (Romaine 1982: 22-5). But the following will be the first published account by myself.

As a characterisation of the linguistic and stylistic markers of Older Scots verse and a survey of their distribution in the corpus of that verse, the following manifestly falls far short of the fully detailed and meticulous account which must some day be presented by someone. Some features, which I have not yet found time to examine, are left unexamined, such as the body of pervasive tags and formulae of different types, some generally distributed and others confined to particular modes: *iwis, bedene, but lese, but layne, in hy, but peir, al and sum, I trow, as I wene, holtis hair,* etc. Other important topics, such as the dictions characteristic of simple and alliterative narrative, have had to be dismissed with no more than a mention. Despite these deficiencies I hope that this partial survey of certain stylistic traits of Older Scots verse may be of use for the time being.

Underpinning this theory of Older Scots verse styles (and a roughly similar theory of prose styles is possible) is the belief that the Middle Scots poets shared a system of modal decorum to which all of them fairly faithfully adhered. So too did their predecessors the Early Scots poets, though their system was a simpler and more limited one. On closer examination it turns out that even such an apparently eccentric work as *Colkelbie Sow* conforms to the Middle Scots system, as C D Jeffery has now shown (Jeffery 1981: 207).

To serve as a frame of reference for the generalisations about distributions of particular types of feature which occupy the remainder of this survey, I propose the following categorisation of Older Scots verse modes, according to criteria of theme, metre and style. In its general outline, this resembles similar schemes expounded by C S Lewis (1954: 68-76) and B Ellenberger (1977: 71-5); and the much earlier one implied by George Bannatyne's division of the poems of his collection (the Bannatyne Manuscript) into five 'parts' (the fourth of these further subdivided).

(i) *Plain narrative verse*, in at first tetrameter ('octosyllabic'), or, later more usually, pentameter, ('decasyllabic') (or 'heroic') couplets, such as Barbour's *Brus*, most of the *Wallace*, the Asloan MS *Buke of the Sevyne Sagis*, Lyndsay's *Squire Meldrum*, and a large body of other poetry. These poems employ, for the most part, fairly plain vernacular language, unpoetic in vocabulary and unelaborate in syntax, except for some of the diction of poetic synonyms shared with alliterative verse, and some favourite formulae and tags used especially in combat episodes. Also to be excepted are the very occasional passages of heightened rhetoric and courtly diction in some courtly, hortatory or didactic prologues and digressions, and occasional courtly laments, such as the passages opening books VI and IX (in Moir's 1889 STS edition) of the *Wallace* (see further p. 21 below).

(ii) *Alliterative verse*, in the three longer narrative poems in the 'Scottish' thirteen-lined rhyming stanza of alliterative 'long-lines' and 'wheel' (*The Buke of the Howlat, Golagros and Gawane, Rauf Coilȝear*), employs an, on the whole, plain vernacular language like that of the plain narrative poems. The alliterative poems, however, are much more pervasively laced with elements of poetic diction from a repertory of words and formulae characteristic of late medieval English and Scottish alliterative verse—'alliterative diction'. They resort frequently to 'straining' or 'extending' the meanings of words. And in syntax they accumulate co-ordinated or appositional redundances—'parallel-ism'—to produce a highly repetitive, diffuse style, advancing the narrative at a very leisurely pace. (The only detailed account of these characteristics of this body of verse is in Mackay 1975.) Sharing these linguistic characteristics of the longer alliterative narrative poems are a number of other poems, either in alliterative long-line and wheel stanzas, such as *Sum Practysis of Medecyne* attributed to Henryson, Douglas's *Prologue* to *Eneados* VIII, and, in an elaboration of this stanza, 'In May in a morning' (one of Bannatyne's 'ballattis of lufe', *Bann. MS* fos. 225b-226a), or in alliterative blank verse, Dunbar's *The Tua Mariit Wemen and the Wedo*; but on account of their content and other features of their style one might rather wish to assign these to other modes following below.

There exist also several poems in either a rather simpler alliterative stanza of 'short lines' or stanzas of regularly alliterated syllabic verse, approximating stylistically to those just specified—Henryson's *Ressonyng betuix Aige and Yowth, King Hart, Tayis Bank* (*Bann.* MS 229a-b), *The Murning Maiden* (*Maitl. F.* cxxx), and others.

(iii) *Elaborate narrative verse*, lexically more wide-ranging, syntactically, rhetorically, and, in many cases, metrically more elaborate than the simple narrative verse—a half-way house between the latter and the narrative of courtly allegories and visions (cf. (vi) below). Examples of this sort of verse are the narrative parts of Henryson's *Fables, Cresseid* and *Orpheus*, the narrative portions of *Lancelot of the Laik*, Douglas's *Æneid* translation, notably wide-ranging and eclectic in language (see Bawcutt 1976: ch. 6), and portions of the latter part of Lyndsay's *The Testament of the Papyngo* (lines 647-1171); and we might prefer to place here rather than in (i) the narrative of Rolland's *Sevin Seages*. All of these are in the accredited 'Chaucerian' metres, either rhyme royal (on which see, especially, Pearsall 1962: 58, and (vi), below), or heroic couplets, and all more or less 'Anglo-Scots' (see section 2).

(iv) *Instructive and hortatory verse*, secular, religious, social or moral, more overtly and straightforwardly didactic than courtly allegory. This includes a number of early works mostly from Cambridge University Library MS Kk 1.5, No. 6 (the *Ratis Raving* MS). These are in octosyllabic couplets, whereas later examples of this mode are mostly in Chaucerian stanzaic metres, or, less often, heroic couplets. Instances include Henryson's *moralitates*, and other parts of Henryson's work, such as the general *Prologue to the Fables* and the introduction to *The Preaching of the Swallow*, as well as the *Contemplatioun of Sinnaris*, several of Douglas's Prologues to the *Eneados* (I, IV, VI, X, XI), Lyndsay's *Dreme* (the 'Epistil' and 'Prologue' excepted), the 'Epistil to the Redar' and the latter part of Lyndsay's *Monarche*, and moralising introductions, digressions and culminations in other works such as *Colkelbie Sow* and *The Quare of Jelosy*, Douglas's *The Palice of Honour* (e.g. lines 1963-2057), and the moralising testaments of Lyndsay (to the *Papyngo* and to *Meldrum*), and that of *Duncan Laideus*. Similar in tone and content to these longer works of instruction are numerous relatively short pieces, notably the majority of those occupying the first two parts of George Bannatyne's collection (*Bannatyne MS*, fos. 1-96), most of Henryson's minor poems, others of Douglas's Prologues and his *Conscience*.

(v) A wide variety of stanza forms, some quite complex and many in shorter lines than the 'Chaucerian' iambic pentameters obligatory for elaborate narrative and courtly verse, characterise reflectively *personal poems* such as Dunbar's 'Into thir dirk and drublie dayis' and most of the other pieces which Kinsley groups together as 'Moralities' in his edition of Dunbar. Perhaps the 'Epistil' to Lyndsay's *Dreme* belongs here, and also *love lyrics* such as Dunbar's 'Sweit rois of vertew and of gentilnes' and most of the pieces, including many by Alexander Scott, in the opening section of the fourth part of Bannatyne's collection, and *simple allegories* such as Henryson's *The Garmont of Gud Ladeis* and Dunbar's *Bewty and the Presoneir*.

These last three kinds of verse, groups (iii), (iv), and (v), largely eschew the stereotyped diction of the simple and alliterative narrative modes, and only incidentally and relatively sparsely draw on the staple vocabulary of the low-life poetry (see section 8). The diction and rhetoric of the courtly poetry (see section 4–7) appear more often, albeit in much less profusion than in the courtly set pieces (group (vi) below), and sometimes appear to be used as it were allusively, as if borrowing or quoting from material which more properly resides within the courtly mode. The content of the abstractly didactic pieces and passages naturally attracts a high density of Latinate vocabulary (see section 6), but Latinisms are quite infrequent in the lyric poems. The degree of syntactical complexity (see section 3) varies, and appears, predictably, to be in general higher in the discursive verse. Conversely, anglicised forms (section 2) seem most favoured by the narrative verse. Over-all the level of style in these three kinds of verse is middle to high, closer to that of the courtly verse than of any other kinds.

(vi) *Courtly verse in the grand manner*, that collection of passages within other poems and entire poems in what C S Lewis calls 'the full-blown high style' (Lewis 1954: 74). Poetry in this manner comprises several elaborate dream-allegories more or less saturated with classical, as well as, rather more incidentally and cursorily, scriptural, allusion (Douglas's *The Palice of Honour* and Rolland's *The Court of Venus*); somewhat simpler love-allegories and dream-visions and 'debates' (such as *The Quare of Jelosy* (in part), the *Lufaris Complaint*, Dunbar's *The Goldyn Targe* and his *The Thrissill and the Rois*, Bellenden's *Proheme of the Cosmographe*, and, among much later examples, the vision in praise of Marie Maitland (*Maitl. Q.* lxix) and E. Melville's *Godlie Dreame*); grandiose panegyrics and laments, such as those by Dunbar on Bernard Stewart and Lyndsay's *Deploratioun*, and, later, Patrick Hume's *Promine*, and the religious counterparts of these, the ballats of our Lady. Almost all of this is in more or less elaborate 'Chaucerian' stanzas, mostly of seven, eight or nine lines of inter-rhyming pentameter lines, such as rhyme royal or the 'Anelida's Complaint' stanza.

Set pieces in the courtly manner are also prefaced or appended to, or introduced into, works mainly in the narrative and didactic modes—as more or less conventional and pretentious prologues and 'prohemes', and conventional panegyrics and hymns, and some 'complaynts' or laments—e.g. to or in *The Buke of Alexander*, Henryson's *Fables* and *The Testament of Cresseid*, the *Wallace*, *Lancelot*, Lyndsay's *Dreme*, his *Testament of the Papyngo*, and his *Monarche*, even *Duncan Laideus' Testament* and Montgomery's *The Cherry and the Slae*.

This sort of verse draws repeatedly on the following pieces of 'business': the zodiacal setting or other astronomical introduction to indicate or reiterate the time of the year or time of day, the landscape and weather setting, most often verdant and summery, occasionally wintry (see (ix) below), most usually in prohemes or introductions but sometimes at later points also, the gorgeous vision following a *chanson d'aventure* adventure or encounter, or as a variant of this, the dream, often allegorical; the presence of Dame Nature; parades of classical gods and goddesses and their retinues of personified qualities; allusions to classical authors such as Homer, Tullius, Ovid, Boethius and (notably by Douglas) others; innumerable catalogues of (mostly attractive or interesting) objects or personages—birds, beasts, flowers, jewels, musical instruments, hunting instruments, deities, personifications, authors, *et al.*

The verdant summer-morning *descriptiones loci amoeni* feature a large number of highly recurrent (many of them virtually invariable or obligatory) clichés of descriptive detail in the equally recurrent formulae in which these are regularly verbalised: the hot beams of rising Phebus dispelling the dew which nevertheless continues to drop down glistening as a balmy liquor, the various colourfully gleaming jewels (beryl, topaz *et al.*) to which the dew or the flowers or the sunbeams are compared, the tender shoots of the trees in which a bird or the birds sing 'from the spleen' or as Venus' choristers, the medicinal nature of the herbage, the floral 'garth' or garden, the mead with its adjoining river the sound of which lulls the poet to sleep and so to dream his beautiful vision peopled by a lady or ladies of ravishing beauty, followed by the allegorical action or the colourfully instructive vision which makes up the body of the poem.

Other recurrent set pieces or topoi of the courtly verse include passages in praise of earlier masters of rhetoric or poetry and panegyrics of noble persons or of the virgin, largely in a series of declamatory or invocatory formulae which describe or address the object of adulation as a lantern, flower or jewel *of* some admirable class of beings or admirable quality (see p. 38 below): such are Dunbar's panegyrics in *The Goldyn Targe,* his Bernard Stewart poems and his *Hail! sterne superne.*

Still another set piece is the interpolated *captatio benevolentiae* or the concluding modesty *envoi,* commonly in a deliberately contrasting style (see section 11).

All of this clearly derives at least in part from earlier works in some of the same stanzas and a similar manner, albeit with rather less profusion of cliché and lower concentration of formulae, by Chaucer (such as *Anelida and Arcite, The Parliament of Fowls* and several of the short poems), Lydgate (whose *Complaint of the Black Knight* is ubiquitous, in its Scottish title 'The Maying and Disport of Chaucer', in the Scottish sources), and Hoccleve (whose *Moder of God* or 'Oracio Galfridi Chaucer' is also current in the surviving Scottish sources). Despite the arguments against the use of the term by Lewis (1954:

74-5) and others in recent decades, I believe there is a good case for applying the designation Scottish Chaucerian, or, still more aptly, Scottish Lydgatian, to this particular branch of Older Scots poetry, since almost all of its typical superficial features result from quite conscious imitation by the Scottish poets of characteristics displayed by these English works, especially those of Lydgate. Though many of these Scots pieces display considerable originality, both in spirit and in technique, this is nevertheless much the most derivative kind of Older Scots poetry.

(vii) *Low-life verse*, Lewis's 'comic poetry' (Lewis 1954: 69 ff.), lies at an opposite pole from courtly verse. This is that varied class of burlesque, comic and vituperative poems, a large sample of which is included by Bannatyne in the third 'part' of his 'book', consisting of 'mirry balletis' (*Bann. MS* 98a-211a). This includes flytings and lampoons—the reverse of the laudatory pieces and passages in the courtly tradition—such as Dunbar and Kennedy's *Flyting*, Dunbar's lampoon on John Damian and most of his *The Tua Mariit Wemen and the Wedo*, and John Roull's *Cursing*. Dunbar's *The Dance of the Sevin Deidly Synnis* also belongs here; and a number of highly realistic pieces with a low-life setting, namely the mock-tournaments and the 'country fair degenerating into a free-for-all' group of *Peblis to the Play* and *Christis Kirk on the Grene*—the reverse of the idealised visions and dreams of the courtly poetry—and the simple rural comedies, *The Wyf of Auchtirmwchty* and *The Wowing of Jok and Jynny*. Like Bannatyne, I would wish to assign also to this class such *double entendre* pieces as Kennedy's *Against Mouth Thankles* (*Bann. MS* 268a, *Maitl. F.* cxxxi), Dunbar's 'Madam, зour men said thai wald ryd', Balnavis' 'O gallandis all', and Robert Sempill's poems on Margret Fleming (*Bann. MS* 123a) and on Jonet Reid (*Bann. MS* 125b).

One must also include here a group of what are superficially highly unrealistic poems, such as *The Droichis Part of the Play*, the *Ballad of Kynd Kittok*, *The Gyrecarling*, *King Berdok* and Lichtoun's *Dreme*—poems, that is, of burlesque and whimsy, which mingle parody of the more far-fetched romances of love and derring-do, mockery of the more preposterous elements of popular folklore (giants, fairies and witches), and a more or less persistent lacing of deliberate nonsense by self-contradictory or merely preposterous statement. But the main point of these poems is to bring all this fantasy down to earth by associating it with the homeliest and most domestic of persons, settings and objects. And they are stylistically of a kind with the other poems of this class.

Many of these poems have approximate antecedents in Middle English: such as the northern alliterative *Tournament of Tottenham* for the mock-tournaments and the small-town fracas poems, Chaucer's *Sir Thopas* for the romance parodies, and Chaucer's, Lydgate's and Hoccleve's passages and poems of personal abuse for the poems of vituperation. But in their language and diction (see sections 8, 9 and 10) these are the most distinctively Scottish among all the kinds of Older Scots poetry, as also are many individual poems in the parochialism or domesticity of their allusions.

In their choice of metres also, the poems of this class have little in common with the courtly verse or with the instructive verse which most nearly resembles it metrically and stylistically. There is a little comic verse, such as Lichtoun's *Dreme*, in heroic couplets, a metre shared with some poems, such as Douglas's *Aeneid* translation, which we might wish to assign to the 'elaborate narrative' class; and Dunbar and Kennedy's *Flyting* is mainly in pentameter lines arranged in a stanza of 'Chaucerian' type. Otherwise the low-life and comic poetry entirely eschews rhyme royal and other 'Chaucerian' stanza-forms characteristic of courtly verse.

The types of verse-line found in this class of poetry range from 'regular' alliterative long lines, e.g. in *Kynd Kittok* or *The Nyne Ordour of Knavis* (*Bann. MS* 157b), through variants of the alliterative long line (by various 'irregular' combinations of first half-line and second half-line types) in some of the speeches of the Pauper and John the Commonweal in Lyndsay's *Satyre* (but we might rather wish to assign these to the following class (viii) of poetic kinds) or in Sempill's 'Crissell Sandelandis' (*Bann. MS* 124a) or in *King Berdok* or in the 'Skeltonics' (which arguably originated with the Scottish poets) of *Colkelbie Sow* and *Lord Fergus' Gaist*, to iambic tetrameters (i.e. 'octosyllabics'), perhaps the commonest line of all, and also trimeters and dimeters, as well as (as we have seen) pentameters.

These various options combine into a varied gamut of stanzas, some but not all of which are to be found earlier in Middle English (mostly non-Chaucerian) poetry: simple couplet and quatrain arrangements of tetrameter lines or the elaboration of the latter in the stanza of *The Wyf of Auchtirmwchty* and Sempill's 'Margret Fleming', and similar arrangements of alliterative lines; tetrameters and trimeters arranged in six- or eight-line tail-rhyme stanzas in a number of poems of this class, or in the linked quatrains of the *Peblis to the Play* stanza; another favourite stanza combines dimeters and trimeters as in Balnavis' 'O gallandis all' and Sempill's 'Jonet Reid'; and there is the regular 'Scottish' alliterative stanza of *Sum Practysis of Medecyne* and its doggerelised variants (for motives of parody, most likely) of *The Gyrecarling* and *Kynd Kittok*.

So strikingly different are these patterns from the staid pentameter stanzas of 'Chaucerian' verse that in Lyndsay's *Satyre* the speeches of the comic and low-life characters stand out at a glance from those of the grand and serious personages. On examination they also prove to differ in content and style in the ways described elsewhere in this essay.

Some of the typical stylistic features of this group of poems (see sections 8 and 9 below) are shared by many incidental 'low-life', and also horrific, passages within other poems, whether comic or not: these are commented on in section 11 below.

(viii) *Verse of denunciation, protestation and petition* for reform or reward, including the poems entitled in original editions and/or by modern editors, 'complaints', 'supplications', remonstrances', 'petitions'. Such are the poems by Dunbar and Lyndsay so entitled, Douglas's Prologue to *Eneados* VIII, pieces or passages of denunciation of critics and sceptics, and many of Bannatyne's 'ballads' of 'remedy', 'contempt' and 'reproche' in the latter half of the fourth part of his book. Most of these are in tetrameter lines in couplets or simple stanzas, or in other 'non-Chaucerian' metres. They are comparatively simple in syntax, and employ a vernacular diction: one less densely northern and Scottish than that of the flytings and other personal invectives, but equally low in Latination and almost devoid of anglicised forms. This is a style which approximates to that of low-life verse.

(ix) The small body of more or less *realistic nature verse,* namely Henryson's description of the seasons and the countryside in *The Preaching of the Swallow* and his brief winter setting of *The Testament of Cresseid,* and the winter scene of Douglas's Prologue to *Eneados* VII. These are virtually free of clichés like those which make up the stereotyped summer-morning descriptions—the *descriptiones loci amoeni*—noticed above as part of the courtly verse gamut. But by the time of Lyndsay (Prologue to the *Dreme*) and Rolland (*Court of Venus* I. 1 ff.) the winter passages too had become stereotyped in descriptive detail and diction (see sections 6 and 7). In the summer descriptions of Prologues XII and XIII of Douglas's *Eneados,* realistic description in country-life terminology is commingled with the conventional rhetoric, imagery and diction of the *locus amoenus* descriptions of courtly verse. Lyndsay similarly laces the winter description of the Prologue to his *Dreme* with *locus amoenus* formulae and diction, ostensibly by way of contrastive reminiscence, as in:

> Oursylit ar with cloudis odious
> The goldin skyis of the orient
> (lines 106-7).

The syntax of these pieces resembles that of the simple narrative verse, and they employ a predominantly, though not exclusively, unpretentious vernacular vocabulary adapted to their particular subject-matter.

The narrative modes and the low-life verse include a considerable amount of more or less realistic dialogue in a level of style not far removed from that of the narrative itself.

I dare say this scheme will accommodate virtually all surviving Older Scots verse down to the reign of James VI, no doubt with some give and take for particular pieces or some hesitation between adjacent categories for others. The various modes, too, have their parodies, such as Dunbar's *Dregy* or his 'Lucina schynning in silence of the nicht'.

A few longer poems, such as Barbour's *Brus* or *Golagros and Gawane,* and many shorter ones, are almost throughout consistent examples of single modes.

Other longer poems, however, are modal medleys with identifiably different verse-kinds succeeding one another by abrupt transitions of style and often of metre (since as we have noted, the various modes each have their preferred verse-forms): such as Holland's *Howlat*, all three of Henryson's major works, *Colkelbie Sow*, *Lancelot of the Laik*, Douglas's *Palice of Honour*, Dunbar's *The Tua Mariit Wemen*, Lyndsay's *Ane Satyre of the Thrie Estaitis*, Rolland's *The Court of Venus* and his *Sevin Seages*.

Many poems or passages which are chiefly of a single mode and in a single manner are not wholly consistently so. The categories are not stylistically watertight; none has an exclusive monopoly of its salient stylistic features. Rhetorical colours and amene diction (sections 4-7 below) are to be met in kinds other than the courtly, albeit in less profusion. In particular, descriptions of heaven or paradise in discursive or narrative verse naturally attract the language, diction and rhetoric most characteristic of courtly verse: for example, Adam and Eve in Paradise in Lyndsay's *Monarche* 785 ff.; an address to a noble patron calls for the grand style of courtly panegyric as at the 'Epistil' to Lyndsay's *The Testament of the Papyngo*; and conversely, mentions of Hell or of horrible and fearsome matters are accompanied by diction and phonaesthetic effects like those of low-life verse and other anti-aureate verse (see further section 11 below). The most densely Latinate kinds of verse (section 6) are the solemn discursive and the courtly; but occasional Latinate expressions occur in virtually all other kinds of verse, the low-life narrative pieces only excepted: this is true even of Dunbar and Kennedy's and others' flytings (see further p. 43 below), since the authors of these are to be taken as educated persons. Equally, although items of heroic (narrative) diction, such as *berne* or *wy* (man, person), or *brand* (sword), are most often found in simple and alliterative narrative verse, and, less regularly, other verse of the more vernacular kinds, there are none-theless also stray occurrences of these items in courtly and didactic or mock-courtly works such as *The Quare of Jelosy* (line 256) or Dunbar's 'Lucina schynning' (line 43). Some similar strayings out of context of l-vocalised and other reduced forms most characteristic of low-life verse are mentioned in section 9.

2 *Anglicised forms*

Anglicised forms—forms imitated from southern English usage where, but not in Scots, they are regular, the typical features of the poems which C D Jeffery calls 'Anglo-Scots' (Jeffery 1978, 1981)—occur as options with corresponding 'native' (northern or Scottish) equivalents in poems of every kind but for the following exceptions: in low-life verse (all but Part I of *Colkelbie Sow*), one alliterative poem (*Rauf Coilʒear*) and a number of early couplet narrative poems (Barbour, the *Legends of Saints*, Wyntoun, the Asloan *Sevyne Sagis,* the *Prestis of Peblis*), anglicised forms are all but absent. These restrictions in their distribution seem securely to identify anglicised forms as literary, non-Scottish, non-vernacular.

In only one of the poems in which they occur at all frequently do most or all of the anglicised forms appear to be non- (or rather post-) authorial. It seems that the quite copious (and not wholly coincident) anglicisations of the two texts of the *Scottish Troy-book* are most or all of them post-authorial (McIntosh 1979 takes a somewhat different view). At least, there is only one anglicised rhyme in the poem which when restored to a Scottish form is impossible to a poem like Barbour's *Brus* in ordinary Early Scots (for example, when one re-places the text's *mo* (for 'make'): *two,* at *Troy-book.* II. 421-2, by normal Early Scots *ma: twa*); the one exception is *slo* ('slay'): *þo* ('then') at II. 2597-8, which looks like a genuine piece of authorial anglicisation. The motive for these anglicisations may have been so that the surviving Scots texts, used to plug gaps in versions of Lydgate's *Troy-book*, should not look too incongruously northern there. They include 'hyper-anglicisms' (see p. 30 below) like *o* (for the indefinite article *a*), *mok* (for *make*), *spok* (for *spake* 'spoke'), *tone* (for *tane* 'taken') and, as we have seen, *mo* (for *ma* 'make'), the southern Middle English form *hem(e)* (for 'them', Sc. *thaim*) otherwise unrecorded in Older Scots, and many other anglicised forms (McIntosh 1979: espec. 13 and 17 n. 2).

In other poems also it is certain that copyists have replaced non-anglicised forms of their original with anglicised ones in their copy—for idiosyncratic or stylistic reasons—and conversely. But it is also true that in every poem which is at all Anglo-Scots, some and often most of the anglicised forms are likely to be authorial. This is evident from the fairly frequent rhymes which will chime only if one of the rhyme-words has the anglicised form (such as *more* or *sore* (Scots *mare* and *sare*) rhyming with, say, *before* or *thairfore,* very frequent in the *Wallace*), or only if one rhyme-word has the distinctively northern or Scottish form and the other the anglicised form (rhymes between (Scots) *glore* and (anglicised) *sore* (e.g. in Dunbar's *Ballat of our Lady*) or (Scots) *donk* and (anglicised) *ronk, bonk, thonk* (Dunbar's *The Goldyn Targe* 93 f.), are of this sort). Sometimes, too, verse-lines demand 'anglicised' inflected verb-forms in *-in* (see pp. 28-9 below) to complete their syllable counts. All of these imply authorial intention.

The different types of anglicised forms are distributed through the Anglo-Scots canon along an 'implicational scale'. The least anglicised poems of all—the early narratives in octosyllabic couplets, namely Barbour, the *Legends of Saints,* Wyntoun, the underlying original of the *Scottish Troy-book,* and the Arbuthnot *Buke of Alexander,* confine their anglicisations to forms such as *one, allone* rhyming with personal names such as *Jhon, Sampsone, Babilone,* and *go* with *Nero, Cupido;* indeed, Barbour offers in all one single example of this, *Jhone: ilkone* (XI. 382, in MS C; MS E has *Jhane: ilkane*). (The form *more* (as against the apparently more regular Scots *mare*), confirmed in rhyme in the same works, has a different explanation as a 'genuine' Scots form, analogous to *lord:* see DOST s.v.).

Almost all the rest of Older Scots verse, other than the exceptions mentioned

at the beginning of this section, employ a much more extensive range of these
'o for a forms'—those words spelled with ⟨o⟩ (or sometimes ⟨oi⟩ etc.) after
southern English forms in o, where the corresponding native Scots word is
spelled ⟨a⟩ (or ⟨ai⟩ etc.) and (in Middle and Modern Scots) pronounced with
the /e/ phoneme: as *quho* for *quha* ('who'), *fro* for *fra* ('from'), *go* and *gone*
for *ga* and *gane*, *one* for *ane* ('one alone', also, as a 'hyper-anglicism', see
below, 'a'), *allone* for *allane*, *anone* for *onane*, *none* for *nane*, *more* for *mare*,
moste for *maste*, *maist*, as well as *bold* for *bald*, *bauld*, *cold* for *cald*, *cauld*, etc.
As we noted above, such forms as these occur frequently in rhyme with, on the
one hand, exclusively northern or Scottish words such as *glore* ('glory'), *schore*
('menace') as well as, on the other, words common to southern English and
Scots ('common British' forms) such as *ho* ('cessation') *expone*, *dispone*,
before, *thairfore*, *ost* ('army'), *bost*, *frost*, *gold*, *fold* and *mold* (both 'earth', in
the tags *on fold* or *on mold*), anglicisms of other types such as *ago*, *tho* ('then'),
forlore ('forlorn, lost'), proper names such as *Jhone* or *Cupido*, and Latin tags
such as *in verbo regio*.

Both throughout the Anglo-Scots canon and even, for two common words,
no and *so*, in those pieces which otherwise eschew anglicised forms, o for a
forms are common *within* the verse-line; in this case we can of course only
surmise whether the choice of the ⟨o⟩ rather than the ⟨a⟩ spelling is the
copyist's or his original's. Within the Anglo-Scots canon itself, they are also
everywhere a regular option in rhyme, varying with native Scottish forms as the
rhyme requirements dictate: in Cresseid's Complaynt in Henryson's *Cresseid*
(lines 407 ff.), we have, on the one hand, (native) *evermair* and *sair* rhyming
with 'common British' *cair* ('sorrow'), *bair* ('bare') and *wer* (past tense of 'to
be'), the three last offering no ⟨o⟩ options; on the other hand, we encounter
(anglicised) *so* and *stro* (Scots *stra* 'straw') rhyming with *tho* and *ago*, and also,
elsewhere in the poem, *moir* rhyming with *befoir* and *thairfoir*.

A large part of the Anglo-Scots canon—poems of the plain narrative mode
such as the *Wallace* and the Asloan MS *Sevyne Sagis*, alliterative narrative such
as the *Howlat* and *Golagros and Gawane*, elaborate narrative such as most of
Henryson, almost all of the didactic and lyric verse such as Dunbar's 'Quhome
to sall I complene my wo' (No. 63 in Kinsley's edition)—confine their
anglicisation to this o for a feature, and in the stylistically more vernacular of
these (those first mentioned, that is) apparently solely as a rhyming
convenience.

Dunbar's and Lyndsay's courtly poems or passages (and Cresseid's
'Complaint' in Henryson's *Testament of Cresseid*), as well as the still more
anglicised pieces mentioned below, add to this several other anglicisation
features. One of these serves also as a valuable rhyme-extending facility,
namely, those forms which add to a verb-stem ending in a vowel the inflection
-*n*, in imitation of the midland and southern Middle English -*en* ending of the
infinitive and the plural present indicative: forms such as *bene* or *beyn*, *seyn*,

sayn for *be*, *se* and *say*, and also, more rarely, *fleyn* for *fley* ('flie'), *leyn* for *le* ('lie'), and *gane* for *ga* ('go'). Examples of this abound in the poems specified, for example in Dunbar's *The Goldyn Targe*, where *bene* ('be' or 'are') and *sene* ('see') rhyme with *amene*, *grene*, *quene*, *schene* etc. Rather more rarely, and this time not as a rule in rhyme, the same poets employ in the same works present indicative verbs inflected in *-ith* (after southern Middle English present tense verbs with *-eth* in the third person singular, and, in some dialects, the plural). In both these instances the Scots poets not infrequently blunder in employing these inflections in persons and numbers which contravene the rules of southern Middle English grammar (e.g. in the first person singular): the Middle Scots poets were less accurate in their imitations of southern usage than a modern philologist might be.

These authors also make use in the same poems of a range of periphrastic constructions with the auxiliary *do*, often or always apparently as a mere metrical convenience (to gain a syllable—stressed or unstressed—and/or to shift the main verb stem into the rhyme position). Some of these constructions are peculiar to Scots, but it is at least a tenable theory that the practice of using *do* periphrastically in these ways has an 'anglicised' origin. There are seven examples in the six stanzas beginning at line 22 of Dunbar's *The Thrissill and the Rois*, such as:

> The lork hes done the mirry day proclame (line 24)
>
> Doing all sable fro the hevynnis chace (line 56)

and

> The birdis did with oppin vocis cry (line 59).

In the same poems we encounter also the repertory of 'Chaucerian' words, borrowed from the English poems of Chaucer, Lydgate and others, and met with in Scots chiefly or only in elaborate narrative and courtly poetry: *frome* (Scots *fra*, 'anglicised' *fro*), *lyte* (Scots *litill*), *morrow* (Scots *morn* or *morning*), *morrowing* (ditto), *tho* (Scots *than*), and *twane* (Scots *twa*). When in *The Thrissill and the Rois* we meet:

> . . . Haill Rois both red and quhyt
> Most plesand flour of michty collouris twane
> (lines 171-2)

and

> And thus I wret as ye haif hard to-forrow
> Off lusty May upone the nynte morrow
> (lines 188-9),

twane and *morrow* (as well as the *o* for *a* forms *both* and *most*) mark these as 'Chaucerian' lines. Commonly associated with these items are the 'native Scots' words *garth* and *to-forrow* and other items of 'consecrated diction' and

'embalmed phrases' discussed in section 7 below. Bannatyne's text of Dunbar's
The Thrissill and the Rois includes one apparent 'hyper-anglicism' (a form
which does not exist in southern English but might have been supposed to do
so on the analogy of regular southern English/Scots correspondences) in *lork*
('lark') (line 24). Lyndsay's printer John Scot (or Lyndsay himself) has another
in *one* for the indefinite article *ane*, in *The Testament of the Papyngo* and the
Monarche (*one* for the *numeral ane* is, conversely, a regular '*o* for *a*' anglicism).
But *o* for the other form of the indefinite article *a* is, however, apparently
confined to the still more thoroughly anglicised *Troy-book* (see p. 27 above),
Colkelbie Sow, *Lancelot* and *The Quare of Jelosy*.

An extensive range of anglicised forms is displayed in *Colkelbie Sow*,
including, in addition to forms already mentioned, *mich* ('much', Scots *mekil*
etc.), *quich(e)* or *quhich* (Scots *quhilk*), and a number of examples of the fem.
pron. *sche* (the only form in rhyme; *scho* occurs as a non-rhyming variant). A
somewhat similar range of anglicised forms is that of a poem very different in
all other respects, *The Kingis Quair*.

The most thoroughly anglicised of all Anglo-Scots poems are two poems
which alternate the elaborate narrative, courtly and discursive modes, *The
Quare of Jelosy* and *Lancelot of the Laik*. To the anglicised forms found in all
other Anglo-Scots poetry, these poems add still others: including *sich* or *such*
(Scots *swilk* or *sic*), *azhane* (Scots *again*), *schall* (Scots *sall*), *shude* (Scots *suld*),
stant (*standis*), the 'hyper-anglicisms' *to* and *tone* (*take* or *ta*, *taken* or *tane*),
mo (*make* or *ma*), *lowe* (*law*: *Quare Jel.* 63), *yf* for *gif* (*give*), as well as both *o*
and *one* indefinite article (on which see above); frequent, though optional, use
of the infinitive and present tense inflection *-in* or *-ing* (also *-en*), which thus
supplies, as needed, an additional unstressed syllable (imitated, like the *-n*
ending on vowel-final stems, from the Middle English inflection *-en* in Chaucer
and other Middle English writers), ('No lady . . . That schall thar for hyme
hating or dispis': *Lanc.* 133, or 'Set oft tyme thai contenyng gret effece', ibid.
140, or, 'To gladin hir and plesyn . . . with thair chere', *Quare Jel.* 129); and
uninflected past participles with or without the prefix *i-*, *y-*, as *y-grave* (*Lanc.*
1798), *iclosit* (ibid. 53), *stond* (ibid. 2029), *y-fret* (*Quare Jel.* 548), *ymurderit*
and yslawe (ibid. 174), (likewise imitated from southern Middle English
usage). The only uninflected past participle at all widespread in Scots sources
(not however in the most vernacular texts) is *forlore* (Scots *forlorin*, 'forlorn,
lost'). Otherwise forms of this sort are confined to this group of ultra-anglicised
poems and to Gavin Douglas.

For most of his canon, with the Prologue to *Eneados* VIII as a notable
exception, Gavin Douglas anglicises much as do Henryson and Dunbar rather
than as do the authors of *The Quare of Jelosy* and *Lancelot*. But he does also
make free and constant recourse to the verb-forms just described, as, for
example, *behaldyn* in 'And frely may behaldyn and espy Tha lakis quhilkis
thame langis to vissy', *Eneados* VI v 73–4; and past participles such as *schaw*

(Scots *schawin*), *ytak* (Scots *taken* or *tane*), *ybe* (Scots *bene*), occur *passim* (see further Bawcutt 1976: 144-5). And he does have instances of the feminine personal pronoun form *sche* (Scots more regularly *scho*) in rhyme, e.g. at *Eneados* XI xi 136.

Without doubt all of these anglicised forms result from an original impetus by Scots poets in the relevant modes to be at one with, imitate and adapt from, in spelling and morphology as in other respects, the English masters whom they so admired and extolled and imitated in other ways (see pp. 22-3), as well as to benefit from the additional rhyming and metrical resources these practices provided. In these imitations they were adapting not so much to the appearance of England-derived manuscripts and prints as to the partially Scotticised Scots copies of the English classics with which they were doubtless more familiar (such as those in Selden B 24, the Asloan MS and the Chepman and Myllar prints). Nor, as we have seen, were they concerned that their imitations should be philologically perfect.

3 Syntax

No variety of Older Scots verse compares for average syntactic complexity with the most syntactically elaborate kinds of prose—the sustained orations in Bellenden's and the Mar Lodge translations of Boece and similar works. But, though of course no kind of poetry has a monopoly of either syntactically complex or syntactically simple sentences, it is a reasonable generalisation that a much higher frequency of complex structures displaying much hypotaxis (i.e. in which the noun-phrase and verb-phrase elements of sentences are modified by words, phrases and clauses) is a normal concomitant of the less vernacular styles, and so is often found in courtly verse (witness, for example, the two opening stanzas of Dunbar's *The Thrissill and the Rois*, which make up what may be analysed as a single sentence through a number of dependent constructions) and didactic or discursive verse (such as *The Contemplacioun of Synnaris*). Equally, it is these less vernacular kinds of prose and verse which more often overtly state the connections between principal statements by dependent phrases or clauses (as 'Quhen this was said, depairtit scho, this quene', Dunbar, *The Thrissill and the Rois* 43) rather than simply imply these by the ordering of statements.

The converse of this could be described as a non-hypotactic syntax favouring simple sentences in parataxis, or co-ordinated by the emptiest connectives, displaying little dependency and modification except what is grammatically obligatory, and with frequent asyndeton (omission of conjunctions of co-ordination and subordination and of relative pronouns, and some other types of ellipsis) and occasional parenthesis. While obviously there is no kind of verse writing which remains consistently at this extreme of baldness, it is towards this pole that the more vernacular kinds of poetry incline—simple narrative and 'oral narrative' verse. (For a much fuller treatment of grammatical tendencies of these sorts in Older Scots writings, see Aitken 1978; and for an account of stylistic variation in the choice of various alternative forms of the relative construction, see Romaine 1982: 166–7.) A cumulation of vocative nounphrases simply in apposition or minimally linked is a natural feature of passages of personal abuse, such as occupy large chunks of Dunbar and Kennedy's *Flyting*.

Asyndeton, including prosiopesis (ellipsis from the sentence of initial words of low information content), and parataxis are common also in the alliterative narrative verse such as Holland's *Howlat* (for example at lines 497 ff.). But the ultimate extreme of a paratactic, asyndetic syntax, with frequent prosiopesis, of quite minimal complexity of sentence-structure, and eschewing overt sentence-linkers, is sustained with high consistency in the narrative of Hary's *Wallace*.

Whereas courtly verse favours as the periphrastic narrative tense of verbs that formed with the auxiliary *did* (cf. p. 29 above), the construction with the auxiliaries *gan, can, couth, coud* (normally, except in the highly 'Chaucerian' or Anglo-Scots *Lancelot*, without *to*) is highly characteristic of the several narrative modes: 'Thay fand the toun and in blythlie couth gang', Henryson, *Fables* 259; 'scho tuke her leif and furth can ga', ibid. 353.

4   Colours of rhetoric

Although most other kinds of Older Scots verse, including simple and alliterative narrative, contain incidental passages of rhetorical display (such as Barbour's celebrated 'Ah! fredome' passage in his Book I), sustained and concentrated use of the stylistic artifices then apparently known as 'colours of rhetoric' (DOST s.v. *Colour* 4) is strikingly a feature of courtly verse, particularly its set-piece stylistic climaxes. 'Colours of rhetoric' ('rethorik colouris fine', Douglas, *Palice of Honour* 819) was, it seems, the designation of the figures of speech listed, named and prescribed in the classical and medieval treatises on poetic or rhetoric (see e.g. Atkins 1943: 200–4, Murphy 1974: 365–74) as supplying elegant 'amplification'. These include elaborate periphrastic metaphors, pathetic fallacies, apostrophes, exclamations and rhetorical questions, the device of paraleipsis (more usually called then *occupatio* or *occultatio*), whereby something is narrated or described under the guise of not doing so (notable examples, among many others, are the long series of these at *Lancelot* 209–298); various repetitive devices, namely, *expolitio* or elaboration, *interpretatio* or repetition of a statement in different words, *repetitio* (i.e. anaphora) or repetition of the same word at the beginning of separate phrases, clauses and sentences, and various other kinds of verbal repetition; and numerous other figures of speech including antithesis and hyperbaton, and, see p. 37, *pronominatio* or antonomasia. Passages copious in these figures are commonly arranged in elaborate syntactical patterns, involving the balancing or repeating of syntactical structures in half-lines, juxtaposed lines, stanzas and successive stanzas—a further addition to the tropes and figures specified in the treatises.

Among the most concentrated displays of these artifices in Older Scots verse, or indeed anywhere, are those in Dunbar's *The Goldyn Targe*, earlier in the Middle Scots period, and Patrick Hume's *Promine*, later; but their profuse occurrence is simply a regular feature of the courtly kind (for their copious use by Douglas see Bawcutt 1967: xlvi–xlviii, and 1976: 57 and 63–4). All of this appears solemnly done, with, unlike Chaucer on occasion, no hint of tongue in cheek.

Concentrated and sustained use of rhetorical colours are conversely not a feature of low-life verse, or, except in isolated passages, of the other kinds of verse in mainly vernacular diction. The simple devices favoured in oral folk-tale and also in low-life verse, some of which, I have suggested, is self-consciously in a folk-tale style (Aitken 1978: 103 ff.), only partly overlap with the gamut of high-style colours. Repetition, simultaneously verbal and of content, is not uncommon in some poems, though not as a rule sustained beyond a single re-statement. But the other devices characteristic of the 'rhetoric' of low-life verse—litotes, certain types of word-order inversion, frequent recourse to the narrative present tense—seem not to be common in courtly verse or other solemn kinds of verse.

5   Unvernacular word-choice of dignified verse

In its diction as in other respects, courtly verse is literary and fairly slavishly derivative from earlier exemplars in the same or similar kinds in Scots and, more especially, in southern English. In direct opposition to low-life verse and, to a lesser degree, the other kinds freely resorting to vernacular diction, it is by intention unvernacular, deriving from literary rather than spoken tradition, directed towards elegant and ornamental expression free from the banal associations of daily speech. So this kind of verse, in particular, and also other sorts of non-narrative serious verse, the instructive and the lyric, are notable as displaying very low incidences of northern or peculiarly Scottish words, which evidently were avoided as inelegant or barbarous. The 189 lines of Dunbar's *The Thrissill and the Rois*, which is not untypical of its kind, contain, by my reckoning, only seven more or less exclusively Scottish or northern words, if one includes the onomatopoeic hapax legomenon *swirk* v., the legal *compeir* v. and the poetic (especially courtly poetic) *garth* n. and *to-forrow* adv., as well as *cluvis* (paws), *dully*, and *skaith*. Even those few northernisms which do occur in this sort of poem are clustered within the brief anti-aureate passages which intentionally point up the typical courtly style by contrast (see further section 11).

6   Courtly diction: Latinate

The unvernacular character of courtly and other non-narrative serious verse results not only from the avoidance of lexical northernisms, but also from the frequent employment of many comparatively recent word-borrowings of Latin and French origin, here designated Latinisms and Gallicisms, the two together being called Latinate diction. These are presumably an important if not the sole constituent of the body of 'heich, pithie and learnit wordis' which James VI recommended for 'ane heich and learnit purpose' in his *Ane Schort Treatise conteining some Revlis and cautelis to be obseruit and eschewit in Scottish Poesie* (hereafter '*Revlis and Cautelis*)' (James VI, *Poems* I. 75). Both as types and as tokens, loanwords of this sort are common in English and Scots by the fifteenth century: Ellenberger counts 830 Latinisms as types contributing 2352 tokens out of a total of (my own conjecture) around 40,000 tokens *in toto* in the Dunbar canon, and the figures for Henryson are similar (Ellenberger 1977: 22); and the Gallicisms mentioned below would doubtless supply at least as many types and tokens again. These words had begun to appear in English in some numbers quite early in the thirteenth century. But the great majority were more recent adoptions and most of those most favoured by our poets date from Chaucer's time onwards, including not a few (over 85 for Henryson and Dunbar according to Ellenberger 1977: 150) which first appear in the Scottish poets' work itself.

Both referentially and morphologically these words were restricted in range. Almost all of them refer to the less basic and general notions in their particular semantic fields: according to Ellenberger (1977: 49) Dunbar's kinship and family terms from this source consist of four items, *genetrice*, *matern*, *matremony*, *successioun*. Whereas French supplied a few conjunctions and prepositions—*except*, *maugré*, *suppose* and others—the Latinisms are exclusively words of semantic weight—nouns (predominantly), adjectives (forming adverbs by native word-formation) and verbs. Though they include a few mono- and disyllabic non-derived forms consisting of the Latin stems only, such as *dulce*, *glore*, *laud*, *sanct*, *trone*, *vult*, *favour*, *defend*, *propone*, *promit*, and a few unchanged Latinisms such as *dirige*, *limbus*, *requiem*, the overwhelming majority are polysyllabic derived forms, displaying the (limited range of) Latin derivational prefixes and suffixes: *com-*, *con-*, *pre-*, *pro-*, etc., and *-abill*, *-all*, *-ance*, *-at*, *-ence*, *-ent*, *-ene*, *-ine*, *-ive*, *-ioun*, *-atioun*, *-ude*, *-our*, *-ment*, etc.

For the most part (an exception is *-at*, F *-é*, as in *ornat*, MF *orné*), these conform to the French rather than the Latin morphological shape (whether or not the corresponding word is actually recorded in MF; generally it is): with, e.g., such suffixes as *-ance* (F *-ance*, L *-antia*), *-ité* (F *-ité*, L *-itas*, *-itātem*), *-ioun* (F *-ioun*, L *-io*, *-iōnem*), etc. It is usually impossible to tell, and scarcely seems to matter, whether it was the existence of a French or a Latin etymon or just the availability of the pattern which instigated the 'borrowing' of any particular item. Perhaps, as Ellenberger argues (1974), more often than not it was Latin.

It seems convenient, in any case, to dub such items 'Latinisms' and to associate with them, as sharing much the same stylistic distributions and connotations, those other items of more or less similar morphological shape, with or without cognates in Latin itself, whose origins are more indubitably Old or Middle French. These 'Gallicisms' include a number of nouns with the suffix -*age* (F -*age*, L -*aticum*, a kind of converse case to that of -*at* above), such as *curage, langage, umbrage, vassalage, visage*. Some words of this sort exist alongside cognates directly (and usually more recently) derived from Latin, like *delit* and *delitabill* beside *delectabill*, *pennance* beside *penitence*, *riall* beside *regall*; and others such as *jugement, penetrive, plesance*.

Doubtless most of both these kinds of words—Latinisms and Gallicisms both—remained markedly literary in their provenance and connotations. They occur only sparsely in the more colloquial kinds of writing (such as low-life verse), but they are profuse in the instructive verse and only less so in most of the courtly verse (with Rolland's *Court of Venus* as perhaps the most Latinate work of all), as well as in all the more literary registers of prose (see Ellenberger 1977: 70 for some frequencies in different kinds of writing). Though this can scarcely have been true of all of them, it is likely that many of these words remained unfamiliar to uneducated persons—the *lewit* or *landwart* or *uplandis* persons with whom the poets pretended with obvious insincerity to class themselves in the modesty passages. Ability to use them freely and comprehend them marked one as a member of the élitist in-group of cultivated persons. In addition, many such words were marked apart from the unlearned vernacular by their morphological forms—the Latin or French derivational prefixes and suffixes and their polysyllabicity. These properties, as well as what possibilities they offered of a range of reference beyond that of their vernacular 'equivalents', helped no doubt to commend them to authors of dignified or pretentious verse, no less than the rhyming convenience which was presented by their limited range of suffixes. In such ways they maintained the dignity of overtone which they had, no doubt, originally derived from their literary and learned beginnings.

So it is unsurprising to find the rhetorical and pretentious courtly verse, especially in its most rhetorical and pretentious passages, employing these words on principle whenever they are available. So in the opening passage of Dunbar's *The Goldyn Targe matutyne* has preference over *morning*, *mansuetude* over *mekenes*, *revest* over *clethit*, *apparalit* over *graithit*, etc. Similarly, Dunbar's *The Thrissill and the Rois*, not the most Latinate of its class, averages a Latinate word every second line or so.

In addition to the general body of Latinate words which are common to the courtly poems and other Latinate kinds of writing (such as didactic verse and prose), the authors of the courtly poems also possessed a special and restricted stock of highly recurrent Latinate expressions, predominantly epithets, belonging to a limited range of semantic fields, on which they drew copiously and repetitively for their conventional set pieces, the *locus amoenus* descriptions, panegyrics, and pseudo-critical passages in praise of the masters of poesy, all three of these sharing this body of diction largely in common. Common Latinisms in this diction are: *angelicall, aurorall, celestiall, celicall*, *etheriall, imperiall, nocturnall, palestrall, regall, terrestriall, triumphall, virginall; incomparable; aureat, deificat, laureat, mellifluat, ornat, purpurat; clarifeit, depurit, poleit, sugurit; eloquent, eloquence, indeficient, orient, redolent, redolence, resplendent, radiant, radiance, reverend, reverence; precellent* or *precelling, preclare; illustir; glorious, radious; cristalline, divine, matutine; regine, rosine; nutritive, restorative; amene, dulce, facound; rethor, rethorik; celsitude, mansuetude, pulchritude; dyademe, paradice; habitakle, signakle; lucern, matern, supern; odour, vapour; clarify, decore, illumine, compile.* Accompanying these are such Gallicisms (mostly di- or polysyllabic), out of courtly medieval French literature, including that of the *Grands Rhétoriqueurs* (on which see e.g. Bawcutt 1967: xxxv–xxxvi), but mostly mediated by the Middle English courtly poets, and equally favoured for Middle Scots courtly set pieces, as *bening, gentil, depaynt, plesant, plesance, polist, tendir, nobill, riall; countenance, portrature; chevallere, genetrice, imperatrice, victrice, salvatrice; chevalrie, gentillesse, gentrise, prowes, richesse; grace, mercy, glore, glorie; liquour, ordour; fluris, flurist, annamalit, annamaling, attemperit, reconfort, revest, endyte.*

These words possessed, to an enhanced degree, the properties of Latinate vocabulary generally. Like the latter, their value included the addition they made to the stock of rhyme-words, specially valuable in the complex inter-rhyming stanzas of this kind of poetry. Notable in this are rhymes between the Latinate suffix *-all* and vernacular words, such as *all, small, wall* with the unvocalised form of this sequence, as *all: imperiall: riall: celicall: terrestriall,* Dunbar *Goldyn Targe* 253 ff.; *small: principall, The Thrissill and the Rois* 176–8; etc. This contrasts with rhymes dependent on l-vocalised forms of the same sequence, characteristic of the low-life poetry (see section 9 below).

Even more than the general body of Latinate vocabulary, the Scots poets derive this more restricted and stereotyped body of diction from their chosen poetic mentors; most of all, it appears, from Chaucer and Lydgate. For the opening and closing stanzas of Dunbar's *The Goldyn Targe,* for example, the dictionaries assign first occurrences in English of the following Latinisms and Gallicisms: to Chaucer *desolat, imperiall, laureat, triumph*; to Lydgate *matutine, celicall, aureat, redolent* (and *redolence*); to Chaucer and Lydgate the figurative use of *sugurit*; to Hoccleve *ornat*; to thirteenth-century Middle English *revest*; to fourteenth-century Middle English *annamalit, cristallyne, illumine, rethor, rethorik, riall* (but with Chaucer and Lydgate among their earliest users, Lydgate first with the figurative use of *cristallyne*); to fifteenth-century Middle English *illuminat* p.p., *terrestriall*; to Henryson *mellifluat*; to Dunbar the earliest figurative use of *annamalit.*

Though many of the items we have discussed in this section were metaphors whose original reference was concrete, perhaps only the most classically minded authors and readers may have remained fully aware of this; perhaps they were for most people nearly as opaque then as they are today. This and the refined associations they had from their normal literary and precious contexts no doubt meant that they were less immediate and sensuous in their connotations than their mono- and disyllabic everyday vernacular equivalents, such as *gilt* or *giltin* beside *aureat*, *hony-swete* (roughly) beside *mellifluat*, *brichtin* or *lichtin* beside *illumine*, *swete* beside *dulce*, *swete-smelland* beside *redolent*, etc.

Thus the imposingly erudite character of this vocabulary and its absence of unrefined homely associations made of its free employment a stylistic elegance, appropriate for a genteel kind of poetry, behind which stood an élitist critical theory of what constituted the best literary language. Equally, referring to the sun as Phebus or Titan or Apollo, the moon as Cynthia or Lucina, the dawn as Aurora, the winds as Eolus, the flowers as Flora, and so on, by the variant of the 'colour' of *pronominatio* or antonomasia favoured in this kind of verse, was another means of exoticising the commonplace. Conversely, the typical diction of low-life poetry was employed for exactly the reverse effects (see section 8).

It is the diction just described that modern scholars appear chiefly to recognise as the 'aureate terms' first referred to by the old makars themselves (as 'termes aureat', also 'poleit termis', 'facound wordis', etc.) (see Ellenberger 1977: 82–4). Whether the makars themselves would have wished to restrict the reference of these expressions to this particular element of the grand style, or to take in also, say, rhetorical colours (section 4) and native courtly diction (section 7) seems moot (see further Zetterstein 1979). Nor is it apparent whether they would have wished to embrace under the same label the corresponding, albeit much less extensive, body of diction consecrated to the conventional winter description, which served as an alternative of different mood to the *locus amoenus* setting: including, from Bellenden's *Proheme of the Cosmographe*, Lyndsay's Prologue to the *Dreme* and Rolland's *Court of Venus*, *boreall*, *boustious*, *penetrative* (and *penetrive*), *perturb*, *poleartik*, *pungitive*, *sabill*, *tempest*. (See further Bawcutt 1976: 64–5.)

7 Courtly diction: native

Latinate diction is not the only kind of special diction used in the courtly poetry. Especially, but not solely, in the summer morning *descriptiones loci amoeni*, the poets draw on a traditional, highly poetic and uncolloquial diction which is nevertheless very predominantly of native origin. It is partly for this reason that the courtly poems overall score a little lower for frequency of Latinisms in Ellenberger's estimates (Ellenberger 1977: 77 and 66–9) than do some straightforward moralising poems such as 'Dunbar at Oxinfurd'.

This non-Latinate courtly diction includes a few words more or less exclusive to the favoured *topoi* (in verse) or to serious poetry more generally, and so they may be reckoned as 'poetic diction', namely *besene* ('arrayed'), *garth*, *gent*, *glete*, *gleter*, *hals* v. ('to greet'), *hew* ('hue'), *lake* ('water'), *leme* ('gleam') *meid* ('meadow'), *schene* ('beautiful, fair, bright'), *strand*, *vale*, *weid* ('clothing'), Alongside these words, the same passages constantly draw on a much lengthier list of non-Latinate words of less restricted distribution, which had nevertheless by long tradition out of earlier English poetry—pre-Chaucerian and Chaucerian—become a regular part of the verdant, summery countryside scenes in verse, words such as *balme, balmy, balmyt, bank, beme, beuch, blome, blomyt, blossom, bruke, clere, fair, fleit, fresch, glaid, herb, hevinly, lusty, mirthfull, soft, stannir, swete*; several words in this set refer specifically to the favourite notions of brightness or shining, *beme, gleme, glance, schine, sterne* ('star') in addition to the more exclusively poetic words with similar reference, *glete, leme*, mentioned above; the effect of variegated light and brightness is heightened with a profusion of names (non-Latinate and Latinate) of flowers, jewels and precious stones, of colour or of colours, singly or in decorative lists, such as *flour, flour delyce, garland, lilly, rose; beriall, charbunkill, cristall, emerant, jem, gilt, gold, goldin, perle, ruby, silver, topace; blew, colour, goulis, grene, red, purpur, quhite*; etc. Many of these words conform to the phonaesthetic requirements of these passages (see section 11) and supply suitable rhymes for them. The words which comprise this diction, especially those consecrated to the *descriptio loci amoeni*, were available both as a set of syntactically 'free' items and also as constituents of the traditional 'embalmed phrases' or conventional, much repeated, formulae, of which the favoured descriptive passages were a tissue—the *fair firthis, grene meidis, cristal knoppis, perly droppis, lemand beriall droppis, silvir schouris, mery foulis, mirthfull morowis, Phebus hemis schene, goldin skyis of the orient, blossom upon spray, dewis donk, stanniris clere as sterne*, leaves etc. floating (*fleit* v.) *in balm*, and the rest (for an idea of the highly traditional character of this phraseology, see, for example, the notes to Dunbar's *The Goldyn Targe* in the STS edition).

The panegyric and the pseudo-critical passages share some of this diction. A favourite formula of these passages has as its grammatical head a term for a shining object such as lamp, lantern or star, or the name of a flower (in general, as *flour*, in particular, as *rose, lilly*, etc.) or the name of a jewel, such as *beriall, charbunkill*, etc., *of* (some class of admired things or beings or some admired quality such as *chevalry* or *gentilnes*) in the general sense 'paragon' (of the class or quality). The same imagery too pervades the pseudo-critical discussions of (say) the rose-garden of rhetoric of which the roses etc. have been plucked in advance by the masters of poetry (e.g. Lyndsay, *The Testament of the Papyngo* 57–60; etc.)

The winter scenes too (see p. 25 above) have their more limited body of non-Latinate diction of favoured words and formulae: *blast, donk, daill, sleit, snaw*, and *penetrative air, frostis penetrive, pungitive wedder*, the *boustious blasts* of *austeir Eolus, mystie vapouris, stalwart stormis, Florais dule wede*, Priapus' *gardingis bair* and *stormy weid*.

8 Vernacular diction and vulgarisms of low-life verse

The most obvious thing about the diction of the low-life verse is that it is, quite unlike that of the courtly verse we have mainly been examining in Sections 5, 6 and 7, much the most densely Scottish of any kind of writing in Older Scots. In part, this follows from what these poems are about. Many of them relate how certain grotesque or rustic or working-class characters have preposterously far-fetched or merely farcical adventures or behave in a boorish or clumsy or uninhibited way, and do this in a homely parochial setting amid everyday objects, livestock and fauna. The poems of vituperation specify directly, in a series of insulting invocations, declamations or descriptive narratives, various repulsive or ridiculous personal traits of the person addressed or described. Since these homely or undignified topics were presumably infrequent in most of the English and other literatures known to the Scottish poets, the only known terminology for them was native, local and colloquial.

More or less by definition this was the kind of vocabulary which contained the highest proportion of northernisms, though of course not all of it was exclusively northern. So the only readily available terms for items like *gusis cro* or *hut* or *bowkaill stok* (lines 3 and 6 respectively of *King Berdok*) or, in the low-life interlude in the *Howlat,* the names of the *tuchet* ('lapwing') or the *gowk* ('cuckoo') (*Howlat* line 821) or that familiar character in the medieval Scottish scene, the vagabond *baird* (*Howlat* 822), or *thevisnek* (the lapwing's cry, *Howlat* line 823), were these purely Scottish terms. At the same time it is doubtless also true that the statement itself in these passages was often deliberately contrived so as to get in as many as possible of these northern terms for domestic objects: *King Berdok's* choice of topics seems to illustrate this, for example.

So in vocabulary this sort of poetry aims at being as thoroughly Scottish and vernacular as possible. And this was more than simple necessity, resulting from the nature of the subjects. The intense Scottishness was no doubt sought after because its local and unliterary associations heightened the desirable down-to-earth effect.

As well as these domestic or culturally Scottish terms, and also of course many 'common British' words used in the same passages for the same sorts of things, there is another semantic class of words which, partly because of the nature of their content, is very copiously represented in these poems: words expressing or implying disapproval or hostility or denoting loud noise and violent or ungainly action. Naturally a good many, though again not all, of these, are exclusively Scottish.

In etymology, the characteristic and criterial diction of low-life poetry, as a predominantly Scottish, or northern and Scottish, vernacular diction, comprises long lists of (invariably mono- or disyllabic) words deriving from the following sources. For items of known derivation, one can list (most of the examples following have been taken from Dunbar's *Flyting*) many mainly or exclusively northern words of Anglo-Saxon origin, such as *ble, brat, derch, dreg, modwart, plat* ('a buffet'), *rerde* ('loud noise'), *swaittis, (upon) wry; elriche, haw* adj., *holkit, sweir; flyte, rare, skyte, thraw, threpe, wary;* others again from Scandinavian, as *craig, gate, gett, carling, lisk, lug, mauch, nowt, skeil, smaik, tedder, waith; bla, blaiknit, boun, ug(sum); flyre, host, rame, rowp, rug, skar, skirl, traik; gar;* from Low Dutch, *cute, dok, dub, gek, loun, scaff, swanky;* from (?spoken) Old French, *aver, barret, botine, cummer* (n. = 'gossip, female crony'), *Mahoun, grunʒe, lunʒe, menʒe; bribour* and *bribry, pelour, trumpour; brangill, cummer* v., *skowder, syle;* from Gaelic, *baird, bledoch, cabrach, catherene, cryne, glen;* as well, of course, as many other words of the same origins of more widespread regional distribution, such as *bich, ers, hairt* (also in the sense 'stomach'), *tedder, lowsy, ruch* adj., *pyke* v.; *grisly, mirk, tyke; hobill; carioun, harlot, hurcheoun, graceles, lipper, luge, port* ('appearance, countenance'), *powder, savour,* (the three last in somewhat specialised senses), *nice, prevy, sawsy, hidwis, petwis, defoul,* and the exclamation *fy!*

In addition to such items of known origin, a strikingly large proportion of the words favoured by low-life and flyting verse have been written off by the etymologists as of unknown or uncertain origin. They include for example (again chiefly from Dunbar's *Flyting*), (nouns) *boy, choll, clod, crele, cufe, dowsy, gane, gild, glar* ('mud'), *gully, irle, larbar, limmer, lokman, nagus, rehatour, scarth, skill, skyre, skrumple, smaik, smy, tod, tramort, wirling; ladry, limmery; caribald, haggirbald, haschbald, luschbald; averill, gruntill; bumbard, dastard, dowbart, scutard; duddroun, ladroun, wilroun;* (verbs) *clasch, glowr, goif, gowk, lounge, roy, scale, skirl, swap, ʒoul; hirkill, hirpill, jingill, rattill, wraggill; bikker, clatter, scunner, skomer;* (adjectives) *glunschoch, harth, queir; limmerfull; bony, gend; gowkit, gukkit, glaikit* (all three = 'foolish'); *swappit; skolderit* ('scorched'). It is a reasonable conjecture that many of these are medieval coinages in folk-speech, and indeed the derivations of some can be so conjectured: *limmer* (from *lim(b)*, e.g. of Satan), *scunner* (from the root of *shun* v.), *dowbart* (? *dulbard*, from *dull* adj. + suffix *-bard*, cf. *coward, dastard* and *-bald* as in *caribald* etc.), *gukkit* (? from *guk-guk* the cry of the cuckoo) and *gowkit* (? from *gowk* the name of the cuckoo), *glaikit* (? from *glaik* 'a flitting sunbeam', itself a coinage on the *gl*-phonaestheme as in *gleme, glete, glitter* etc.), *skolderit* (? connected with *scald*, with frequentative suffix). Several nouns and verbs seem to be echoic or onomatopoeic in origin, *clasch, roy, skirl, swap, clatter, rattil.* The frequentative endings *-ill* and *-er* are active in forming verbs of this set. The suffixes *-ard, -bald,* (? and *-bard:* see above), *-roun* and *-it* form abusive descriptive terms (*-bald* and *-roun* virtually restricted to this body of diction in this kind of verse), and *-ry* forms pejorative collective nouns, such as *harlotry, ladry, limmery, lounry.* Some items, as was pointed out above in passing, are simply specialised applications of existing words of already identified (known and unknown) origins.

The flytings and lampoons include many novel abusive compounds—those on the verb-noun pattern of *byt-buttoun*, (perhaps) *crawdoun*, *hurlebehind*, *lik-schilling*, *nipcaik*, *rak-sauch*, others formed on agent-nouns like *girnall-ryvar*, *muttoun-dryvar*, and others of various formations such as *gallow-breid*, *purs-pyke*, *tramort*, *widdefow*, *chitterlilling*, *wallidraggil*.

The literary 'embalmed phrases' of the courtly descriptions are matched in the low-life verse by formulae and proverbial clichés, no doubt out of everyday informal parlance, such as *to lauch one's hairt sair*, *to get one's paikis*, *to mak biggingis bair* or *waistie wanis* ('to impoverish oneself'), *to brek* someone's *gall* ('to break his spirit'), *he had na will to mow*, *it was na mowis*, *the gallowis gaipis* (for someone), *quhat man settis by* (one's adversary)?, *quhat* or *quhare devill?*, (one's adversary or butt is) (some notoriously disreputable individual's) *air*, (to sink in something) *up to the ene* (= 'eyes').

Many of the words and phrases distinctive of the low-life poetry are special in their lexicographical histories (as distinct from their etymologies), appearing fleetingly or intermittently on record. Of those whose origins are known (such as *flyre* and *carling* and *lug* and *smaik* from Scandinavian) a high proportion (*carling* and *lug* and *smaik* in this instance) are unrecorded or all but unrecorded between the source language and their emergence in the low-life Scottish poetry. The same is true of several of the words listed above as of Anglo-Saxon origin, such as *elriche*, *haw*, *plat*, *swaittis*: these remain unrecorded between Old English and their re-emergence in Older (sometimes Middle) Scots. A still higher proportion of the items of unknown origin make their first or almost their first appearance in the Scots poetry. Some of these have a later history in English, though often, as with *lounge*, *queir* and *up to the ene*, only after a long interval of a century or more. Some do have a continuous history in Scots. Others are ephemera which fail to outlast the sixteenth century—*gane* ('face'), *gend* ('silly'), *larbar*, *smy* and others.

Many of these words too are rare in Older Scots itself. Some are hapaxes or occur only twice or three times in the low-life poetry only. Others are found also in a quite restricted set of other contexts: violent or condemnatory passages in other verse and prose, and passages of alleged direct speech cited in court records and in certain works of narrative prose in later Middle Scots, beginning with Knox's *History*. An example of the latter sort is this passage from the *St Andrews Kirk Session Register* (1561, SHS 4, 106–7):

> Wyliam Mortoun of Cambo oppinlie in the public essemble manest boistit and injurit the said minister in the pulpet, saying thir wordis following or sicklyik in effect: My brother is and salbe vicar of Crayll quhen thow sall thyg thy mayt fals smayk. I sall pul the owt of the pulpet be the luggis and chais the owt of this town.

This passage is typical of many similar incidental prose passages of 'flyting and bairdrie' which crop up in the court records through the sixteenth and seventeenth centuries, for this activity was very common in the streets and even, as we see, in the churches of sixteenth-century Scotland, as well as in the poetry.

The discontinuous lexicographical history and general rarity of some of these words can be simply explained from the fact that the kind of detailed attention to domestic operations, intimate personal characteristics and physical traits given in this class of poem does not happen in any other kind of Older Scots writing: an example is the process of butter-making described in *The Wyf of Auchtirmwchty* but nowhere else in Middle Scots, so that the terms *bledoch* (buttermilk) and *ʒyrn* (curdle) occur only there. But the rarity of other words of this diction has a less trivial explanation. They belonged to an essentially colloquial or slang register and so were appropriate only in writings which imitated this, like the prose passage just quoted and the low-life verse itself. Their emergence into the limelight of literature had to await the appearance of this copious body of writings in an exaggerated vernacular or colloquial style.

A glance at virtually any portion of the poems or passages specified will readily confirm these generalisations. In the low-life interlude in the *Howlat* (lines 794–845), for instance, what appear to be colloquial register items are *flyrand* (*flyre*, 'to grimace, especially jeeringly') (all its occurrences seem to be in flytings or flyting-like contexts), *gukkit* (rather similarly distributed), *hiddy-giddy* (only in a few comic and earthy poems) and *smaik* 'a rascal' (in verse-flytings and reported prose-flytings). *Smad* (a LG word meaning 'to stain, smut, begrime') occurs only here in Older Scots but is quite common in Modern Scots.

As a small specimen of verse-flyting we may take the following from Dunbar's *Flyting with Kennedy*, lines 121–8:

> Lene larbar, loungeour, baith lowsy in lisk and lonʒe,
> Fy, skolderit skyn, thow art bot skyre and skrumple;
> For he that rostit Lawarance had thy grunʒe,
> And he that hid Sanct Johnis ene with ane womple,
> And he that dang Sanct Augustine with ane rumple
> Thy fowll front had, and he that Bartilmo flaid;
> The gallowis gaipis eftir thy graceles gruntill,
> As thow wald for ane haggeis, hungry gled.

In this passage occur, *inter alia*, a collection of favourite flyting expressions for 'the face', viz. *grunʒe*, literally, 'a snout', used contemptuously in flytings for the face of a person, *gruntill*, mostly 'a pig's snout,' here used like *grunʒe*, and *front* 'the forehead of a person or front part of anything' and in flytings (for the first time here) 'a person's face'. Besides these, *larbar*, *loungeour* (the first occurrences of this rare slang word, *lounge*, belong to Dunbar's *Flyting*), the cliché *the gallowis gaipis eftir* and the abusive use of the adjective *graceles* are all apparently colloquialisms. *Skyre* as a noun of obscure origin and meaning is found only here and *skrumple* as a noun (its origin is uncertain) only here in Older Scots: the same word is not uncommon in Modern Scots, meaning 'something dried up or burned to a crisp.' Items with a frequentative ending like this seem also to be favourites in flytings and the like; and indeed what we might call the sound effects, as well as the diction itself, of the passages we have just considered, are also typical of this kind of poetry (see section 11).

By way of comparison, the reported prose-flyting cited above from the St Andrews Kirk Session Register has, in *thyg,* a chiefly northern and Scottish word for 'to beg', and *smayk,* the flyting word which we identified above. *To pul* another out of a place *be the luggis* is presumably a colloquialism; at least, *lug* itself, applied to the human ear, seems from the hostile or contemptuous contexts in which it regularly occurs, to have had slangy overtones.

In view of all that has now been said, it will not surprise the reader that the Latinate diction, 'consecrated' or merely 'general', and the native amene vocabulary which we have identified in the courtly poetry are almost totally absent from most low-life poetry. This is unquestionably true of the more rustic and (seemingly) unpretentious of these works, such as *Peblis to the Play, Christis Kirk* and *The Wyf of Auchtirmwchty,* and the other works of this sub-set. As befits their educated contestants, a small proportion of Latinisms and Gallicisms is indeed present in the flytings and lampoons of such learned protagonists as Kennedy, Lyndsay (who did not forget that he was addressing the King), and Polwart, and (even fewer) Henryson, Dunbar and Montgomery (Dunbar's *Flyting* is among the least Latinate of his works, though even less so is his *Twa Cummeris,* Ellenberger 1977: 68).

Except in parody of courtly diction ('Boece said, of poyettis that wes flour', *King Berdok* line 47), the only body of poetic diction which does occasionally supply a few items to low-life and flyting verse is the native diction most characteristic of alliterative verse, in a few of its synonyms for 'man', such as *berne, freke, sege,* and in a few tags such as *on raw* (all of these, for example, in Dunbar's *Flyting*). In the tournaments, the 'fair and fracas' poems, and the burlesques, this is sometimes presumably mock-heroic or by way of parody.

So the vocabulary of the low-life verse is vernacular, domestic, vulgar and ribald, favouring words whose distribution and meaning suggest slang or colloquial overtones, mono- or disyllabic rather than polysyllabic, predominantly northern and Scottish in provenance, of vernacular spoken rather than literary origin, un-Latinate, and in all of those ways the opposite of the courtly and to an only slightly lesser extent the instructive and the lyric kinds of Older Scots verse.

9 *Reduced forms*

Unlike all other kinds of Older Scots poetry, these low-life poems do not display, in rhymes or elsewhere, any of the anglicised forms described in section 2 above, and their copyists also, sensitive to stylistic proprieties, normally impose none on them (with the sole exceptions of the all-pervasive spellings *no* and *so*). Low-life poetry does, nevertheless, have its own formal stylistic markers. Whereas those of 'Anglo-Scots poetry' are more or less sporadic and sometimes inaccurate imitations of spellings and inflections seen (on the written page by the eye) in the prestigious writings of Chaucer and the other English paragons of 'lusty fresch endyte', low-life poetry's formal markers mimic in writing recent innovations in the pronunciation of spoken Scots (as heard in everyday local speech by the ear). All of them involve phonetic reduction, the shortening of fuller forms of words by the vocalisation or loss of consonants. All were probably still only optional in speech, existing alongside alternative full-form options, as indeed most continue to do in modern Scots today. Specifically, these are *aw, caw, gaw* etc. beside *all, call, gall* etc., *haus* beside *hals* ('the throat'), *now* beside *noll* ('the head'), *bowt* beside *bolt, fow, pow* beside *full, pull,* among the forms which resulted from l-vocalisation in early fifteenth-century Scots. Other reduced forms result from the loss of intervocalic and word-final *v*, such as *deill* beside *devill, ein* and *eining* beside *evin* and *evining, gein* beside *gevin* 'given', *ha, ge, lo* beside *have, geve, luve,* and *ser* beside *serve*; forms due to loss of (originally voiceless) *th*, namely *mow, uncow,* and *no,* beside *mouth, uncouth* and *noth* or *nocht*; others similarly losing final *f* or *v* in *himsell, thairsell(is)*; various other reductions including *en* and *sen* beside *end* and *send*; and *beid, dude, ford, kend,* etc. for *be it, do it, for it, ken it,* etc. All of these forms occur in low-life verse in general, including both narrative and invective passages. Only the reduced pronoun-verb operator phrases *Is, weis, ʒeis* for *I sall, we sall, ʒe sall* and *Ile, ʒele* for *I will, ʒe will* appear to be confined to dialogue. (For a fuller list of all of these forms, and others like them which are not similarly stylistically restricted, see Aitken 1971: 195-7, and for specific examples in context, see the various entries in DOST.)

When the Older Scots poems were written these forms were comparatively recent innovations in speech. They remained unacceptable—presumably as colloquial modernisms—in written usage generally, and certainly for the most formal and dignified styles of verse and prose, throughout the Older Scots period. Indeed they failed to emerge into regular written use until the appearance of the modern Scots dialect verse of Allan Ramsay and his followers (including Robert Burns) in the eighteenth century. In written Older Scots they are largely restricted to overtly colloquial verse, to certain narrative poems, and to more or less 'illiterate' prose (such as some ill-spelled private letters of the sixteenth-century and other irregularly spelled Older Scots writings). Blind Hary's *Wallace,* the Asloan MS *Sevyne Sagis* (full listings are given in van Buuren-Veenenbos 1982: 98-101 and 123), Gavin Douglas's *Aeneid* translation, William Stewart's *Chronicle* and Rolland's *Sevin Seages,* which I classed in section 1 in the simple or the elaborative narrative kinds, share with low-life verse the practice of employing l-vocalised and other reduced forms for rhyming purposes, but in their case do so even in quite serious and dignified passages. The few rhymes requiring reduced forms of this sort in Douglas's *The*

Palice of Honour, however, all occur in what we might accept as 'appropriate' contexts: of fear (*my sell*, line 306), of irritation and contempt (*stupefak*, line 1460), and in a list of low-life and fantastic poems (*fow*, line 1714). The same explanation does not seem to apply to the substantially larger number of such rhymes in John Rolland's *The Court of Venus*, no doubt inspired by and imitated from *The Palice of Honour*: *fow* (Prol. 82, I. 564), *haid* (have it, I. 122), *kend* (ken (know) it, III. 611), *dude* (do it, IV. 121), *zour sell* (yourself, III. 352), *twell* (twelve, III. 660), *thame sell* (themselves, IV. 514), *stupefact* (rhyming with *bak, slak, wndertak, lak,* III. 152). Perhaps we should regard this as an extention by Rolland of a licence which he imagined he had observed in Douglas's poem.

In the low-life poetry generally these forms occur fairly frequently, albeit optionally, as spellings and in rhymes. Sometimes the copyist presents us with a full-form spelling where the rhyme demands the reduced form (there are examples in *Kynd Kittok* line 13 (Ch. & M.) and *The Wyf of Auchtirmwchty* lines 9, 10, 33, 50 (Bann.)). Six of *The Wyf of Auchtirmwchty's* 60 rhymes, indeed, are reduced forms. They were evidently regarded as typical of 'flytingis and invectives' by King James VI, who in his *Revlis and cautelis* specifies for that sort of writing words which are 'cuttit short and hurland ouer heuch' ('cut short and hurtling over precipice') (James VI *Poems* I. 75).

10 *Stylistic opposites*

We have now noted several striking stylistic contrasts between the extremes in the gamut of Older Scots verse kinds—the courtly and the low-life: the one kind favours some phonological anglicisation, a prevailingly complex syntax, a plethora of rhetorical colours, an avoidance of northernisms of vocabulary, a profusion of Latinity generally and of consecrated Latinate diction in particular, as well as a body of 'amene' poetic diction of native etymology; the other is in general syntactically direct and uninvolved and practises much asyndeton, is virtually free of the prescribed rhetoric so profuse in courtly verse, has a densely vernacular word-choice, including some vulgarisms, and uses (in spelling and rhyme) colloquial 'reduced forms'. The two kinds stem from widely separate traditions, the one highly literary, the other with evident colloquial and oral reference. We have noted in section 1 (especially pp. 19, 20, 21, and 24) that the two kinds also contrast quite strikingly in the metrical forms which each favours.

It is naturally possible also to compile a list of pairs or sets of synonym alternatives in Middle Scots, one or more of each set being favoured by serious prose and dignified verse, and another favoured by the more vernacular kinds of writing or in more vernacular passages. The dignified alternatives are in some cases Latinate, but in other cases of native etymology, opposed to a more vernacular or vulgar, though equally 'native', synonym. In pairs like the latter, for example, the first appears to have had more solemn overtones: *knaw* and *ken, ere* and *lug, fox* and *tod, hound* and *dog* (or, more abusively, *tyke*). Old French supplies the more dignified alternative in the sets *pas* and *gang* ('to go'), *promise* and *hecht* and *requeist, ask* and *speir*. A particularly revealing set already encountered is that of the synonyms for 'face': the dignified (and Latinate) *visage* (e.g. in Dunbar's *The Thrissill and the Rois* lines 11, 148) or *countenance* (ibid. 89, 93), the 'common core' item (of Old French origin) *face* (ibid. 55), and the vernacular (and more or less abusive) *front, gane, gruntill, grunȝe, snout* (in Dunbar and Kennedy's *Flyting* and similar works) (for references to and derivations of these, see section 8). The *amene redolence, odour sweit* or *dulce odour* of courtly poetry has its low-life verse opposite in such expressions as *foul stink*.

11   *Style-switching and -drifting and Phonaesthetics*

Style-switching was hardly an invention of the Middle Scots poets. Their English and Scottish predecessors and some English contemporaries knew something of this, especially the northern English. Well-known noisy passages interrupt calmer narrative or dialogue in *Purity, Sir Gawain and the Green Knight, The Destruction of Troy, The Awnturs of Arthur,* many of the northern miracle plays and many other narrative and, especially, alliterative poems in English. In Scots, Wyntoun has a number of violent and noisy passages, including a highly alliterative flood (following the northern Middle English *Cursor Mundi*) at I. 397–409. But since they enjoyed an even more extreme range between the diction of ugsome and violently abusive northern and Scottish vocabulary and the neutral or 'British' or literary-Latinate vocabulary of the courtly and instructive passages, as well as the peculiarly Scottish formal contrasts between the reduced forms of low-life verse and the full forms of the more dignified kinds of verse, it is especially in the Middle Scots poets, from Holland on, that the distance between the stylistic poles is greatest and the stylistic contrasts accordingly potentially most striking. Furthermore, to these contrasts there is added contrast in onomatopoeic effect between 'ugsome' and 'amene' passages. In Holland's opening six stanzas, the first three stanzas are in 'amene' style, with some 'native courtly' and a little Latinate vocabulary, displaying complex interlinkings of alliteration on 'liquid' consonants, rhyming in *-ene, -ede,* and other 'calm or gentle' phonaesthemes, whereas the second three stanzas on the Howlat's repulsiveness contrast in all these respects (Mackay 1975: 250–7). Holland may have learned this technique from the opening lines (lines 1 to 5 versus 6 to 11) of *The Quatrefoil of Love,* a north midland Middle English antecedent and, in part, model for his own poem (see Mackay 1975: 49–51).

Passages featuring tight clusters of northernisms of vocabulary and 'ugsome' sound-effects, such as those which characterise the low-life and abusive poetry, also occur, usually quite briefly, in most poems of the courtly and the elaborate narrative classes. These are the passages which introduce unpleasant or noisy characters and episodes like the incident of the bard and the fools in the *Howlat* (stanzas 62–5); Cresseid's leprosy and the descriptions of Mars and Saturn in Henryson's *Cresseid*; the terrible desert and 'grisly flood' in Part I and the 'loch of cair' and the shipwreck in Part III of Douglas's *The Palice of Honour* (lines 136–62 and 1315–77); the noisy departure of the ladies in Dunbar's *The Goldyn Targe* (see below); mentions of Hell (as at *Eneados* VI Prol., stanza 3, or Lyndsay's *Monarche* 5998 ff.) or descriptions of fearsome Underworld episodes or characters in *Eneados* VI; Lyndsay's version of Noah's flood in the *Monarche*, lines 1406 ff.; reproaches to the Empress and reproachful parts of the *moralitates* of Rolland's *Sevin Seages*; and the poets' descriptions of their own alleged barbarousness of language in the modesty *envois* or other *captationes benevolentiae*. Alliteration is rarely absent for long from any kind of Older Scots verse; but passages of these sorts are among the most heavily alliterated.

As well as anti-aureate passages like these embedded in what are mainly courtly or elaborate narrative poems, there are a few examples also of courtly or spoof-courtly passages in mainly comic or low-life settings: for example, when the three minions in Lyndsay's *Satyre*, whose talk is normally in the full colloquial manner, break into courtly diction to describe the attractions of Dame Sensuality (lines 331 ff.).

An unusually effective and highly revealing example of this kind of thing is the startlingly sudden departure of the allegorical ladies at lines 235–52 of Dunbar's *The Goldyn Targe*, that archetypal specimen of the courtly love allegory.

The passage is worth actual quotation here:

> In twynkling of ane eye to schip thai went,
> And swyth up saile unto the top thai stent,
> And with swift course atour the flude thay frak;
> Thay fyrit gunnis wyth powder violent
> Till that the reke raise to the firmament;
> The rochis all resownyt wyth the rak,
> For rerde it semyt that the raynbow brak;
> Wyth spirit affrayde apon my fete I sprent
> Amang the clewis, so carefull was the crak.
>
> And as I did awake of my sueving,
> The joyfull birdis merily did syng
> For myrth of Phebus tendir bemes schene;
> Suete war the vapouris, soft the morowing,
> Halesum the vale depaynt wyth flouris ying,
> The air attemperit, sobir and amene;
> In quhite and rede was all the felde besene
> Throu Naturis nobil fresch anamalyng,
> In mirthfull May, of eviry moneth Quene.

The first of these two stanzas, much the most violent of the poem, contains nine northern words (out of a total of about 25 in the entire poem of 31 stanzas). In the second stanza we return to the languorous dream-world of the *locus amoenus* of courtly poetry, with its own very poetic diction free of northernisms.

Furthermore, the first stanza is dominated by voiceless plosives, notably /k/, in word-initial and word-final position, in rhyme and alliteration, and is heavily alliterated for effect of movement (*swift course*), action and violent noise. The second stanza, conversely, features front vowels, continuant consonants (nasals, liquids, sibilants), fewer consonant clusters (none obstruent), much less alliteration, and then only on the phonaesthetically 'amene' consonants /m/, /n/ and /s/, and constant variation in vowel quality. From these passages and others it is evident that there were quite different sets of sound-sequences favoured in, on the one hand, passages which aimed at noisy, violent or generally unpleasant effects, which are also typically anti-aureate in their diction, and on the other those in the calm and melodious mood which predominates in the courtly poetry. Some others of the noisy and anti-aureate sets appear in the passage from Dunbar's *Flyting* cited on page 42 above (among many others in that and similar works), as well, of course, as in the 'ugsome' passages listed on page 47.

The question of what specific features of the phonology of words and sentences constituted the sound-sequences appropriate for one or another purpose—for example, the fact, for such it apparently was, that the phonaestheme -*ene* was highly appropriate in rhymes in melodious passages, whereas the constituents of the word *skrumple* (see pp. 42-3 above) were evidently the reverse—would take us into what are for me difficult and complex problems of historical semantics and literary history. But for aspiring theorists of such phenomena, Middle Scots poetry would serve as an excellent testing-ground. A useful beginning is Bawcutt's account of the techniques in this respect practised by Gavin Douglas in his *Eneados* (Bawcutt 1976: 155-8).

12 Conclusion

It is evident that the theory of three levels of style of classical and medieval poetic and rhetoric is quite inadequate to account for the modal variety we have just considered. But it may be that, as was suggested in section 4, the practice of 'rhetorical colours' for elegant amplification does owe something to the precepts of the theorists of poetic as well as to imitation of admired predecessors.

Evidently, however, convention and imitation exerted far more potent control of the practice of the medieval Scottish poets. Whereas the earlier of the Middle Scots poets, such as Holland, must have depended on models from furth of Scotland, a later poet such as Lyndsay could well have learned all of his conventions (whether or not he in fact did so) from the considerable body of native Scots performance which by his time was available.

REFERENCES

References to original texts employ either the styles of the *Dictionary of the Older Scottish Tongue* (see its Registers of Titles of Works Quoted, especially that of vol. III), or the full names of authors and full short titles of individual works.

Aitken, A J 'Variation and variety in written Middle Scots', in *Edinburgh Studies in English and Scots,* eds A J Aitken, Angus McIntosh, Hermann Pálsson, (London: Longman, 1971) pp. 177-209

Aitken, A J 'Oral Narrative Style in Middle Scots', in *Actes du 2ᵉ Colloque de Langue et de Litterature Écossaises (Moyen Age et Renaissance)*, eds J -J Blanchot and C Graf, Université de Strasbourg, 1978, pp. 98-112.

Atkins, J W H *English Literary Criticism. The Medieval Phase.* (Cambridge: Cambridge UP, 1943)

Bawcutt, Priscilla *The Shorter Poems of Gavin Douglas.* STS, (1967)

Bawcutt, Priscilla *Gavin Douglas.* Edinburgh: Edinburgh UP, (1976)

Ellenberger, B 'On Middle English Mots Savants', *Studia Neophilologica* **46**, (1974) pp. 142-50

Ellenberger, B *The Latin Element in the Vocabulary of the Earlier Makars, Henryson and Dunbar.* Lund Studies in English 51: (CWK Gleerup, 1977)

Jeffery, C D 'Anglo-Scots Poetry and *The Kingis Quair*', in *Actes du 2ᵉ Colloque de Langue et de Litterature Écossaises (Moyen Age et Renaissance)* eds J -J Blanchot and C Graf, Université de Strasbourg, 1978, pp. 207-21.

Jeffery, C D '*Colkelbie Sow*: An Anglo-Scots Poem', in *Proceedings of the Third International Conference on Scottish Language and Literature (Medieval and Renaissance)* eds R J Lyall and Felicity Riddy, (Stirling, Glasgow, 1981) pp. 207-24

Lewis, C S *English Literature in the Sixteenth Century excluding Drama.* (Oxford History of English Literature: Oxford UP, 1954)

McIntosh, A 'Some notes on the language and textual transmission of the *Scottish Troy Book*', *Archivum Linguisticum* **10** (new series), (1979) pp. 1-19

Mackay, Margaret A *The Alliterative Tradition in Middle Scots Verse.* University of Edinburgh PhD thesis, 1975

Murphy, James J *Rhetoric in the Middle Ages.* (Berkeley: University of California Press, 1974)

Pearsall, D A *The Floure and the Leafe* and *The Assembly of Ladies,* ed. D A Pearsall, (London: Nelson, 1962)

Romaine, Suzanne *Socio-historical linguistics, its status and methodology.* (Cambridge: Cambridge UP, 1982)

Van Buuren-Veenenbos, Catherina C *The Buke of the Sevyne Sagis.* (Leiden: Krips repro meppel, 1982)

Zettersten, A 'On the aureate diction of William Dunbar', in *Essays presented to Knud Schibsbye,* eds Michael Chesnutt, *et al.* Copenhagen: Akademisk Forlag, pp. 51-68.

THREE

The Biography of Alexander Scott and the Authorship of *Lo, quhat it is to lufe*

John MacQueen

First, a word of explanation. The immediate occasion for this essay—far removed from the respect and affection which I feel for David Murison—is Mrs Felicity Riddy's review (*Scottish Literary Journal*, Supplement no. 12, Summer 1980, 89–90) of the Scotsoun Makars Series cassette SSCO43, *Poems of Alexander Scott*, to which I contributed an introduction. In the course of her review, Mrs Riddy attached importance to an earlier adverse review (*Notes and Queries*, January 1972, 32–6), by Professor Denton Fox, of my book *Ballattis of Luve* (Edinburgh, 1970), and my British Academy Warton Lecture 'Alexander Scott and Scottish Court Poetry of the Middle Sixteenth Century' (delivered 1968, published 1969). Among much else, the lecture offered a reconstruction of Alexander Scott's biography, which in turn the book expanded, while an appendix to the lecture advanced evidence in support of my earlier contention[1] that Scott was in fact the author of the well-known lyric, 'Lo, quhat it is to lufe', usually attributed to Sir Thomas Wyatt. In March 1972 I refuted Professor Fox's main points in a letter which the then editors of *Notes and Queries* courteously declined to publish. At the time I felt that an adequate response was to send copies privately to Professor Fox and a few friends whose opinion I valued. Mrs Riddy's review shows that I misjudged the situation. The present article has grown from my letter, but includes a good deal of new material. My hope is that it makes a positive contribution to studies in sixteenth-century literary and linguistic history, appropriate to the interests of the recipient of this volume.

I begin with the biography of Alexander Scott. Professor Fox's dislike of my reconstruction is based, first, on the belief, derived from Chicago New Criticism, that any biographical approach to literature is necessarily improper, that the poetic text must be autonomous; secondly, and no doubt as an indirect consequence, on the assumption that the historical circumstances of the sixteenth century were identical with those of the twentieth. 'As a whole', he thus comments, 'the proposed biography would fit only a man who jumped from place to place, and from post to post, with a most unlikely alacrity.' But of course this is not so. Pluralism was a marked, indeed a notorious, characteristic of the pre-Reformation church in Scotland as elsewhere. 'Beneficis ar nocht leill devydit', says Dunbar,[2] 'Sum men hes sevin, and I nocht ane.' To give only one instance, Patrick Paniter, James IV's secretary, at various times held the following benefices: 'the rectory of Fetteresso, the vicarage of Kilmany, the chancellorship of Dunkeld, the archdeaconry of Moray and the rectory of Tannadice, together with the abbey of Cambuskenneth.'[3] Possession of a benefice implied no more for the holder than receipt of a salary. Residence was unnecessary; resident deputies were cheap and easy to obtain. The career which I proposed for Scott is typical of the early and middle sixteenth century.

Professor Fox commented on the legitimisation in 1549[4] of the two sons of Alexander Scott, prebendary of the Chapel Royal at Stirling: 'A more likely surmise, I should think, was that the legitimisation occurred because the father was a priest.' In the records the absence of a title before the father's name shows that he was *not* a priest. Laymen, or those in minor orders, often held ecclesiastical benefices of considerable importance and value. Patrick Paniter, whose career I have already mentioned, was not a priest. The career of this Alexander Scott (a musician, as his position in the Chapel Royal indicates), and of his two sons, can be traced with considerable clarity as far as the death of the father in 1582 or 1583.

Professor Fox further comments: 'Professor MacQueen also tries to arrange Scott's poems in some sort of chronological sequence, in order to construct Scott's spiritual biography.' I may, or may not, have constructed Scott's spiritual biography, but that was not my primary intent. One of the major movements of the sixteenth century, unmentioned by Professor Fox, was the Protestant Reformation. As I frequently state in *Ballattis of Luve*, one of the main purposes of my Introduction, and of the entire collection, was to show the effect of the Reformation on the development of one kind of literature in Scotland. It so happens that the surviving poems of Alexander Scott very directly illustrate that effect. Even if we ignore everything else, the poem on the death of the Master of Erskine at Pinkie, the poem 'Of May', and the poem addressed to Queen Mary on her return to Scotland, are internally dated in sequence, and show the gradual increase in Reformation ideas and influences. Professor Fox puts forward the alternative hypothesis that the poems as a whole are the work of several men, all possessing the same name, but differing widely in temperament and opinion. His place clearly is with the more extreme chorizontes.

So far as sixteenth-century Scottish poets are concerned, Professor Fox's statement that 'the attributions in the Bannatyne MS are far less reliable than Professor MacQueen suggests' rather misses the mark. One might suggest that Bannatyne was in a better position than Professor Fox to assess the reliability of his attributions. He did not, one presumes, choose names absolutely at random: a manuscript attribution is evidence for the fact that someone with a particular name, often contemporary with Bannatyne, was believed by Bannatyne to have written poems or songs, one at least of which he was including in his anthology. It may be possible to identify the man who, in Bannatyne's opinion, was the author. If only one or two poems are credited to him, we are left dependent on external evidence, which is seldom forthcoming, to confirm or contradict the attribution. Where a substantial number of poems, attributed to a single author, have survived, internal stylistic evidence may allow us to accept unity of authorship. (This I believe to be true of Scott.) If the documentary evidence suggests that in sparsely populated sixteenth-century Scotland (where, too, half the people spoke not Scots but Gaelic, a point to which I shall return) a man, whose name corresponds to Bannatyne's attribution, had a career which equipped him to write the verses attributed to his namesake, it requires no great brilliance of induction to bring an unbiased reader to the conclusion that the poet and the man in the records were probably one. Professor Fox would seem almost to think that sixteenth-century Scotland contained as many people as the modern United States.

Finally, despite Professor Fox, there are no 'traditional datings for the sixteenth-century Scots poets'.

One further biographical observation may be added. It has sometimes been regarded as improbable that Alexander Scott's date of birth should have been so early as c.1515, which I proposed. Scott died in 1582 or 1583 and, if I am right, he would then have been 67 or 68—by the standards of the time not excessively old. Among contemporary men of letters, George Buchanan, for instance, was born in 1506 and died in 1582 at the age of 76, while Sir Richard Maitland of Lethington was born in 1496 and died in 1586 at the age of 90. Of the older generation, sir John Fethy (?1480–c.1570) may have had as long a life as Maitland. John Major (1467–1550) died at 83, and Sir David Lindsay (?1486–1555) at almost 70. Longevity, one might almost say, was characteristic of sixteenth-century Scottish authors. We have no precise knowledge of the date at which Scott was born; it is clear that he did not die young, and if we allow him the conventional three score years and ten, the assumed date of his birth would be 1512 or 1513. The estimate which I have put forward may be too conservative.

The biography of Scott may therefore be stated as follows. He was born no later than 1515. In 1539 he was attached to the Chapel Royal at Stirling, in which capacity he received the revenue of the parsonage of Ayr. In 1540 he may have been in Paris. Between 1539 and 1548, still as a Chapel Royal musician, he received the revenue of the parsonage of Balmaclellan. In 1547 he wrote the commemorative 'Lament of the Maister of Erskine'. Perhaps as a reward, in 1548 he became organist of the Augustinian priory of Inchmahome, with a canon's portion, and travelled with the future Regent Mar, Maister Johne Erskin, prior of Inchmahome, younger brother of the Master of Erskine, to

France, perhaps as one of the entourage accompanying the young Queen Mary. In 1549 his sons John and Alexander Scott were legitimised, probably when Scott married their mother. Before 1560 Scott had lost or given up the benefices attached to the Chapel Royal, and had become associated with the Augustinian house of Inchaffray, probably as organist, from which he received a canon's portion. As was usual, the portion continued to be paid after the Reformation. Between 1555 and 1560 Scott wrote 'Of May', a poem with distinctly Protestant undertones. In 1562 he wrote his longest poem, 'Ane New Yeir Gift to the Quene Mary, quhen scho come first Hame; 1562', which un-mistakably is the work of a Protestant. In 1567 and 1570 he purchased lands in Fife and Perthshire respectively. In 1567 his younger son Alexander, pre-sumably as a Protestant minister, received the half-parsonage and vicarage of Coylton in Ayrshire. The minister was married, and had a son, also called Alexander, grandson of the poet. In 1580 the minister and his wife, supported by the poet, purchased land in the barony of Cumnock, Ayrshire; the minister died shortly thereafter. In June 1582 the poet made arrangements for the payment of an annual rent on his Perthshire estate, but by July 1583 he was dead, and the obligation had passed to his surviving son, John.

Some of the adverse criticism directed towards book and lecture was provoked by the suggestion, or demonstration, that the long-standing attribution to Wyatt of 'Lo, what it is to love' (I retain for the moment the more generally familiar convention of spelling), the first part of poem 87 in the most available edition to preserve original spelling, that of Kenneth Muir,[5] would not bear scholarly examination. In the Bannatyne MS, fo. 286 a-b, 'Lo, quhat it is to lufe', is ascribed to Scott, and in the appendix to the Warton Lecture (pp. 114-16), I put forward seven points to support the attribution, and to show that Wyatt's part in the composition of the poem was secondary, and at most cosmetic. The first three cleared the ground by emphasising the general value of the Bannatyne MS, its particular authority for Scott, and the extent to which Scott's authorship was biographically plausible. The second four were concerned with internal details—the fact that the poem is closer to Scott's stylistic norm than to that of Wyatt; that it reads like a song, as Wyatt's second and third parts do not; that the author of the third part writes as the voice of common humanity replying to an individual other than himself;[6] and finally that the rhyme *wise/advice/dice* fits more readily into a Scots than an English context. My concluding sentence runs: 'The likeliest solution would seem to be that Scott wrote "Lo, what it is to love", and *either* that Wyatt made a personal reply *or* that he utilized a song by Scott as the basis for a more extended poem of his own.' (If, as I suspect, the latter is the more likely, Wyatt need not have known Scott personally, nor even known that the song was by Scott. The only necessary presupposition is that the song should have attained some popularity in English as well as Scottish circles. Many channels were open between the court of James V and that of his uncle, Henry VIII.)

One or two points should now perhaps be added. The first is that Professor Fox in his review seems unable to grasp the philological point of the discussion of rhyme. It fits more readily, as has been noted, into a Scots than an English context. Precise parallels are to be found in poems attributed to Scott; none in poems attributed to Wyatt. (Not all the Wyatt attributions, by the way, are certain[7]—the manuscripts leave considerable room for doubt.) As might be expected, Wyatt's natural tendency is to rhyme the adjective 'wise' with words ending in the voiced *s* sound; in difficulties he, or at least some poet of his circle, is prepared to admit rhymes in voiceless *s* in company with others in voiced *s*. In the two later poems of the series as developed by Wyatt, the rhymes *wise/devise/dise* are governed by the scheme of the first poem, and so do not form independent evidence. In a curiously contorted footnote, Professor Fox quotes one example in which Wyatt rhymes the adjective with one word ending in voiceless and one in voiced *s*. It is unfortunate that his other two examples involve not the adjective but the substantive 'wise', which has a different etymology and a different phonological history, and which therefore is entirely irrelevant to the argument.

The most suspect feature of the Bannatyne text is the false internal rhyme in line 15, 'now thus, now *than*, so gois the *game*,/Incertane is the dyiss', where, although corruption has occurred, the text preserves the gambling metaphor, lost, or at most subliminally present in the Egerton reading, 'Now thus, now than,/Now of, now an,/Vncerteyn as the dyse' (19-21). Line 21 here is inserted in Wyatt's hand; Mr Mason has commented on the oddity of the form *an*. A straightforward emendation, justifiable in terms of minim confusion, 'so gois the gaine' (*gaine*, 'advantage, profit') retains the metaphor, and at the same time restores the Bannatyne rhyme scheme to the accuracy one associates with Scott. Mr Mason's suggestion[8] that Wyatt had before him a text other than Bannatyne may thus possibly, but not necessarily, be accepted; his deduction that the stanza in Bannatyne is an imperfect understanding of an English original reverses the most probable interpretation of the facts. It is Wyatt who seems to find difficulty in understanding a Scots original, difficulty which might be explained if we were to assume that the text from which Wyatt worked contained the corruption of *gaine* to *game*, which his ear found offensive, but which he was unable to emend, and which as a consequence he completely erased, abandoning the gambling metaphor, and introducing the *an* form.

The poem appears in Egerton with no apparent indication that the author is anyone but Wyatt (it is indeed attributed to 'Tho.'). Other poems in the manuscript are in Wyatt's hand or have been corrected by him, and, as has been mentioned, he has inserted a line in one stanza of this poem. The general authority of the manuscript has never been doubted. It is therefore the more surprising that the poem contains corrupt readings, for which in one instance, as has just now been shown, Wyatt was himself responsible. In the couplet

> Love is a fervent fire
> Kendeld by hote desire
> (i. 33–34)

another seems completely to have escaped his attention. In Bannatyne, the corresponding lines preserve the more difficult reading

> Lufe is ane fervent fire
> kendillit without desire
> (7–8)

a reading which, despite the superficial difficulty, it is easy enough to defend. In either version, the poem turns on the paradoxes of love—'ane pure (poor) tressour without messure', 'to rege with gud advyis'. 'Kendillit without desire' follows the same pattern: the reference is to the archetypical courtly love situation in which the young sceptic by a kind of spontaneous combustion is suddenly and against his will ('without desire') stricken by love, as Troilus was when he saw Criseyde in the temple:[9]

> So ferde it by this fierse and proude knyght:
> Though he a worthy kynges sone were,
> And wende nothing hadde had swich myght
> Ayeyns his wille that shuld his herte stere,
> Yet with a look his herte wax a-fere . . .
> (*Troilus and Criseyde*, I. 225–9)

In this context, 'kendeld by hote desire' is much weaker, probably derived from scribal misreading or mishearing; alternatively, it may even be a deliberate 'correction' made by someone who was unable to comprehend the meaning of the original—someone who saw the paradox, but not the resolution. If the poem were in fact by Wyatt, he would have been unlikely to have overlooked so total a reversal of his own meaning.

In the Bannatyne text, the preposition 'without' is twice used in a single stanza, once (*kendillit without desire*, 8) to introduce an adverbial phrase modifying a past participle used adjectivally, once (*tressour without messour*, 11) to introduce an adjectival phrase qualifying a noun. This idiom is characteristic of Scott; I have noted 23 examples of the prepositions 'without' and 'withouttin' in approximately 2000 lines of his surviving work. Of these, 9 introduce phrases used adjectivally to qualify nouns, 2 are used predicatively, and 5 introduce adverbial phrases modifying an adjective or past participle used adjectivally. Only 5 times is it used in the normal way to introduce an adverbial phrase modifying a verb or adverb. The 2000 lines contain in addition more than 20 examples of the preposition *but*, 'without', used generally to introduce an adjectival phrase qualifying a noun. Examples are: 'I am thy awin trew liege without tressone', ("Up, helsum hairt", 12), 'Ane hairt it is without dissait', 'ane mirthless hairt withouttin mesour', 'ane hairt withouttin fenyeit fabill' ("The answeir to the ballat of hairtis", 16, 20, 22), 'wappit without recure'

("Oppressit hairt indure", 2), 'way justice equale without discrepance', 'wordis without werkis', 'weilfaire without wo' ("Ane New Yeir Gift to the Quene Mary", 29, 109, 175), 'Lordis but ressone' ("Of May", 21), 'Ane hairt but solace' ("The answeir to the ballat of hairtis", 35), 'weill but wo' ("Favour is fair", 22), 'langour but releif' ("A Complaint aganis Cupeid", 15). Wyatt obviously does not ignore *without*, but his usage does not parallel Scott's; in more than 6000 lines I have noted 49 occurrences, of which 39 correspond to modern usage, 4 introduce phrases used adjectivally to qualify nouns, 2 are used predicatively, and 4 introduce adverbial phrases modifying an adjective. Wyatt does not use *but*, 'without'. The two poets thus differ strikingly both in the distribution and in the usage of the words.

It is possible, indeed, that Scott's usage reflects a Gaelic substrate in his language. The preposition *gan*, later *gun*, 'without', is used in Gaelic verse, much as Scott uses the Lowland equivalents. Compare, for instance, two stanzas from the beautiful *A phaidrín* ('O rosary')[10], which Aiffric nic Coirceadail composed about 1465 on the death of her husband Niall Óg, chief of Clann Neill and constable of Castle Sween in Knapdale, Argyll:

> *A h-éagmhais aon duine a mháin*
> *im aonar atáim dá éis,*
> *gan chluiche, gan chomrádh caoin,*
> *gan ábhacht, gan aoibh i gcéill.*

> *Gan duine ris dtig mo mhiann*
> *ar sliocht na Niall ó Niall óg;*
> *gan mhuirn gan mheadhair ag mnáibh*
> *gan aoibhneas an dáin im dhóigh.*
> (29-36)

For want of one man all lonely am I after him, without sport, without kindly talk, without mirth, without cheer to show.

Without one man to whom my mind draweth of the stock of MacNeill since young Neil is gone; ladies lack mirth and joy (literally, 'without mirth, without joy at ladies'); I am without hope of gladness in song.

Three centuries later Alasdair Mac Mhaighstir Alasdair (*c.*1690-*c.*1770) used the same idiom[11] to describe Inverey in Knoydart:

> *Baile gun ghlaistig, gun bhòcan*
> *'S coisrigte gach crann is fòid deth,*
> *Gun deanntag, gun charran, gun fhòtus,*
> *Lom-lan chluaran, lilidh, 's ròsan.*
> (37-40)

A township with no she-devil or hobgoblin, and consecrated is each tree and turf of it; without nettle, without spurrey, without refuse; brimfull of corn-marigold, lily and rose.

Inchmahome and Inchaffray, the two Augustinian houses with which Scott had connections probably involving residence, were both in the sixteenth-century Scottish Gaeltacht, on the south-eastern boundary of which stood Stirling and the Chapel Royal. At that time the population of Stirling must have been substantially Gaelic-speaking, as must, it is perhaps worth noting, those of Ayr and Balmaclellan, with which Scott had connections not necessarily involving residence. Perthshire, in which Scott eventually purchased land, was mainly Gaelic in speech, and there is even a reasonable possibility that Fife, where he also bought land, retained some Gaelic.

Whether or not the Gaelic parallels are important, the fact that one out of four stanzas of the Bannatyne version contains two phrases, one adjectival and one adverbial modifying a participle used adjectivally, introduced by 'without', is reasonable additional evidence that Scott rather than Wyatt was the author of the poem.

In Egerton, the corruption of 'without' to 'by hote' may be the result of scribal accident. The order of stanzas, however, is also different, and this appears to be a deliberate alteration. If Bannatyne is read in isolation, the order of stanzas is logically and poetically satisfying in a way appropriate for a song. The first, 'Lo, quhat it is to lufe', leads by way of the painful paradoxes of love, clearly and effectively to the conclusion, 'Fle alwayis from the snair'. By putting this last stanza second, and concluding with the paradoxes of love in reverse order, Wyatt, or the Egerton scribe following his authority, weakened the immediate effect. When the poem is regarded as the first movement of a three-part variation, the change gives the opportunity of an effective conclusion with a dismissive variation of the fire image:

> Such fire and suche hete
> Did never make ye swete,
>   For withoute payne
>   You best obtayne
> To good spede and to great;
>   Who so doeth playne,
>   You best do fayne
> Such fire and suche hete.
> (iii. 33-40)

(The stanza incidentally is additional proof that Wyatt himself accepted the reading 'by hote desire'. 'Hete' in the first and last lines is derived from 'hote' in i. 34, and 'hote', as has been shown, is a corrupt reading—additional proof that Wyatt cannot be the author of the first movement in its basic form. The alteration in stanza order depends on a corruption in the text forming the basis of the variations.) It is improbable that a group of stanzas composed as the first part of a set of variations should be so easily transposable to make sense as an isolated lyric; the reverse process is more readily comprehensible.

I have already commented elsewhere[12] on the additional stanza found in Wyatt. Mr Mason seems to accept my argument.[13]

It is now more than fifteen years since I first proposed the acceptance of the Bannatyne attribution. During the period, I have seen no evidence to make me retract. The statement by Professor Rebholz,[14] 'The first part of this three-part argument may be a revision and expansion of the Scottish poem, but it is equally probable that the Scottish version derives from the English', is simply inadequate. The priority of Wyatt is no longer a tenable hypothesis. One side-effect of this paper is to throw new light on Wyatt's method of composition as well as on the cultural relationship between Scotland and England in the first half of the sixteenth century. The likelihood that some influence would pass from north to south should perhaps have been more readily anticipated. In the previous century, after all, the accomplishment of Scottish poetry had substantially exceeded that of English.

NOTES

1   'Some aspects of the Early Renaissance in Scotland', *FMLS* III, no. 3, July 1967, p. 219
2   Poem 39, lines 46-7, James Kinsley (ed.), *The Poems of William Dunbar,* (Oxford, 1979), p. 120
3   Matthew Mahoney, 'The Scottish Hierarchy, 1513-1565', in D McRoberts (ed.), *Essays on the Scottish Reformation,* (Glasgow, 1962), p. 56
4   *Registrum Magni Sigilli, 1546-1580,* no. 395
5   *Collected Poems of Sir Thomas Wyatt* (London, 1949; Muses' Library edition, 1963). The edition by Muir and Patricia Thomson (Liverpool, 1969) is more difficult to obtain, and has received much adverse comment. Richard Harries (ed.), *The Canon of Sir Thomas Wyatt's Poetry* (Cambridge, Mass., 1975), contains an elaborate version of the Egerton text. Editions in modernised spelling are Joost Daalder (ed.), *Sir Thomas Wyatt. Collected Poems* (London, 1975) and R A Rebholz (ed.), *Sir Thomas Wyatt. The Complete Poems* (Penguin Books, 1978).
6   I now accept the view that the third poem is a reply to the second in the sequence. I am not certain that it is intended to be in the same *persona* as the first.
7   See, apart from the editions mentioned above, H A Mason, *Humanism and Poetry in the Early Tudor Period* (London, 1959), pp. 168-78; John Stevens, *Music and Poetry in the Early Tudor Court* (London, 1961), pp. 110-11, 405; Raymond Southall, *The Courtly Maker* (Oxford, 1964), Appendix A, 'The Egerton Manuscript Collection of Early Tudor Poetry, *c.*1530-1542'; H A Mason, *Editing Wyatt* (Cambridge, 1972).
8   *Editing Wyatt,* pp. 118-22
9   F N Robinson (ed.), *The Works of Geoffrey Chaucer* (2nd edn, Boston, 1957), p. 392. Compare in Southall, op. cit. chapter III, '"Troilus and Criseyde": A Point of Departure'.
10 W J Watson (ed.), *Scottish Poems from the Book of the Dean of Lismore* (Scottish Gaelic Texts Society, Edinburgh, 1937), pp. 60-5
11 A MacDonald and A MacDonald (eds), *The Poems of Alexander MacDonald,* (Inverness, 1924), p. 272
12 Warton Lecture, p. 115
13 *Editing Wyatt,* p. 121
14 *Sir Thomas Wyatt. The Complete Poems,* p. 428

FOUR

Language Choice in the Reformation: The Scots Confession of 1560

Mairi Robinson

To my first kindly mentor in lexicography, as an affectionate thank-offering

The leaders of the Scottish Reformation are often said to have played a major part in the decline of the Scots language among its native speakers and writers. This essay will examine one of the few indigenous documents of the Reformation in Scotland, the Scots Confession of Faith of 1560, in an attempt to see whether any new insights can be gained into contemporary linguistic attitudes.[1]

The Scottish reformers are well known for having been content with documents compiled elsewhere rather than making up native Scottish versions for the use of the infant Scottish Protestant church. For example in the 1550s and indeed into the 1560s Protestants in Scotland had used King Edward VI's Second Prayer Book as their service book. This was later replaced by a version, only slightly changed, of the 1556 Service Book of the English Protestant exiles in Geneva;[2] and the adoption by the Scots of the Geneva translation of the Bible into English is of course notorious.

But indeed it was perfectly natural that the reformers should have considered an English translation of the Bible to be satisfactory for Scots-speaking Protestants. The reasons for this are clear. Scots and English have had much in common at all periods of their history, from their joint ancestry and from their constant contact with each other. One of the results of this was that within the various options available in the sixteenth century, it was still possible for Scots to be *written* in a very similar orthography to English, even though the *spoken* forms of English and Scots had already diverged considerably. This meant that what was written as English could be and was pronounced as Scots and therefore was regarded as being Scots, although it could at the same time quite happily be accepted as English. The terms 'English' and 'Scots' were being used interchangeably to describe the language of Lowland Scotland by the mid sixteenth century.[3]

One small piece of evidence confirming this is to be found in the Act of

Parliament allowing the use of the vernacular Bible in 1543, which was expressed in these terms:

> It is statute and ordanit that it salbe lefull to all our souirane ladyis lieges to haif the haly write baith the new testament and the auld in the vulgar toung in Inglis or scottis of ane gude and trew translatioun and that thai incur no crimes for the hefing or reding of the samin.[4]

Here 'Inglis or scottis' may be intended as alternative descriptions of the same thing; but even if they are being thought of as distinct, they are nevertheless both included in the overall description 'the vulgar tongue'. In the entry for 19 March 1543 authorising the proclamation of the Act at the Mercat Cross, it is described as

> The Act maid for having of the new testament in Inglis wulgare toung with certane additionis.[5]

And in 1558, the *'First Oratioun and Petitioun of the Protestantes of Scotland to the Quein Regent'* was largely concerned with the provision of more parts of religious observance 'in the vulgare toung',

> as we haif, of the Lawes of this Realme, after long debaite, obteaned to reade the Holy bookes of the Old and New Testamentes in our commoun toung, as spirituall foode to our soullis.[6]

This can only mean English as there was no Scots version of the Bible available,[7] and it therefore seems as if written English was regarded as being 'our commoun toung' by Scots in 1558. This, indeed, continued to be the case for some time longer. In the eighteenth century in particular the Scottish literary tradition is well provided with clear examples of English spelling being used where Scots pronunciation is intended. Nowadays, however, we do not regard it as appropriate to pronounce this 'common English' otherwise than with our version of an *English* pronunciation. For anything to be pronounced in a Scots manner today we feel it has to be spelt in one of the other, more restrictedly Scots, options. And these kinds of option were also available in sixteenth-century Scots.[8]

It still had the option of using the orthographic system of early Scots of the fourteenth and early fifteenth centuries, which in many respects was similar to that of Middle English. It had also developed new spelling conventions which had come about partly as a response to changes in pronunciation in the fifteenth century. Furthermore, it was of course affected by contact with contemporary English spelling conventions, now that English printed books were so readily available. And it is at this period that English spelling is beginning to stabilise, partly because of the desire for standardisation by English printers, with the enormous increase in material coming from the English presses. Some sixteenth-century Scots writers seem to have rationalised the rather free spelling system which resulted from this, to the extent of imposing a consistency of their own on their text, while others vary quite arbitrarily from moment to moment in their choice within the options. Both of these types are to be found in the versions of the Confession.

In the Scots Confession, it is possible sometimes to see how Biblical English, having been *pronounced* as Scots, is then *written*, partly at least, in a restrictedly Scots option by the Scottish scribe or printer. Echoes of many different English translations can be detected throughout the Confession,[9] but there are also a few extended quotations where a direct comparison can be made with the original. For example, at the end of the Title there is a quote from Matthew 24: 14 in some versions of the Confession.

The English translations for this verse are divided in their renderings of the Greek word for 'gospel'. Some have 'gospel', the native English calque for the Greek; others have 'glad tidings', thereby translating the word afresh. The Confession is using one of the versions with 'glad tidings'. The proof of this is not merely that all the Confession texts have variants of these actual words: after all, the author(s) of the Confession could at a pinch have been re-translating too. But if the Confession's English translation had used 'gospel', this would, I think, have been given by the Confession's author(s) as 'evangel'.[10] 'Evangel' is used at least three times in the Confession itself (and at these points, genuine English editions[11] of the Confession give 'gospel'), for example in the Salutation, the Preface, and Chapter 21. 'Evangel' seems to have been the regular preferred choice in sixteenth-century Scots. Indeed the vast majority of the examples of fifteenth- and sixteenth-century use of the word in OED are from Scottish authors. It seems to have lost popularity in England during those two centuries, although it had been found earlier and was to return later; and it was one of the examples in the sixteenth-century controversies in England as to whether or to what extent the introduction of Latinate terms was acceptable in English.

The use of the phrase 'glad tidings', then, shows that either Tindale (whose New Testament had been circulating in Scotland since 1526) or the Geneva Bible (the New Testament of which had been published in 1557) is the source. Perhaps the fact of the *chapter* number only being given makes Tindale more likely—verse numbering in the Bible was only introduced in 1551, with the text continuous and the numbers in the margin; the Geneva Bible was the first both to number the verses and to break up the text into separate paragraphs for each verse.

To come now to the complete quotation:

Tindale 1534:[12] And this gladtidingees of the kyngdome shalbe preached in all the worlde for a witnes vnto all nacions: and then shall the ende come.

Scot:[12] And this glaid tydingis of the Kingdome salbe preached throuch the heale warld for ane wytnes vnto all nationis: And than sal the end cum.

Knox E:[12] And this glaid tydingis of the kyngdome sall be precheit throwch the haill warld, for a witnes unto all natiouns, and than sall the end cum.

L1561:[12] And this glaid tydinges of the kingdom shalbe preached throught the hole world for a witness to all nations and then shall the end cum.

It is interesting to see how the different scribes and printers have 'naturalised' Tindale's English to their own personal style. All the versions above have some words in common Scots/English, such as *and*, *this*, *of*, *the*, *end*. For the other words, however, while Scot and Knox E almost exclusively choose Scots forms, each only having one English or common Scots/English feature (Scot's is *preached*, Knox's *a*), L1561 shows no such homogeneity. On the Scots side he has *glaid*, *cum* and *throught* (which exhibits the Scottish scribal habit of adding a final -*t* to words ending in -*ch* or -*th*); but as examples of English or common Scots/English use he has *tydinges*, *shal* (twice), *preached*, *hole*, *world*, *a*, *nations*, *then*. Because of the text being originally English, no conclusions can be drawn about whether or not there is anglicisation on his part, but it can be said that the Scot and Knox texts seem to prove that the Tindale was being pronounced in Scotland as Scots, not English, and also that they do not seem to be uneasy about departing from the written English form.

Why then, if it was perfectly natural that English versions of the Bible and Service-Book should be acceptable in Scotland, did the Scottish reformers nevertheless make up their own Confession of Faith? The answer seems to be that it was usual among reformed churches for each to make its own statement of doctrine.[9] Each of these was regarded as particular to its time and place, and they could be (and frequently were) modified with the passage of time. It should be noted that the Scots Confession never seems to have been used as part of the worship of the church—it is rather long at 25 substantial chapters; instead the Apostles' Creed and the Confessions contained in the Service-Books were used. The Scots Confession was used, however, as a test of doctrinal orthodoxy, both on its own in the 1560s and 1570s, and as part of the Negative Confession in the 1580s and beyond.[13]

The matter of the authorship of the Confession is perhaps not wholly clear. Knox says in his account of the composition of the Book of Discipline,[14]

> Commissioun and charge was gevin to Mr Johne Winram, Suppriour of Sanctandrois, Maister John Spottiswoode, Johne Willok, Mr John Douglas Rectour of Sanctandrois, Maister Johne Row, and John Knox, to draw in a volume the Polecey and Disciplyn of the Kirk, as weill as thei had done the Doctrin.

On the other hand, Sir Thomas Randolph, the English ambassador in Edinburgh, writing to Sir William Cecil at some length about the Confession,[15] describes it as having *an* author, and also as having been submitted to certain lords 'to see their judgementes' and to William Maitland of Lethington and John Winram, who found its language too extreme; they moderated its tone, and advised the omission of the section on the civil magistrate (which was not done).

Here we have a conflict between Knox's six authors and Randolph's one. It certainly seems unlikely that Winram would have been vetting the document, far less disapproving of it, if he had been one of its authors. On the other hand it was usual for Reformation confessions to be composed by more than one person. Perhaps it may be that one of the six men mentioned by Knox was the chief draughtsman, but that the others were also involved in its composition, perhaps by supplying individual chapters or (like Winram) acting as critics.

Whatever the exact truth about its authorship may be, the approval of the Confession by parliament was regarded as a necessary first step towards the establishment of the Protestant faith,[16] and the Confession was accordingly presented to parliament. Knox and Willock laid it before the Lords of the Articles and the bishops on 14 August 1560;[17] it was later brought before the Estates, where no theological objection was made to it; and it was voted on article by article and passed on 17 August 1560, as 'hailsome and sound doctrine groundit upoun the infallable trewth of Godis word'.[18] The acts of this 'Reformation parliament' were never ratified by Queen Mary, and it was not until the first parliament of the infant James VI, in December 1567, that the proceedings of August 1560 were legalised.

Before we proceed to look at the early versions of the Confession in detail, a few fairly general remarks about its language might be helpful. The most immediately obvious point is that there is very little specifically Scots vocabulary, morphology or syntax in any version of the Confession. For vocabulary, we have already noted the use of *evangel*; there is also *contrare* as a preposition = 'against', in the Preface, and *mun* = 'must', occasionally, but otherwise the only lexical Scotticisms are Scots or northern cognates or variants such as *sick, mekle, quhilk, admoneis*.

The only Scots morphological features to be found in the Confession are the renderings of inflections. Thus the Scots inflection for plural nouns, *-is*, and for past tenses and past participles, *-it*, are both found, but usually in apparently random distribution with the common Scots/English variants. For the third person singular of the present tense of verbs we find Scots *-is*, common Scots/English *-s* and southern English *-eth*. The pervasiveness of the southern form is no doubt partly due to so much of the Confession being exact or approximate quotation from various English translations of the Bible. Its occurrence in all except the parliamentary texts suggests that it was in the original draft, but not in the parliamentary record. The distinctively Scottish form of the plural of *this, thir,* is found, but in most of the versions it is only in the Colophon; and this cannot have formed part of the original text of the Confession, but comes from the parliamentary record (see Appendix §II). The only other place where *thir* is found is in fact in the parliamentary editions, particularly in chapter 14. Otherwise *these* is always used. And finally there are no examples at all of the Scots present participial ending *-and*.[19]

Nor indeed is there very much distinctively Scottish syntax. There are several examples of concord of adjectives with their nouns, always with *uther*, in *utheris Realmeis* in the Salutation, *utheris places* in chapter 18, and *utheris magistratis* in chapter 24, though these do not all occur in all versions; and also several examples of plural subject + inflected verb, in chapters 13 and 21, again not all occurring in all texts, but with every version having at least one example.

The linguistic levels which exhibit the greatest variety between the texts both in the choice between Scots and English and within Scots itself are orthography and to a lesser extent phonology. It will therefore be mainly with these two levels that we shall be concerned in our investigation. We shall also try to establish as far as possible the derivation of each version, since the linguistic choices being made in each case must have been conditioned to some extent by the exemplar being used.

The manuscripts of the Confession

The original manuscripts of the proceedings in parliament no longer exist for either 1560 or 1567. That there probably was an official copy made in 1560 is suggested by Randolph's statement in his letter to Cecil of 19 August,

> That all these things were done by common consent the Duke gave a piece of silver (as the order is) to the Clerk of Register to have an instrument of the same.[20]

James MacGill, the Clerk Register, signed the 1568 edition of the Acts of the 1567 parliament as having been extracted from the book of the Acts of Parliament by him, which should mean that there was an official manuscript copy for 1567: unless of course the 1560 record was merely transferred to this new date, as this 1567 parliament was explicitly confirming the unratified legislation of the 'Reformation parliament'.

The most significant surviving manuscript containing the Confession is that of Knox's *History of the Reformation*, known as the Laing MS, or MS of 1566, now in the possession of Edinburgh University Library, which I have called Knox E.[21] Dickinson[12] describes this manuscript very fully,[22] and from him we learn that this part of the *History* was probably written by Knox in the early months of 1566. The number of recopyings may make the actual date of the manuscript itself somewhat later than spring 1566, but perhaps only by a few months. However, documents seem to have been added to Knox's text from originals, so it is possible that the source for the Confession was a copy dating from 1560. Dickinson also establishes that the manuscript as we have it is a recopying of a first copy; and this seems to be true of the Confession as well, as it appears to be already fully embedded in the text of the *History* from which this copy was made, and connects without a break to the surrounding material. This is important, as Dickinson has shown that the scribe he calls A wrote the previous copy. Two scribes are responsible for the extant text of the Confession:

scribe C, probably Richard Bannatyne, Knox's secretary, who wrote fos. 224^r–228^v, i.e. from the Title to near the end of chapter 11, and scribe A himself, probably John Gray, Clerk to the General Assembly from 1560 to 1574, who wrote fos. 229^r to the end.

Here we have an interesting situation. The manuscript is certainly at several removes from the original, but the fact of the change in scribes may enable us to see more easily which features are scribal idiosyncrasies and which perhaps belonged to the exemplar being used. On the whole C more frequently chooses the Scots option than does A. For instance, scribe C has to a greater extent selected specifically Scots orthography, such as his much more frequent use of digraphs in -*i*; but A has plenty of Scots spellings too, as *thairfoir, greattare*; and both A and C have one example of *ane* as the indefinite article before a word beginning with a consonant; Scots phonology is revealed in *yit, na, lauboured*; Scots morphology in plurals in -*is*; and Scots cognates are chosen in *sick, mun, mekle*. (Most of A's examples are taken from chapter 18.)

These points of agreement lead us to the hypothesis that the underlying text is fairly strongly Scots. The points on which C and A differ can tell us the kinds of words likely to be good indicators of sixteenth-century language choice. Some specific points of divergence are:

> C: *haif, haid, quhilk, alssua*, past tenses in -*it*.
> A: *have, had, which, also*, past tenses in -*ed*.

Some of these divergences may be accidental, due to the smallness of the sample—for instance immediately after the Confession A uses *haif*. But *quhilk* and -*it*, *which* and -*ed* occur sufficiently frequently and consistently to be significant. And a further point to be made about A's choice of language is that we may perhaps assume that A was likely to have exhibited the same characteristics when writing the previous draft as he shows in this one. Thus it seems probable that A wrote *which* and -*ed* in the previous copy, and therefore that it is C who is introducing the *quhilk* and -*it* in this copy. Here again we have evidence that it was just as possible for sixteenth-century Scots writers to scotticise as it was for them to anglicise.

The other manuscript of Knox's *History* which is of some significance is that in the possession of Glasgow University Library, which I shall call Knox G. Laing assigns it to the 1580s.[23] If that date is correct, it was not seen by Knox himself, unlike Knox E, of which it is a transcription. In fact Knox G contains very little of the Confession, only from the Title to the end of chapter 4.[24] When we investigate what Knox G can tell us about language choice in the 1580s, we are at once helped by also still having its exemplar, Knox E, which at this point is being written by scribe C, the more Scots of the two Knox E scribes. Thus we can see that Knox G chooses the 'English' option rather than Knox E's more specifically Scots one in

Knox G	*Knox E* (scribe C)
-ed past tenses and participles (usually);	*-it* (always)
-eth 3rd person singular present tense (sometimes)	*-s*, *-is* (always)
vther Realmes	*vtheris Realmeis*
if	*gif*
haue	*haif*
danger	*daingear.*

But conversely he chooses the more Scots option in

Knox G	*Knox E*
wiss	*wische*
lang	*long*
neuir	*neuer*
spellings with *i*-digraph overwhelmingly the commoner	spellings without *i*-digraph about equal in number to spellings with
nouther	*neither.*

And of course in most words Knox G has the same as Knox E, whether in following an English or a Scots option. It would appear, then, that this scribe, writing about twenty years later than the Knox E scribes, both exhibits less internal consistency than they do, and also shows no sign of standardisation of any kind, including anglicisation.

The manuscript nearest in time to the composition of the Confession which is now extant is probably that to be found in the Public Record Office in London,[25] which I shall call PRO. This is a copy of the Confession sent to Cecil[26] by either Maitland of Lethington[27] or Randolph,[28] probably during August 1560. Perhaps it is Maitland's copy, as Randolph describes his as 'written in such haste that I am ashamed to present it', and this manuscript is quite tidily and clearly written. It has not, so far as I am aware, been used in the production of any edition of the Confession, but is obviously of considerable interest as being so close in time to the first appearance of the Confession.

It is written in a Scottish hand and its orthographic and phonological character is on the whole very Scots, with for example *quhilk, quha, fra, nocht, wardly*; but it also shows signs of anglicising, as in its frequent verbal past tenses and past participles in *-id*, which seem to be a compromise between Scots *-it* (the other form found in this version) and English *-ed* (which is not found here). It also has a higher than average partiality for the southern English third person singular ending *-eth*. Another example is *hoill* = 'whole', for which the native Scots would be *haill*. Here the English member of the phonological pair is chosen, but it is then given a typically Scots spelling with *-i* digraph. Again it vacillates between English and Scots in, for example, the use of *church* in the titles of chapters 5, 16, and 25, but *kirk* within the chapters themselves (compare Knox E (both scribes) and Scot, who have *kirk* in all instances, and L1561 and Hall,[12] with *church* in all instances). As a whole, this manuscript gives the impression of being somewhat schizophrenic linguistically. Perhaps the circumstances of its composition may have something to do with that, if the scribe knew that it was intended for England. If so it is interesting both that he should have thought it necessary or at least desirable to anglicise his text, and also that he should have done it so ineffectually.

The editions of the Confession:
1. Editions of 1561

To turn now to the most important sixteenth-century printed editions of the Confession. These come into two main categories which it may be easier to discuss separately, though there is some inter-relationship. Firstly there are the three editions of 1561, two produced in Edinburgh and one in London. The Edinburgh editions were printed by John Scot[29] and Robert Lekpreuik respectively, and the London edition by Rouland Hall.

It may at first sight seem strange to find John Scot as the printer of one of these editions. He is the only printer known to have been working in Scotland during the previous decade, and was therefore responsible, not only for the few literary works published in that period, but also for the more numerous items published by or in support of the Catholic Church, such as Archbishop Hamilton's Catechism of 1552 and his 'Twopenny Faith' of 1559, and Quintin Kennedy's 'Ane compendious tractive . . .' of 1558. And Scot was again printing Catholic apologetic after 1561, for in 1562 we find him as the printer of Ninian Winzet's controversial works 'Certane tractatis for reformatioun of doctryne and maneris . . .' and 'The last blast of the trompet . . .'. Indeed, if Leslie is to be believed[30], it was while Scot was in the act of printing the latter that his premises were broken into by the magistrates of Edinburgh with their officers, the copies of the book were seized and Scot himself dragged off to prison. After this, he does not seem to have been able to take up his profession again in Scotland until 1568. But in 1561 he brought out an edition of the first Protestant propaganda document, the Confession of Faith. He also seems to have used the same source as Knox and PRO, from the correspondences between the texts,[31] which would suggest that an official version was made available to him, perhaps even Knox's own draft (see Appendix §II). It also seems possible that he was made a burgess gratis by act of the Town Council of Edinburgh on 11 July 1560,[32] just after the 'Reformation parliament' had begun to sit, on the 10th. Perhaps his services were being secured by a timely sweetener.[33] If that is so, the good relations between Scot and the Protestants do not seem to have lasted long: he was soon printing Catholic tracts again, and in the meantime Lekpreuik seems to have been brought in as a reliable printer for the Protestant propaganda machine.

Scot's edition shows signs of having been prepared in a hurry—it has many misprints, and some errors which look like the result of carelessness or haste, such as transpositions and omissions of letters, dittography, and omissions of words and phrases. Its language is fairly strongly Scots, with Scots phonological options such as *resavit, innimeis,* Scots orthography in *seid, maid,* Scots renderings of inflectional endings in *utheris, knawin, followis,* and Scots cognates in *sick* and *quhilk.* Most of these features are also found in Knox E and PRO. Scot too is fond of past tenses and participles in *-id,* which occur intermittently, but not in the same places as in PRO.

The second Edinburgh edition of 1561 is that printed by Robert Lekpreuik, which I shall call L1561. Nothing is known of Lekpreuik before 1561, but in that year he printed three works in Edinburgh which show him to be a supporter of the Protestant cause: the Confession; an English translation of the French Protestant Theodore de Bèze's 'Ane Oration . . .', which is a theological address; and Robert Norvell's 'The meroure of an Chrstiane' (*sic*), religious verse by a close friend of Knox. Lekpreuik seems to have enjoyed the confidence of the Protestant leaders from the start, for all his first productions in 1561 already bear the imprint *cum privilegio,* which almost certainly implies that he had been authorised to print by parliament. We lack the Act which confirms this to be so, but that is not surprising, as so few of the records from this period have survived.

Lekpreuik certainly had at least one powerful patron in Alexander Clerk, for a contract between Lekpreuik and Clerk in 1564 does survive[34], in which Clerk undertook to put up the money to buy new types and paper in return for half the profits from Lekpreuik's printing of *The Forme of Prayers . . .*.[35] Clerk, who like Robert Norvell and Knox had been in France in 1559, was a wealthy Edinburgh merchant known to the English Secretary Cecil by early 1561, and on close terms with Randolph, the English ambassador;[36] altogether a very important man in the politics of Reformation Edinburgh. With connections like these, and with the granting of parliamentary privilege to print, it seems probable that Lekpreuik's edition of the Confession was in some sense officially approved. But I shall leave more detailed discussion of his 1561 edition until we come to his 1568 parliamentary edition, and pass on in the meantime to the last of the 1561 editions, the London edition by Rouland Hall.

Hall is clearly based on the same source as L1561: indeed it is probably taken directly from the printed version of L1561 itself, as its page layout is even the same as L1561's; it shares with L1561 the same series of differences from the Scot/Knox/PRO group,[31] and has a few more textual differences of its own, apart from those resulting from its choice of English instead of Scots. But its chief differences are linguistic, and in this area Hall always chooses the English option, changing the wording completely where this is the only way to make a comprehensible English text. The main interest for us in the Hall version is in seeing how much alteration he thought necessary to achieve this, thus

	L1561	*Hall*
orthography:	operatioun, holl	operation, whole
phonology:	awne, yit	owne, yet
inflections:	forbodin	forbidden
vocabulary:	euangell,	gospel, spreads
	sparsis contrar	abrode against
use of inflected	all others realmes	all other realmes
adjective		

For Hall as the source of Waldegrave's 1581 edition, see Appendix §V.

The editions of the Confession: ·
2. The Parliamentary Editions

The second main category of printed texts of the Confession is those contained in editions of the Acts of Parliament. In none of these except APS are the proceedings of the 1560 as well as the 1567 parliament given.[37] The Confession therefore appears for the first time in the proceedings of James VI's parliament of December 1567, in which the legislation of the 'Reformation parliament' was confirmed. The first printing of this was Lekpreuik's edition of April 1568 (which I shall call L1568).[38] There were two more sixteenth-century editions of the Acts of this parliament: John Ross's in 1575 (which I shall call Ross) and Robert Waldegrave's of 1597, prepared by Sir John Skene (which I shall call Skene).

It is *a priori* likely that the source of these editions is the parliamentary record. Furthermore, these editions agree with L1561 in their differences from the Scot/Knox/PRO/group.[31] As we may also infer from L1561's having been granted parliamentary privilege that it too was likely to have had the parliamentary record as its source, and since it is quite likely that the record originally made in 1560 was used for the 1567 parliament (see p. 64), we can be fairly confident that it was indeed the same parliamentary record which was used as the source for both L1561 and the sixteenth-century editions of the Acts of Parliament.

In addition, it seems probable to me that both Ross and Skene were using the printed text of L1568 as their source (see Appendix § III.), and so have nothing to tell us about the archetype of their group. What they can show, however, is whether there was any specific development in language choice later in the sixteenth century. In fact the main change seems to be that anglicisation does increase in the later editions, but in two different ways. Ross anglicises in a haphazard manner, sometimes adhering very closely to L1568, and at other times, as in the example from chapter 6 given below, moving quite far from it. Skene on the other hand anglicises a little all the time, and is also more consistent, for instance in regularly giving past tenses and past participles in *-ed* rather than L1568's *-it*.

L1568, however, I think *was* using the manuscript of the parliamentary record (see Appendix § IV). It may be worth spending a moment or two here examining how faithful a transcriber of the manuscripts of the parliamentary records Lekpreuik usually is when printing the Acts. Very few of the original manuscripts of Parliament survive for this period, and even fewer correspond with those actually printed by Lekpreuik. One of these is printed in Lekpreuik's edition of the Acts of Queen Mary and her predecessors, published in 1566. It is for 15 March 1543 (APS II. 424b). Here Lekpreuik's own preference is clearly for digraphs in *-i*, as *weill, seilis, keiparis, quhairfoir* against the manuscript's *wele, selis, keperis, quharefore*, and for *-ȝie* against *-ȝe* as in *failȝie, assolȝie*; both of these types of preference could be attributed to the twenty-year gap between the manuscript and 1566, as both characteristics are increasingly prevalent as the sixteenth century proceeds. It is of course noteworthy that it is the more up-to-date *Scots* option that Lekpreuik chooses here, and not an English option. Other preferences that he shows, for each of which there are several examples in this Act, are: *not* for *no*ᵗ, *els* for *ellis*, *thay* for *yai*, *chancellar* for *chanceler*, *souerane* for *souirane*. Many of these, though not all, could be interpreted as moving away from the restrictedly Scots towards the common English option. This is confirmed by his alterations of the 28 August 1571 record in his 1573 edition, where for example he has *haue* for *haif*, *richteously* for *richtuouslie*, *ratifyit* for *ratefiit*. However, in nearly every case, for the 1571 as for the 1543 record, he retains *-is* plurals, and in every case he keeps the 3rd person singular present verb ending *-is*, and the past tense/past participle ending *-it*. The overall effect is very strongly Scots. And as a fairly similar effect is produced in L1568, perhaps we can safely assume that this is by a similar amount of change from his exemplar. But in L1561, clearly Lekpreuik was not using the same system at all.

We had a brief glimpse of L1561's strange mixture of English and Scots in the Biblical quotation on page 62. Now let us see a little more of it, in comparison with the other versions. If we take some of the words which show variation between the texts in chapter 6:

Scot:	quhen, awin glorie, warld, quho tuke, sick utheris, ather/eythir.
Knox E	(N.B. at this point the scribe is C, the more Scots of the two) quhan, awin glory, warld, quha tuik, sick vtheris, either.
PRO:	quhan, awin glorye, warld, quho took, suche vtheris, eyther.
L1561:	quhen, awne glorie, world, who tuke, suche others, eyther.
L1568:	quhan, awin glorie, warlde, quha tuik, sic utheris, outher.
Ross:	quhen, owen glorie, worlde, who tuke, suche vtheris, ether.
Skene:	quhen, awin glory, warld, quha tuke, sic vthers, either.

We can turn this information into more objectively assessable figures if we adopt the fairly simple system of assigning one point for every feature, whether it be Scots, English, or common to both. Thus each word will have four points assigned to it, one each for phonology, orthography, morphology and lexis. For the chapter 6 sample above, this yields the following:

	Scots	English	Common
Scot	14	1	21
Knox	14	1	21
PRO	9	6	21
L1561	3	9	24
L1568	17	0	19
Ross	6	8	22
Skene	11	2	23

This sample is of course far too small to be able to do more than give a sketchy indication of differences between the texts. However, the first point which can be noted is that common English/Scots features form the largest group in all the texts. Secondly, the ratio of Scots to English varies enormously between the texts, from 3:9 to 17:0; and this variation comes almost wholly from the areas of spelling and phonology. It is also clear that L1561 has by far the lowest 'Scots quotient', while L1568 has the highest.

If we were correct in our analysis of Lekpreuik's usual practice when transcribing the parliamentary records, we can infer that the parliamentary record in this case was very similar to or perhaps even slightly higher in its Scots content than L1568. This of course need not mean that the original of the Confession was equally high in Scots—the parliamentary scribe was very likely to be 'normalising' his source as far as possible to his own usual fairly dense Scots. But it does mean that L1561's source was very Scots in style, and that he has converted this into a much more anglicised text.

I would tentatively suggest that perhaps L1561's extraordinary mixture of language is due to his not yet being in the habit of printing in *Scots*. The Confession, after all, was almost certainly Lekpreuik's first attempt with a Scots text. He had probably just arrived in Scotland from abroad, where his previous experience as a printer was highly unlikely to have made him accustomed to the conventions of Scottish typography. But he *was* likely to be familiar with English conventions even if it was not England in which he had been working, because of the sheer quantity of books being produced in English by this time. Perhaps this indeed is the explanation of why so many apparently glaringly obvious Scotticisms survive in Lekpreuik—that he was not consciously trying to suppress Scots at all; but that his knowledge of written English was so much better than his knowledge of written Scots that he constantly fell into the habits of English. His other Scots work in 1561, the Norvell poems, is also very anglicised, and shows some of the same 'hybrid' features that are found in

L1561, such as the use of *an* as the indefinite article before consonants. But from the evidence of his 1563 *Scots* books, he had by then thoroughly mastered the conventions of Scots. This is particularly clear from his edition of John Davidson's 'Ane answer to the Tractiue . . . be Maister Quintine Kennedy', which is a dialogue between Kennedy and Davidson, both of them in Scots, and also in 'The Ressoning betuix the Abbote of Crosraguell and John Knox', where Kennedy's contributions are given in Scots, and Knox's in a faintly scotticised English. By 1566, as we have seen, when he prints the Acts of Parliament, he is confidently and correctly modernising the Scots of twenty years earlier.

What then can these versions of the Confession tell us about the linguistic attitudes of the reformers, and in particular about their position in the Scots versus English controversy? In the first place, there is no sign of editorial control by the leaders of the Reformation over the language of any of the versions of the Confession. Nor do they seem to have been imposing any particular linguistic line on the original draft. In vocabulary the authors of the Confession have almost always selected the neutral common Scots/English item, and in grammar there is little that is specifically Scots. In phonology and spelling, however, the original draft would appear to have chosen the Scots option rather more frequently, if the immediately derived texts, Scot, Knox and PRO, may be taken as a reliable guide. The most obvious feature in almost all the extant versions is that shared by other sixteenth-century works, namely a great deal of variation in orthography, both within Scots and between Scots and English, and some variation also in phonology between Scots and English. Some of the versions show a little consistency, but this is confined to one or two minor points, such as preferring either *-it* or *-ed*, or preferring spellings with *i*-digraph to those with final *-e*. This stylistic pattern of superficial consistency is also to be found in other sixteenth-century writers. The only version of the Confession in a consistent style is L1568, and this is the one which we have shown to be closely derived from the parliamentary record. That genre of prose was one of the few to have a well-established model to follow in sixteenth-century Scots. Indeed, the absence of a coherent style in all of the versions except L1568 is, I think, a symptom of the ailing state of Scots prose at this time. The subsequent and continuing failure to remedy this by developing imitable models for all types of Scots prose guaranteed its eventual demise. The evidence from the 1560 Scots Confession of Faith, however, does not support the idea that the reformers had any particular love of English for its own sake, or any positive antagonism to Scots. In fact they do not seem to have been initiating any new trends at all.

APPENDIX: Textual variants and the inter-relationships of the texts

§ I

The manuscripts and editions of the Confession fall into two main groups, which for convenience I shall call the Scot group, containing Scot, Knox E and G and PRO, and the Lekpreuik group, containing L1561, Hall, L1568, Ross and Skene. The main pieces of evidence which point to this two-fold division are as follows:

1   Numbering of chapters. There is no such numbering in the Scot group. The Lekpreuik group does number the chapters, *and* makes an error. L1561 and Hall jump from chapter 12 to 14; L1568, Ross and Skene jump from 13 to 15. The difference can be easily explained by the later editions having gone on numbering correctly for one further chapter without checking the exemplar; then at the next chapter noticing the actual number given as xv and giving that. Modern editions usually do number the chapters, and any such numbers given here are corrected numbers.

2   The Title. The two groups have slightly different Titles (PRO has no Title). Laing, II. 93-4 gives an example of each, i.e. Lekpreuik's Title as well as Knox's.

3   Chapter 14 (Laing, II. 106). Knox E has 'geve we may *ganestand* it' and 'the transgressing of any other commandiment in the First or Second Table, we confesse and affirme to be syn, by the which Goddis *hote displeasour* is kendilled against the proude and unthankfull world'.

   (a) *ganestand* Knox E, PRO; *gainstand* Scot; *withstand* L1561, Hall, L1568, Ross, Skene.

   (b) *hote displeasour* Knox E, PRO, Scot; *hate and displesour* L1561, Hall; *hait and displesoure* L1568; *hait and displeasure* Ross; *anger and displesure* Skene.

In (a) we can see clearly the split between the two groups.

In (b) I take it we see the descendants of *Goddis hait displesour* (a conclusion also arrived at by the editor of APS 1560). The Scot group or its source has anglicised this to *hote displesour*. The source of the Lekpreuik group has misheard or misread the phrase as containing the English noun 'hate', and has added 'and' to give some sense. Skene however has realised there was something wrong with the phrase in its new form and has emended it to *anger and displesure*.

4   Chapter 21 (Laing, II. 115). Knox E has 'Christ Jesus, in his *naturall* substance'.

naturall Knox E, Scot, PRO; *Eternall* L1561, Hall, L1568, Ross, Skene. *Eternall* is theologically correct here; the error has arisen from the words being near anagrams, and has been confirmed by the discussion earlier in the chapter of transubstantiation, in which the phrase 'Christis naturall body' was used.

5   The final Biblical quotation (Laing, II. 120). Knox E has 'lett all Nationis *atteane* to thy trew knowledge'.

atteane Knox E, Scot, PRO; *cleue*, *cleif* L1561, Hall, L1568, Ross, Skene. This again shows the split between the two groups clearly.

6   The Colophon (PRO has no Colophon). The date of the Act being read in Parliament is wrongly given as 17 July 1560 in Knox E and Scot. The Lekpreuik group correctly has 17 Aug 1560.

§ II

I should also like to suggest that the Scot group derives from a draft of the compilers before it went to parliament; either the final draft, or perhaps Knox's own. Such a draft would not originally contain the Title or Colophon, as both of these refer to its passing by parliament, and in this basic form I think it was copied by PRO (see §I.2 and 6). In addition I would suggest that the Scot group's versions of both the Title and the Colophon (with wrong date) were taken from the parliamentary record when it was first made up, that the record was subsequently changed, and that it is the later version which is found in the Lekpreuik group. I think that the Title was changed principally in order to remove the statement of the Confession having been *ratified* by the Estates, as this would certainly have been regarded as provocative; the final version of the Title is more bland. So far as the Colophon is concerned, the manuscripts of the records elsewhere show errors in date, which are usually scored through and corrected later; in this case the error could be due to the Parliament's actually having begun in July.

§ III *L1568 the exemplar of Ross and Skene*

1   The identical and wrong chapter numbering of L1568, Ross and Skene, which is also different from that of L1561 (see §I.1), make it more likely that the later parliamentary editions were copying L1568 rather than looking at the manuscript (which presumably contained L1561's error).

2   Chapter 14. Where L1561 has 'to *suffer* innocent blode to be shed', L1568 and Ross have *lufe* and Skene *let*. I think this results from the archetype giving *suffer* in abbreviated form with a back-curving stroke for the final -*er*; L1568 misreads the initial *s*- as *l*- (as he also seems to do in chapter 7 where I think his *all* should be *als* = 'also'); he then has *luff* + the curving stroke, which he either does not notice or thinks is merely an ornamental flourish, since he already has sense of a sort. He then gives the word in his own spelling, *lufe*. Ross just follows this reading, but Skene again realises the sense is not right, and guesses an emendation, not the kind of emendation that would have been suggested by the letters themselves, but an emendation *ad sensum* to *let*. I should have thought it very likely that if Skene had had the manuscript before him, he would not have made that emendation.

3   The Preface is missing from all three parliamentary editions, but not from any of the other versions. This is not in itself a proof that the later versions are taken directly from L1568: for if it was felt inappropriate to give it in 1568, because of its specific application to the period immediately before 1560, it should have been thought even more inappropriate for 1575 and 1597. But its absence in all three editions does add weight to the probability that Ross and Skene were copying direct from L1568.

§ IV *The MS of the parliamentary record, not L1561 or Hall, the source of L1568*

1   The misreadings by L1568 given in §III.2 show that the actual manuscript itself was L1568's source.

2   Chapter 8. Knox E has

quhatsoever we have *lost* in Adam.

lost Knox E, Scot, PRO, L1561, Hall; *tint*, *tynt* L1568, Ross, Skene. This I take to mean that the Scot group's source had *lost*; the Lekpreuik group's source, the parliamentary record, had *tint*, but L1561 followed by Hall anglicised this to *lost*, while L1568 transmitted it without alteration.

§V   *Hall the source of Waldegrave's 1581 edition*
1   Hall has *gospel* at all points where the other early texts have *evangel* (see p. 61).
2   In the Preface (Laing, II. 96) Hall has *spreads abrode against* where the others have *sparsis contrar* and variants.
3   Also in the Preface (Laing, II. 96) Hall omits a substantial clause and removes the next clause to make the necessary correction of grammar.

All three of these features and many more points of purely linguistic variation in Hall are also found in Waldegrave's 1581 edition of the Confession, contained within his edition of the Negative Confession. Waldegrave, then, is directly derived from Hall. It is worth remembering that it is this 1581 edition by Waldegrave which is so roundly condemned by John Hamilton for its Englishness, both in its language and in the fact of its being published in London (*Catholic Tractates of the 16th century*, ed. T G Law, (S.T.S. 1901), p. 105). Here we have a further level of Englishness, that the text of the 1561 Confession contained in Waldegrave is from the English edition of 1561.

NOTES

1   The idea that the Scots Confession might be worth examining for this purpose was suggested to me by a paper given by Rev. Dr Ian Hazlett of Glasgow University to the first meeting of the Scottish Society for Reformation History in May 1981. I am most grateful to Dr Hazlett, both in general for providing the initial stimulus and for many specific points of information about the Confession, and also to several other members of the Society, who have been most generous in the help and advice they have given, in particular Dr John Durkan, Dr Michael Lynch and Rev. Dr Duncan Shaw. I should also like to thank Dr Lynch and Mr A J Aitken for their helpful comments on the first draft of this paper. I gratefully acknowledge the assistance given by the Carnegie Trust for the Universities of Scotland and by the Scottish National Dictionary Association Ltd towards the expenses of the research.
2   *The Forme of prayers and Ministration of the Sacraments etc used in the English Church at Geneva* . . . published in Scotland in 1562 in reduced form, and again in 1565 in a form 'approved and received by the Church of Scotland', including the complete 150 Psalms (for the first time in any edition), both editions published in Edinburgh by Robert Lekpreuik; the 1565 and subsequent editions have been variously entitled at various times, either officially or unofficially, 'The Psalm Book', 'Knox's Liturgy', 'The Book of Common Order'.
3   See J D McClure, 'Scottis, Inglis, Suddroun: language labels and language attitudes' in *Proceedings of the Third International Conference on Scottish Language and Literature (Medieval and Renaissance)*, (Stirling/Glasgow 1981), eds. R J Lyall and F Riddy, pp. 52–69.
4   APS II. 415, for 15 Mar. 1543
5   APS II. 425. Few of the early translations contained all of the Old Testament, hence perhaps the change in description between the 15 Mar. and 19 Mar. entries.
6   Laing, I. 303–4 (see note 12)
7   Murdoch Nisbet's Scots version of the New Testament, made around 1520, had never been published.
8   For a full discussion of these options see A J Aitken, 'Variation and Variety in

Written Middle Scots', *Edinburgh Studies in English and Scots* (1971), eds. A J
Aitken, A McIntosh and H Pálsson, pp. 177–209.

9   Hazlett. See note 1

10   Cf. Nisbet's version of this verse, which is based on Purvey's revision of Wyclif.
     Purvey and Wyclif have 'gospel'; Nisbet has 'euangel'.

11   i.e. Hall, Waldegrave, Vautrollier (see next).

12   See end-list for a full description of abbreviated references.

13   G D Henderson, *The Scots Confession*, (Edinburgh, 1937), pp. 15 ff.

14   Laing, II. 128

15   Cal. State Papers Scot. I. No. 902

16   Cal. State Papers Scot. I. No. 880

17   Cal. State Papers Scot. I. No. 881

18   Laing, II. 93

19   W Dunlop in his version of the Confession in *A Collection of Confessions of Faith*
     II. (Edinburgh, 1722), does give present participles in *-and*, but he shows other
     signs of deliberate archaising, including the erroneous hyper-Scotticism *despichtfull*
     (cf. Knox E *dispytefull* (Laing, II. 95)); so this feature probably does not derive
     from some other unknown early source.

20   Cal. State Papers Scot. I. No. 889

21   The Confession is at fos. 224^r–239^r. This manuscript is the main basis of Laing's
     text of Knox and also is one of the sources of the APS 1560 text.

22   Dickinson, I. *Bibliographical Note*, pp. lxxxviii to cix

23   Laing, II. pp. xxxiii–xxxv

24   The Confession in Knox G occupies from fo. 152^r to fo. 153^r, and chapter 4 ends at
     the foot of 153^r. 153^v is blank. At the top of 154^r we find 'This oure confessioun was
     publiclie red . . .'. These are the words immediately following the complete
     Confession in Knox E. I suspect that this indicates that the scribe of Knox G was in
     doubt whether he needed to complete the Confession, because printed editions of
     it were available. His leaving 153^v blank suggests that he was awaiting further
     instructions from his client. If this is so, it seems probable that nothing further was
     ever added. It is certainly the case that Knox G was in this state in the early
     eighteenth century when Robert Wodrow saw it. He has a note to this effect in the
     margin of the early seventeenth century quarto manuscript of Knox's *History*
     owned by him (Laing's MS IV, N.L.S. Wodrow MSS Quarto VIII), at the end of
     chapter 4. Whether or not, then, it has always been incomplete, Knox G certainly
     did not contain the rest of the Confession in Laing's day. Laing nevertheless ascribes
     variants in the later part of the Confession to Knox G (see in particular chapter 22).
     His actual source at this point was almost certainly the 1732 edition of Knox's
     History, which claims to be based largely on Knox G, and which Laing describes as
     so faithfully giving the text of Knox G that 'an entire collation . . . might only
     have exhibited slight occasional changes in orthography'. I rather think the 'might
     have' gives the game away, and that Laing began a transcription by which he found
     the 1732 edition to be so close to Knox G that he did not, in fact, collate the whole,
     but then used the 1732 edition as his source of information for the rest of the
     manuscript, including the Confession.

25   I am most grateful to Jane Dawson for providing the reference for this document
     (see References, p. 78).

26 Cal. State Papers Scot. I. No. 882
27 See his letter of 15 Aug. in Cal. State Papers Scot. I. No. 880
28 See his letter of 19 Aug. in Cal. State Papers Scot. I. No. 886
29 The edition now seems to exist only in a single copy in the possession of the British Library, Catalogue No. G. 11837, which is reproduced in facsimile as no. 555 of *The English Experience*, (Amsterdam/New York, 1972). Laing does not seem to have had access to a copy; his only information about the edition is bibliographical (Laing II. 120). Scot's edition is the basis of another highly regarded modern edition (see e.g. A C Cochrane, *Reformed Confessions of the 16th century* (London, 1966), p. 162), that of Theodor Hesse, in *Bekenntnisschriften und Kirchenordnungen der nach Gottes Wort Reformierten Kirche* (ed. W. Niesel), Heft 2 (Munich, 1938), pp. 79–117. Unfortunately Hesse's information about the other Scots versions of the Confession is derived wholly from Laing, and therefore also contains Laing's errors. In addition he fails to give all the correct information supplied by Laing, and also misreports him, e.g. by giving readings as being only in Knox which are also in L1561 and Hall.
30 John Leslie, *De Origine, Moribus et Rebus Gestis Scotorum* (Rome, 1578), p. 584
31 For details of these correspondences, see Appendix § I.
32 Dean of Guild Register, fo. 51^v: I am extremely grateful to Dr Michael Lynch for this information. The only other John Scot known to have been in Edinburgh at the time was an apprentice, who is not likely to be the person in question here.
33 Wheeling and dealing of this kind by a committed Protestant faction in order to gain the services and perhaps the loyalty of a printer seems a quite likely scenario for Reformation Edinburgh. Cf. Lynch, *passim*.
34 Scottish Record Office, Edinburgh Burgh Register of Deeds, 1561–70, B22/8/1, fos. 117^v–118. I am most grateful to Dr John Durkan for drawing my attention to the contract, and for providing me with a transcript.
35 See note 2. This was indeed Lekpreuik's first work printed in roman type rather than black-letter.
36 Lynch, p. 281
37 APS 1560 is in fact a conflation of APS 1567 with (mainly) Knox E.
38 L1568 is the main source of APS 1567.

REFERENCES

APS: *The Acts of the Parliaments of Scotland,* eds T Thomson and C Innes, (Edinburgh, 1814–75)

APS 1560: The version of the Confession given in APS II. pp. 526–34, for 17 Aug. 1560

APS 1567: The version of the Confession given in APS III. pp. 14–22, for 15 Dec. 1567

Cal. State Papers Scot.: *Calendar of the State Papers relating to Scotland and Mary, Queen of Scots* 1547–1603, eds J Bain and others, (Edinburgh, 1898–)

Dickinson: *John Knox's History of the Reformation in Scotland,* ed. W C Dickinson, (Edinburgh, 1949)

Hall: *The Confession of the Faythe and Doctrine beleued and professed, by the Protestantes of the Realme of Scotlande* . . . (London, 1561). (S.T.C. 22017)

Hazlett: W I Hazlett, *The Scots Confession of 1560: texts, sources and theologies* (unpublished). See note 1

Knox E: Manuscript of Knox's *History of the Reformation*, in Edinburgh University Library, Catalogue No. La. III. 210

Knox G: Manuscript of Knox's *History of the Reformation*, in Glasgow University Library, Catalogue No. MS Gen. 1123

L1561: *The Confessione of the fayth and doctrin beleued and professed by the Protestantes of the Realme of Scotland* . . . (Edinburgh, 1561) (S.T.C. 22018)

L1568: *The Actis of the Parliament of* . . . *Iames the sext.* (Edinburgh, 1568) (S.T.C. 21880)

Laing: *The Works of John Knox,* ed. D Laing. (Edinburgh, 1846–64)

Lynch: Michael Lynch *Edinburgh and the Reformation.* (Edinburgh, 1981)

Nisbet: *The New Testament in Scots,* ed. T G Law. (S.T.S.) 1901–1905

PRO: Manuscript of the Confession in the Public Record Office, London, Catalogue No. S.P. 52/5, fos. 22^r–31^r

Ross: *The Actis of the Parliament of* . . . *Iames the sext.* (Edinburgh, 1575) (S.T.C. 21881)

Scot: *The Confessioun of faith professit and belevit be the Protestantes within the Realme of Scotland* . . . (Edinburgh, 1561) (S.T.C. 22016)

Skene: *The Lawes and Actes of Parliament, maid be King Iames the First, and his successours* . . . (Edinburgh, 1597) (S.T.C. 21877)

Tindale 1534: W. Tindale, *The New Testament.* (1534)

Vautrollier: John Knox, *The first booke of the History of the Reformation of religioun within the realme of Scotland* (also second and third books, incomplete, 1587) (S.T.C. 15071)

Waldegrave: *The confession of the true and Christian fayth according to Gods word, and actis of Parliament* . . . (London 1581) (S.T.C. 22022)

FIVE

The Vernacular Revival and the Poetic Thrill: A Hedonist Approach

Thomas Crawford

1

It is not my intention in the present essay to write yet another historical survey of verse written in Scots in the eighteenth century. I shall rather try, in a very limited way, to establish some of its specifically poetic qualities without worrying too much about its limitations. My methods will be synchronic, not diachronic, and the language of this school of writers will be treated solely as a literary medium. In spite of my title, the approach will not be entirely subjective, but will be based partly on the still useful view of Russian Formalism and the American New Criticism of the nineteen-thirties that poems are 'autotelic' and self-subsistent, and partly on the older opinion that what is important is the amount and type of pleasure they give to readers or hearers. The 'language poets use' is deemed good or bad because of the pleasure or discomfort it causes in the best readers, reciters and hearers in the speech-community, who experience these effects because they have learned to respond actively to certain codes of what may be called aesthetic language. (In most cases, aesthetic language is merely ordinary language organised for artistic purposes.)

Poetical writing by Scots from the second decade of the eighteenth century to the death of Hogg in 1835 can be regarded as a double system with both parts interacting. On the one hand is the resurgent poetry in English by those who emigrated to the south, like Thomson, Mallet, Smollett and Falconer, and those who stayed at home, like Robert Blair, John Home and Thomas Blacklock. On the other hand was the poetry of the Vernacular Revival. To make matters more complicated, Thomson and the others belong in a sense to English literature considered as a system as well as to Scottish, just as Henry James and T S Eliot belong to English literature as well as to American; to make them more complex still, the major figures of the vernacular movement not only wrote poems in what looks like English on the printed page, but made

Scots-English and English-English do for them what aureation did for the makars—they used, that is to say, both systems. Furthermore, there was still a third system, that of popular song and balladry, interacting with both the vernacular and the Scots-English movements. As early as 1666 Pepys records Mrs Knipp singing 'her little Scotch song of "Barbary Allen"' (*Diary*, 2 Jan. 1665-6); the Aberdeenshire-born counter-tenor John Abell brought Scots songs to London after 1679, and his songs as well as those of earlier and later immigrants stimulated English hack writers to publish pseudo-Scots songs about pastoral Jockys and Jennys and Scotch Moggys of the type printed in Tom Durfey, *Wit and Mirth: or, pills to purge Melancholy* (1699). A number of these Durfey songs came back to Scotland to enter a period of oral transmission which turned them into something like genuine folk songs,[1] while English broadside ballads like 'The Babes in the Wood' and a number of Robin Hood ballads[2] formed part of the popular repertoire along with such pieces as 'The Life and Age of Man' which Burns remembered his mother singing to his grand-uncle whose 'most voluptuous enjoyment was to sit down & cry' while she did so.[3] The language of one part of this poetical 'system' of popular song—the ballad part—is treated elsewhere in this volume by Hamish Henderson (pp. 100-128). The popular song system was also a double one, in which vernacular Scots and Scots-English (with many of its songs imported from England) interacted. And the fact that music is inseparable from song meant that in the popular song system Gaelic was able to make a marginal contribution, through tunes of Gaelic origin, both Irish and Scottish. The other point at which Gaelic culture touched the interacting binaries, Scots and Scots-English,[4] was at the English pole, in Macpherson's Ossianic concoctions, based ultimately on Gaelic fragments, crossed with European primitivist and sentimentalist concepts, and expressed in a poetic prose drawing its rhythms in part from the Authorised Version of the Bible (which of course was by the mid eighteenth century thoroughly integrated into the speech and thought of the Scottish people) and in part from English translations of Graeco-Roman epic.

2

The most distinctive—though not necessarily the most intense—pleasure that can be derived from the poetry of the Scottish Vernacular Revival is got from verse whose language fits in with the ordinary meaning of the term 'vernacular': that is, where the language reproduces the features of everyday speech. Where vocabulary is the strongest component of such poems, our pleasure comes from the imagination—the historical imagination; from a willed 'feeling into' the experience of the community whose vocabulary we have learned as detached observers during our first reading of the poem. The best example is probably Burns's 'The Auld Farmer's New-Year-morning

Salutation to his Auld Mare, Maggie'.[5] Our final response is to the total experience conveyed in the poem, which is that of the shared working life of man and horse; the structure is thus biographical, derived from their twin interacting lives, embodied in an address with some sentimental[6] overtones, a gentle wistfulness for struggles past and gone (lines 91-6). Counterposed to the retrospective regret is an intense awareness of past *action*, which saves the poem from sentimentality in the bad sense; the actions are conveyed in verbs which are partly onomatopoeic:

> (i) How thou wad prance, an' snore, an' screigh
> An' tak the road!
> (lines 45-6)

> (ii) Thou never lap, an' stent, an' breastet,
> Then stood to blaw;
> (lines 81-2)

Thus the sound system of Scots co-operates with lexis (nouns and verbs of the agricultural vocabulary) and colloquial syntax to sustain our delight in these two lives, each the mirror of the other, presented with the utmost economy and skill. In Ramsay's elegies on Maggy Johnston (1718: ?written 1711), John Cowper, Kirk-Treasurer's man (1718: ?written 1714), and Lucky Wood in the Canongate, an ale-seller (1718: ?written 1717); and also in the 'Last Advice' of Lucky Spence, 'a famous bawd who flourished for several years about the beginning of the eighteenth century' (1718),[7] the source of interest is again the celebration of characters. But our pleasure comes also from the recognition of idiom and the rising and falling intonations of a speaking voice.

It is in 'Lucky Spence' that Ramsay's poetry of intonation reaches its peak, with a 'poetic thrill' that, however different from the thrills and terrors of the Sublime, is yet at the comic level concerned with the infliction of pain:

> There's ae sair cross attends the craft,
> That curst Correction-house, where aft
> Vild Hangy's taz ye'r riggings saft
> Makes black and blae,
> Enough to pit a body daft;
> But what'll ye say.
> (lines 49-54)

That Ramsay himself was aware of what I have called the poetry of intonation is proved by his own note on line 54: 'The emphasis of this phrase, like many others, cannot be understood but by a native.' This brings us to a crux in the evaluation of colloquial poetry. How can Americans, or Australians, or English people, react fully to this stanza of 'Lucky Spence's Last Advice'? How can Americans, or Scots, or people from the English provinces react fully to the end of the second section of 'The Waste Land', containing such lines as:

It's them pills I took, to bring it off, she said . . .
You are a proper fool, I said.
Well, if Albert won't leave you alone, there it is, I said,
What you get married for if you don't want children?
(lines 159, 162-5)

They must make the same sort of effort as Germans and Italians do in order to catch the nuances of standard English or American-English intonations. With present technology, this involves hearing 'but what'll ye say' and 'It's them pills I took, to bring it off, she said' several times on cassette, pronounced by the right sort of Edinburgh and London speakers, thus registering a permanent mental impression of how the lines might sound.

In their four 'Familiar Epistles' sent to each other from 26 June to 4 August 1719, William Hamilton of Gilbertfield and Allan Ramsay reach a still higher level of colloquiality, perhaps because their letters are not monologues but at least in part imaginary conversations in verse. Thus in 'Answer II, Edinburgh, August 4th, 1719', Ramsay reports a dialogue between his muse and himself in which the muse commands:

> Swith to Castalius' fountain-brink,
> Dad down a-grouf, and take a drink,
> Syne whisk out paper, pen and ink,
>   And do my bidding;
> Be thankfou, else I'se gar ye stink
>   Yet on a midding.
>   (lines 19-24)

Ramsay's own gloss for 'dad down a-grouf' is 'fall flat on your belly'. Using Ramsay as his model, Burns takes Ramsay's type of colloquiality much further, and not just in epistles. The dialogue part of 'Death and Doctor Hornbook', a narrative poem, is built out of similar racy, proverbial and semi-proverbial expressions to those used in 'Lucky Spence': the difference is that Ramsay achieves perfect fusion between speech and stanza-form only occasionally, whereas Burns does it consistently; and also it is only rarely that Ramsay finds expressions as fitting, and therefore as beautiful, in their context, as these:

> 'Fient haet o't wad hae pierc'd the heart
>   Of a kail-runt'.
>   (lines 101-2)
> 'Waes me for Johnny Ged's-Hole now . . .
> Nae doubt they'll rive it wi' the plew;
>   They'll ruin Johnie!'
>   (lines 133, 136-7)

Burns could have said of 'Waes me for Johnnie Ged's-Hole now' what Ramsay did of 'But what'll ye say': 'the emphasis . . . cannot be understood but by a native', for the effect comes in the first place from intonation. The difference is partly rhythmic, as can be seen from the scansion suggested above, and partly semantic. The Ramsay question means something like 'so what?', 'It's all the same', 'ça ne fait rien'; it conveys an emotional attitude to life in general, and is again rather colourless apart from the intonation. Burns, however, takes a phrase derived from 'a common Indo-European interjection used as a natural exclamation of lament' (NED), often in Scots applied to a person ('Waes me for Prince Charlie', W Glen, *Poems* (1874), p. 121), and uses it of a person's possession or product. Further, that person's name has itself conceptual status—it has something of the value of a common noun, as well as of a proper noun, since it was the country name for the gravedigger (Burns's own gloss). But there is also a kind of metonymy present, involving metaphor as well: 'Ged is Scots for pike, whose greed is as the grave's',[8] and Death's greed is by association attributed to the gravedigger.

As already suggested, it is in epistles that the colloquial mode reaches its peak. Fergusson's two examples, the 'Answer to Mr J.S.'s Epistle' and 'To Andrew Gray', though vigorous, are relatively undistinguished; however, we may compare the 'dad doun a-grouf' stanza of 'Answer II to Hamilton of Gilbertfield', already quoted, with stanzas 6 and 7 of the 'Second Epistle to J. Lapraik':

> Sae I gat paper in a blink,
> An' doun gaed stumpie in the ink:
> Quoth I: 'Before I sleep a wink,
>   I vow I'll close it;
> An' if ye winna mak it clink,
>   By Jove I'll prose it!'
>
> Sae I've begun to scrawl, but whether
> In rhyme, or prose, or baith thegither,
> Or some hotch-potch that's rightly neither,
>   Let time mak proof;
> But I shall scribble down some blether
>   Just clean aff-loof.
>   (lines 31-42)

Remarkable though the Ramsay stanza is, and however striking the 'dad down a-grouf' expression is in itself, the Burns lines are again superior. Once more, this is partly a matter of rhythm, the management of enjambement and the pauses at the end of lines, and partly that Burns creates a subtle interplay of contrast between himself and the Muse. 'I' is active in getting paper, but the pen goes into the inkhorn as if of its own accord, and is personalised through a term, 'stumpie', that has almost the force of a proper noun—a nickname; its diminutive ending conveys an affection for the writing-instrument that recalls a farmer's feeling for his beasts ('The Auld Farmer's New-Year-morning Salutation', 'The Death and Dying Words of Poor Mailie, the Author's only

Pet Yowe', 'Poor Mailie's Elegy'). The whole stanza creates a remarkably vivid impression of what it feels like to be 'in a writing mood'. Further, Ramsay's Muse is in complete command, and even threatens that the poet will end up on a dung-heap if he doesn't do what she wants, whereas Burns if necessary is prepared to master her. His drive to dominate is perfectly rendered by his use of 'prose' as a verb. Yet the active decision to write results in practice in will-less spontaneity; the poet is excitedly carried along in a flood of words of whose import he is not quite sure; the twin poles of the contradiction are 'I' and 'aff-loof'.

3

Everything I have said so far goes clean against the view which stresses the artificiality of the language of the vernacular revival.[9] We have been too often misled by the propaganda of the revivalists themselves: in order to further their aims they claimed to be going back to the language of the past, not reproducing contemporary language.

What recent writers on the period have done is to stress the role of consciousness in the revival.[10] It is, of course, only an apparent paradox that spontaneity and colloquial ease and vigour were the qualities most valued by the movement; these were precisely the qualities *consciously* aimed at. Apart from sundry lyric stanzas, the poets used principally six verse forms taken over from the seventeenth century. Three of these—common measure with its freer variant the ballad stanza, the octosyllabic couplet, and the pentameter couplet—are also popular English forms. A further three, 'Standard Habbie' (the Burns stanza), the 'Christ's Kirk on the Green' stanza, and the 'Cherrie and the Slae' stanza, may, whatever their antecedents, be treated as specific to Scotland. The last of these carries with it something of the artificiality of the poem by Alexander Montgomerie which gives it its name, a long dream-allegory which was actually sung and may even have been danced as an action-song with costume.[11] When Ramsay used it in 'The Vision', the result was grave and deliberately old-fashioned. It is again used solemnly and reflectively by Burns in the 'Epistle to Davie', and only by a tremendous technical tour-de-force is he able to make it express the energy and abandon of his anarchic beggars in 'Love and Liberty' (lines 1–28, 236–49). But the other two verse forms, 'Standard Habbie' and the 'Christ's Kirk' measure, with its variants, seem almost to contain within themselves the values of a plebeian colloquiality very different from, say, the aristocratic colloquiality of Pope's 'Epistle to Dr Arbuthnot' ('Shut, shut the door, good John! fatigu'd I said'), or Byron's *Don Juan*. Kenneth Buthlay has suggested that the two short lines of the Habbie stanza may 'correspond to some characteristic turn of speech in Scotsmen's use of their vernacular'[12], while others have seen a link with dance steps or the

'Scotch snap' in fiddle-music. Following the precedent of its sixteenth-century originals, the 'Christ's Kirk' stanza was used in poems of boisterous group celebration, rustic brawls, or 'Donnybrooks'.[13] The short line at the end of the stanza again reminds one of certain musical effects: it is as if the leading dancers have come all the way to the end of the row, or a new couple are about to enter the centre of the ring:

> An it be true that some Fowk says,
>   Ye'll girn yet in a Woody;
> Syne wi' her Nails she rave his Face,
> Made a' his black Baird bloody,
>   Wi' Scarts that Day.[14]

In 'The Christmass Bawing o' Monymuss' (1739) John Skinner adds north-eastern phonological features to his Lothian model, though his vocabulary, densely dialectal as it seems, contains few words that would be unknown in central parishes. In stanza 13 'bierly' and 'fow' (how) reproduce north-eastern pronunciation, and 'staffy-nevel job' (a set-to with cudgels and fists) is perhaps a local dialect expression:

> His cousin was a bierly swank,
>   A stier young man heght Robb,
> To mell wi twa he wadna mank
>   At staffy-nevel job:
> I wat na fow, but on a bank,
>   Whare thrangest was the mob,
> The cousins bicker'd wi' a clank,
>   Gart ane anither sob
>   And gasp that day.
>   (lines 109–117)

The Standard Habbie stanza was used more often in poems which concentrate on an individual person or—as in epistles—on a relationship in which the personalities of writer and recipient are vividly realised. This is partly because the original 'Habbie Simson' was an elegy which celebrated the achievements and character of an individual, and of course the other elegies and mock elegies which followed of necessity had an individual at their centre, even when they were concerned with an animal. Often, however, the community is powerfully present in the background: all the ceremonials and entertainments of Kilbarchan in 'Habbie Simson', all the personalities of the Mauchline Kirk Session and Ayr presbytery in 'Holy Willie's Prayer', and all the solid reality of Edinburgh in Fergusson's poems written in this measure. The original 'Christ's Kirk' set out to portray a community happening, though with individuals brought forward briefly for our perusal; and the community therefore remains central in most of its successors, as is evident from their titles—'Leith Races', 'Hallow Fair', 'The Ordination', 'The Holy Fair'. Our pleasure is in the energy

of violent motion or mental conflict within a group, and in the overall structure
of the contest or calendar custom portrayed.

4

At the level of individual lines or stanzas, the keenest pleasure is often produced when a spark crosses the gap that separates the ordinary vernacular of
every day from some other linguistic system, even when that system can be
regarded as subsidiary to general Scots, such as an occupational vocabulary or
even an 'in-group' jargon. Sometimes the surprise is an entirely comic product
of that 'willed spontaneity' which was such a feature of the movement, as in
macaronic verse like the seventeenth-century 'Polemo-Middinia', attributed to
Drummond of Hawthornden, or this stanza from Ramsay's second answer to
Hamilton of Gilbertfield:

> *Quisquis vocabit nos* vain-glorious,
> Shaw scanter skill, than *malos mores,*
> *Multi et magni* men before us
>   Did stamp and swagger,
> *Probatum est, exemplum* Horace,
>   Was a bauld bragger.
>   (lines 55–60)

This rather puerile virtuosity presumably formed the model for Burns's
exquisite deflation of the jargon of small-time pharmacists and quacks in
'Death and Doctor Hornbook'. In Burns the macaronics are integrated with the
character of Hornbook, as satirised: they are simultaneously part of the satirical
deflation, and funny in themselves (lines 121–6). The comic interplay between
Scots and Italian musical terms in the fifth recitativo of 'Love and Liberty' is
equally fitted to the high-pitched vigour of the fiddler. In Fergusson's 'Hallow
Fair' the gap is between eighteenth-century vernacular Scots and the regional
dialect of Aberdeen ('Come ye to me fa need', line 38) and conventional
Highland-English ('She maun pe see our guard', line 94; 'Pring in ta drunken
sot', line 96).

But some of the most vivid effects occur where the gap crossed is that
between the Scots and the English systems, particularly where the gap is
cultural as well as linguistic. These may be comic, as in the celebrated reductive
idiom, which is often seen as a blemish.[15] The main poets of the revival,
including Burns, were keenly aware of linguistic decorum which the reductive
idiom deliberately breaks. In Fergusson's 'Braid Claith' it is used ambivalently
to criticise the bourgeois persona of the poem, who in stanza 1 advises all
aspirants to poetic fame to give up the struggle and buy themselves a good
suit—the outward sign of respectability—instead. It is this persona who uses
Hudibrastic rhymes and the brutish image of 'snout on' to denigrate

would-be Scottish poets and men of science, and England's culture heroes as well (lines 49-50), whereby unconsciously giving himself away exactly as Holy Willie did by asking God to curse the generous, liberal Gavin Hamilton's 'kail and potatoes'. The reduction in 'Holy Willie's Prayer' is of the person and doctrine satirically attacked, and proceeds by means of terms familiar within the community, not extraordinary ones like Ramsay's dog-Latin. In cases where Burns himself, and not any persona of his invention, employs reductive techniques, they can sometimes blunt his social criticism, as David Craig has pointed out[16]; but at other times they can be most successful, as in the treatment of the royal family near the end of 'A Dream' (lines 109-17).

Interaction between the vernacular system and the English and Scots-English can produce effects ranging from the crudely parodic to the sublime. One type of contact is where the pentameter couplet, which had been used for example in Gavin Douglas's *Eneados* in the sixteenth century, is written with the contemporary English heroic couplet in mind, as in *The Gentle Shepherd* or Fergusson's two eclogues. In content *The Gentle Shepherd* is just as indebted to English models as 'Auld Reikie': it seeks to provide a more down-to-earth model for the realistic pastoral demanded by some French and English theorists than southron dialect imitations could achieve.[17] Ramsay's indebtedness to Gay's burlesque *Shepherd's Week* is curious: he saw that linguistic effects which in England could only be used for humour, could in Scotland be transformed into a serious presentation of rural life. Ramsay's shifts from Scots to what looks like English and back again in his treatment of Sir William Worthy raise problems of general application to Scottish writing in the eighteenth century. It has often been said—with qualifications like 'largely' or 'more or less'—that Worthy speaks in Scots when he visits his former estate incognito, and in English when he is being himself, and when soliloquising; and it has been stated too, that when Peggy thinks forward to her possible future status as a laird's wife she uses English, but on all ordinary occasions, Scots.[18]

Within Ramsay's drama Sir William speaks a single idiolect. Its unity is hidden by the inconsistencies of eighteenth-century Scots orthography, which is so uncertain as to give us little help in deciding how a word is to be pronounced. There are signals of a Scots pronunciation both in Sir William's final adjuration to his tenants and in his self-communings; they are just as natural, and therefore just as Scots, to Sir William, to his tenantry ('the society within the work') and to Ramsay's original audience, as are the denser Scottish passages when he is in disguise. This is confirmed by the colloquiality of 'now all's at rights' in line 230, the last line given to him in the play. As for Peggy, we must admit that her genteel future casts a shadow backwards over her language, rendering it latterly insipid—but not less Scottish in pronunciation. Take the lines:

My heart was like to burst; but now I see
Thy generous thoughts will save thy love for me.
With patience then I'll wait each wheeling year,
Hope time away, till thou with joy appear;
And all the while I'll study gentler charms,
To make me fitter for my traveller's arms:

(IV. ii. 166–71)

Peggy is doing exactly what Burns does in the 'But pleasures are like poppies spread' section of 'Tam o' Shanter' (lines 59–72); she is modulating into a type of expression which is not un-Scottish, though if we apply a test of strict verisimilitude it would not be 'natural' to girls of her upbringing; the lines distance her in mood as well as matter from her immediate surroundings. But whereas the Burns half-paragraph is a sheer delight,[19] our excerpt from Peggy is at best competent. It is where Ramsay employs a much denser Scots that he achieves originality in the pentameter couplet, as in Patie's description of a light-hearted amorous contest and yielding (I.i.121–34). Alexander Ross's couplets in *Helenore* show less Augustan influence than Ramsay's, and indeed he openly acknowledges his debt to the older Scottish tradition of Gavin Douglas, as well as directly to Ramsay (line 26). Just as Skinner injected north-eastern features into his poem in the Christ's Kirk stanza, so Ross introduced them into his narrative. His Muse, Scota, has a north-eastern pronunciation, and so too does his heroine, as in this account of a dream:

I thought that we were washing at our sheep
Intill a pool, an' O! but it was deep.
I thought a lad therein was like to drown;
His feet yeed frae him, an' his head yeed down;
Flaught-bred into the pool my sell I keest,
Weening to keep his head aboon at least:
But ere I wist, I clean was at the float;
I sanna tell you what a gloff I got:
My eyn grew blind, the lad I cudna see,
But ane I kent na took a claught of me,
An' fuish me out, an' laid me down to dreep.
Sae burden'd was I, I coud hardly creep.

(lines 1120–30)

'Yeed', 'keest' and 'fuish' are Northern forms, and 'flaught-bred' (with out-stretched hands or arms, like a bird) and this sense of 'gloff' (sudden shock) may also be regional. Our pleasure is rather like our response to some very simple lyrics, or to ballad narrative: it comes from the directness and vividness of her speech, the starkness of the story line, the absence of ornamentation. Ross's couplets are less indebted to contact with the English and Scots-English system than either Ramsay's or Fergusson's, though of course *Helenore*, as a whole, being a pastoral narrative, touches it at the level of genre.

M P McDiarmid is certainly correct when he says that in the opening inter-change in the 'Eclogue to the Memory of Dr Wilkie' Fergusson gives the couplet 'a polish and sweetness never achieved by Ramsay', and that his use of it in verse argument as in 'The Mutual Complaint of Plainstanes and Causey' and 'The Ghaists' marks another advance on Ramsay[20]—and, of course, on Ross. It is, however, with Fergusson's modification of the Spenserian stanza that the most original interaction between Scots language and an English verse-form takes place. By the mid eighteenth century the Spenserian stanza aroused very different expectations from those suggested by Standard Habbie, the Christ's Kirk stanza, or even the couplet. These, for Fergusson's contem-poraries, were primarily the slow, grave reflection of Canto I of Beattie's 'The Minstrel', published just two years before 'The Farmer's Ingle' first appeared in Ruddiman's *Weekly Magazine*, and the celebration of humble virtues in Shenstone's 'The Schoolmistress' (1742), about which the author says in his advertisement that he endeavoured there to imitate Spenser's 'language, his simplicity, his manner of description, and a peculiar tenderness of sentiment remarkable throughout his works'.[21] By choosing the Spenserian stanza for a poem entitled 'The Farmer's Ingle' Fergusson signalled that he was attempting something 'sage and serious' within the pastoral kind—that he intended the realistic imitation of everyday life. In Fergusson's poem the language is of course not Spenserian English but Scots—a demotic Scots which, because of the rhythmic pressure of the stanza and the inversions occasionally compelled by the rhymes, seems slightly distanced from actual speech and therefore more in accord with the notion of the revival's poetic language as an artifical construct than anything we have considered so far.

The occasional genuine or apparent Spenserian echo adds to this impression: 'For cleanly house loes he, tho' e'er sae mean' (line 18), 'Careless tho' death shou'd make the feast her foy' (line 81: only the sound of 'foy' is Spenserian, the word in its sense of 'farewell feast' being found all over the British Isles), 'And a lang lasting train o' peaceful hours succeed' (line 117). As for 'tender-ness of sentiment', this is most evident in Fergusson's compassion for the senile grandmother in the passage beginning 'O mock na this, my friends! but rather mourn' and ending with the antithetical metaphor, 'The mind's ay cradled whan the grave is near' (lines 68–72). To me, this is the best line in the poem, giving a pleasure which I instantly recognise as poetical. Others are 'And gar their thick'ning smeek salute the lift' (line 13: note the Scots-English literary word 'salute'); 'And ca' the leglen's treasure on the ground' (line 98: the effect of Scots-English 'treasure' is parallel to that of 'salute' in the previous example); 'The leaden god fa's heavy on their ein' (line 102: the contrast is now more complex: a stock southern literary periphrasis for Morpheus is equated with the process of falling asleep conceived as an action, so that 'fa' and 'heavy' acquire literal solidity); 'Yet thrift, industrious, bides her latest days' (line 73: the semi-personification of thrift, and the placing and semantic cross-reference of 'industrious', seem borrowed from English Augustan practice); 'The cruizy too can only blink and bleer' (line 104), potent with the alliteration of everyday speech. Crucial to the poem's structure are two stanzas of poetic adjuration whose language can best be described as an attempt at a national standard Scots—stanza 5, strategically near the centre, beginning 'On sicken food has mony a doughty deed' (line 37), and the final stanza, beginning 'Peace to the husbandman and a' his tribe' (line 109).

In 'The Cotter's Saturday Night' Burns employs, apart altogether from his description of the interior, no less than three kinds of rhetoric of address: (1) the rhetoric of tender sentiment, as in Shenstone (stanza 9, beginning 'O happy love! where love like this is found!' line 73), passing into the moralistic frenzy of stanza 10, beginning 'Is there, in human-form, that bears a heart' (line 82); (2) the rhetoric of Protestant individualism in the century of sentimentalism (stanza 17, beginning 'Compar'd with this how poor Religion's pride', line 145); and (3) synthesising the first two, a patriotic rhetoric resembling Fergusson's (stanzas 19 and 20, beginning 'From Scenes like these, old Scotia's grandeur springs', line 163) and moving in the final stanza to a prayer ('O Thou! who pour'd the patriotic tide', line 181) in much more public-sounding diction than would have been employed by the 'priest-like Father' whose family devotions are at the centre of the poem.

None of these three kinds of Burnsian rhetoric attempts to be a standard Scots, such as we find Fergusson aiming at in his two commenting stanzas. They are variants of a Scots-English rhetoric more likely to have been uttered in real life than the language of stanza 5 of 'The Farmer's Ingle'. It seems to me to have the eloquence of the 'sonorous and well-rounded periods which were the contemporary ideal of public oratory',[22] or of ministers of the gospel writing and delivering 'sermons of the heart'.[23] One feels that in the rhetorical stanzas of 'The Cotter's Saturday Night' Burns is imitating real or possible forms of discourse in Scots-English, while Fergusson is creating an ideal rhetoric in an imagined national Scots. There are only three passages of direct speech in 'The Cotter's Saturday Night' marked off by quotation marks: five lines of sentimental reflection on innocent young love, uttered by Burns himself or his persona at the end of stanza 9 (lines 77-81), which demand only a faint Scottish pronunciation, like that perhaps of George Dempster or Hugh Blair among Burns's older contemporaries, and the two direct utterances given to 'the priest-like Father', which must be broadly pronounced, since in the first of these he is given the markers 'mind' and 'gang' to show that his speech is fully Scottish (lines 50-4). And the key line of the poem, which rarely fails to send a shiver down my spine when I recall it, must be pronounced with strongly Scottish sounds: 'And Let us worship God! he says with solemn air' (line 108).[24]

It also follows that stanzas 12-16, the real centre of the poem, describing the little family singing metrical psalms to Scottish tunes like 'Dundee', 'Martyrs' and 'Elgin', the readings from the Old and New Testament and the final prayer, must be broadly pronounced ('Nae' and 'hae' in line 117 provide additional markers—'Nae unison hae they with our Creator's praise'). Despite their appearance on the printed page they are just as Scottish in language as anything else in Burns, or Fergusson, or Ramsay: there is nothing in principle which would have prevented them from being uttered by that very same Auld Farmer who so movingly greeted his auld mare Maggie at New Year.

When the central religious section of 'The Cotter's Saturday Night' is put beside the religious stanzas in Shenstone's 'The Schoolmistress' which so clearly influenced Burns, it is obvious that Burns has instilled a sense of nationality lacking in Shenstone. Here are the relevant lines in 'The Schoolmistress':

> Here oft the dame, on Sabbath's decent eve,
> Hymned such psalms as Sternhold forth did mete . . .
> Sweet melody! to hear her then repeat
> How Israel's sons, beneath a foreign king,
> While taunting foemen did a song entreat,
> All for the nonce untuning every string,
> Uphung their useless lyres—small heart had they
> to sing . . .
>
> And, in those elfins' ears, would oft deplore,
> The times when Truth by Popish rage did bleed,
> And tortious death was true Devotion's meed;
> And simple Faith in iron chains did mourn,
> That nould on wooden image place her creed;
> And lawny saints in smouldering flames did burn:
> Ah! dearest Lord! forfend thilk days should e'er return.
>   (lines 118-19, 122-6, 129-35)

The only patriotic references in Shenstone are one insignificant mention of St George (stanza 18), another of Admiral Vernon (stanza 27), and some insipid suggestions that there might be future bishops, chancellors and major poets like Milton and Shakespeare among the schoolmistress' charges (stanza 28). The sublimity in Burns's poem is made possible by the development of what in Shenstone are mere hints, expressed in language which is *nationally* Scottish—because of everything that Protestantism, individual religious experience, and the Authorised Version of the Bible have meant for the Scottish people. 'The Cotter's Saturday Night' does not so much touch English culture at the level of language (even 'Anticipation forward points the view', line 42, must be broadly pronounced in its context) as in the stanza form, mediated by Fergusson's daring use of it in 'The Farmer's Ingle', and Shenstone's sentimentalism. It is this interaction which makes possible the high poetry it occasionally achieves.

5

Found as far back as Barbour's *Brus*, the octosyllabic couplet is even more
'native to Scotland' than the pentameter couplet. Prior's and Swift's octosyllabics may indirectly have helped Ramsay to establish the easy tone of his fables
and of such tales as 'The Monk and the Miller's Wife'. In 'Tam o' Shanter'
contact with the English/Scots-English system is mostly a matter of genre-
elements (mock-heroic), and the same is true of 'The Twa Dogs' (the Horatian
satirical spirit). In Fergusson's 'Auld Reikie' the contact is pervasive: the
poem's very organisation was suggested by Gay's *Trivia: or the Art of Walking
the Streets of London* (1716), and the polish of his couplets owes something to
his English predecessors. The subject is first of all a community as in the
original 'Christ's Kirk' poems—that of the capital city, itself composed of
many subordinate communities. As in both the 'Habbie' and the 'Christ's
Kirk' poems we have looked at, there are subsidiary portraits of individuals and
types—the bruiser, the macaronies (fops), barefoot housemaids and stairhead
critics, the worn-out whore, the idealised country beauty (lines 211-8), and
such a dignitary as good Provost Drummond. The poet's shifting attitudes to
the sights and sounds of an average day do not involve the warm intimacy of so
many of the Standard Habbie poems: there is a certain aloofness from the
inhabitants of the city he loves, reflected in the poem's language. This is not
the place for a detailed comparison between Gay and Fergusson, but what can
be attempted, as a demonstration of how the contact between the Scots and the
English/Scots-English system works, is an examination of Gay's, Ramsay's and
Fergusson's treatment of that ever-recurring urban type, the Whore.
      First, Gay:

> 'Tis she who nightly strowls with saunt'ring pace,
> No stubborn stays her yielding shape embrace;
> Beneath the lamp her tawdry ribbons glare,
> The new-scower'd manteau, and the slattern air;
> High-draggled petticoats her travels show,
> And hollow cheeks with artful blushes glow;
> With flatt'ring sounds she sooths the cred'lous ear,
> My noble captain! charmer! love! my dear!
> In riding-hood near tavern-doors she plies,
> Or muffled pinners hide her livid eyes.
> With empty bandbox she delights to range,
> And feigns a distant errand from the *'Change*;
> Nay, she will oft' the Quaker's hood prophane,
> And trudge demure the rounds of *Drury-lane*.
> She darts from sarsnet ambush wily leers,
> Twitches thy sleeve, or with familiar airs
> Her fan will pat thy cheek; these snares disdain,
> Nor gaze behind thee, when she turns again.
>   (*Trivia*, III. 267-84)

The portrait is of a horrible, garish deceiver: adjectives and nouns with pejorative associations build up the picture—'tawdry', 'slattern', 'hollow-cheeks/artful blushes', 'flatt'ring', 'feigns', 'prophane', 'wily leers', 'familiar airs', 'snares'. And there is an unpleasant mingling of humour with the venereal disease likely to afflict the country visitor who has anything to do with her:

> Ah hapless swain, unus'd to pains and ills!
> Canst thou forego roast-beef for nauseous pills?
> How wilt thou lift to Heav'n thy eyes and hands,
> When the long scroll the surgeon's fees demands!
> Or else (ye Gods avert that worst disgrace)
> Thy ruin'd nose falls level with thy face,
> Then shall thy wife thy loathsome kiss disdain,
> And wholesome neighbours from thy mug refrain.
>
> (III. 299-306)

Gay's moralism has no trace of sympathy for the prostitute. In Ramsay's 'Lucky Spence's Last Advice' the dramatic monologue technique transforms the same elements of deception, robbery of clients and venereal disease into a vigorous acceptance of the horrible as a necessary part of the Whore's life, which in turn becomes a distorted image of the entire human condition:

> Forbye, my looves, count upo' losses,
> Ye'r milk-white teeth and cheeks like roses,
> Whan jet-black hair and brigs of noses,
>   Faw down wi' dads
> To keep your hearts up 'neath sic crosses,
>   Set up for bawds.
>
> (lines 61-6)

We are not told whether Ramsay felt any pity for the girls: what is presented is the torture in the Correction House (lines 49-54), and the bawd's own low-life stoicism—all these evils must be borne, because they are inevitable:

> Nane gathers gear withouten care,
> Ilk pleasure has of pain a skare;
> Suppose then they should tirl ye bare,
>   And gar ye fike,
> E'en learn to thole; 'tis very fair
>   Ye're nibour like.
>
> (lines 55-60)

The position is identical with that put forward by Imlac in Dr Johnson's *Rasselas*: 'Human life is everywhere a state in which much is to be endured, and little enjoyed' (chapter 11). There is, however, a definite note of pity in lines 55-60 of the 'Elegy on John Cowper, Kirk-Treasurer's Man', where the 'poor jade' is sent to the House of Correction at the foot of Leith Wynd to spin

> With heavy heart and cleathing thin,
> And hungry wame,
> And ilky month a well-paid skin,
> To mak her tame.

Fergusson's first mention of the prostitute is in the 'Answer to Mr J.S.'s Epistle':[25]

> And frae ilk corner o' the nation,
> We've lasses eke of recreation,
> That at close-mouths tak up their station
> By ten o'clock,
> The Lord deliver frae Temptation
> A' honest fock!
>
> Thir queans are ay upon the catch
> For pursie, pocket-book, or watch,
> An can sae glibb their leesins hatch,
> That you'll agree,
> Ye canna eithly meet their match
> 'Tween you and me.
>   (lines 55–66)

There is here none of Ramsay's savage vigour; the tone is entirely satiric, with an irony subtler than Gay's ('of recreation'—a term with genteel associations; 'o' the nation'—indicating the extent and social roots of prostitution): and there is criticism of religious hypocrisy in the use of the 'Scotch Presbyterian eloquence' in lines 59–60, carrying the suggestion that the 'unco guid' may sometimes actually go so far as to *yield* to such temptation. In 'Auld Reekie', however, moralising is combined with a humane pity for an ex-whore turned ballad-singer and bawd:

> Near some lamp-post, wi' dowy face,
> Wi' heavy een, and sour grimace,
> Stands she that beauty lang had kend,
> Whoredom her trade, and vice her end.
> But see whare now she wuns her bread,
> By that which Nature ne'er decreed;
> And sings sad music to the lugs,
> 'Mang burachs o' damn'd whores and rogues.
> Whane'er we reputation loss,
> Fair chastity's transparent gloss!
> Redemption seenil kens the name
> But a's black misery and shame.
>   (lines 87–98)

Even more subtly than in the 'Answer to Mr J.S.'s Epistle', Fergusson conveys in lines 95–6 an oblique critique of bourgeois hypocrisy, the morality of 'Thou shalt not be found out'. It is the loss of reputation, not of innocence, that is important; by implication, a whole system of social ethics is blamed for the Whore's fate; Fergusson has gone back to Gay, it is clear, bypassed both his and Ramsay's references to venereal disease, and aroused our sympathy for the prostitute as victim, in the tradition of English and European sentimentalism. Like Henryson, however, in 'The Testament of Cresseid', he does not minimise the whore's criminality: her 'evil' is clearly stated to be 'vice'.

6

Up till now I have concentrated on the general pleasure to be derived from the poetry of the Vernacular Revival—that is, the pleasure to be got from the structure of a given poem as a whole. What of the particular pleasures—the *frissons* which raised the bristles on A E Housman's beard when he recollected lines as he shaved?[26] The 'pure-poetry effect' is sometimes relatively independent of context, and sometimes entirely the result of it. We do not need to know more than 'A rose-red city half as old as time' (J W Burgon, *Petra*, line 132) to respond, but we can never have any sort of physiological reaction to 'And never lifted up a single stone' unless we know its position in Wordsworth's 'Michael'. Context is necessary for single colloquial idioms to have this effect ('Waes me for Johnnie Ged's-Hole now'), and most of my own pleasure, at least, in the genre poems, satires and epistles of the revival is of the general sort. When I remember a line like 'Now auld Kilmarnock cock thy tail' (Burns, 'The Ordination', line 46), I react because of my previous experience of the whole poem. Yet when Edwin Muir produced samples of what he considered Burns's greatest lines,[27] they were more isolable than these—though not completely separable from the works from which they come:

> And sae I sat, and sae I sang
> And wistna o' my fate

> But seas between us braid hae roar'd

> And I will love thee still, my Dear,
> Till a' the seas gang dry.

> Had we never lov'd sae kindly,
> Had we never lov'd sae blindly!
> Never met—or never parted,
> We had ne'er been broken-hearted.

It is most striking that all the lines Muir singles out for their poetic quality come from songs. Two other points are worth pondering—first, this selection of Burns's 'greatest' lines, by a major poet of acknowledged sensitivity and critical power, seems to call in question such a statement as David Craig's 'we must conclude that touching up songs was a second-rate job for an eighteenth-century poet of any quality';[28] and, second, none of Muir's examples are in a 'dense' vernacular, but are equally divided between a thin Scots and Scots-English.

If Muir had been writing about eighteenth-century vernacular poetry as a whole, and not just about Burns, he would no doubt have included as pure poetry lines from songs which draw on a magical fund of common symbolism, like the following stanza from a broadside concerning 'A bonny Lad of High Renown/who Liv'd in Aberdeen's fair town':

> My Love and I's like a Mine of Gold,
> planted in an island in the Sea,
> Where Boats and Barks and Men make bold
> in that curious island for to see.
> My Love and I's like a Mine of Gold,
> all Cloathed o're on every side,
> Where Boats and Barks and Men make bold
> by that overflowing of the Tyde.[29]

I would myself extend the canon beyond song to include vignettes and images from satirical, realistic and descriptive poems, like the following:

(1)   The lasies are raiking awa,
        In petty-coats white as the lilly,
        And biggonets prind on fou braw
                (Ramsay, 'The Marrow Ballad', lines 6-8)

(2)   See, how she peels the skin an' fell,
        As ane were peelin onions
                (Burns, 'The Ordination', lines 104-5)

(3)   How haps it, say, that mealy bakers,
        Hair-kaimers, crieshy gezy-makers,
        Shou'd a' get leave to waste their powders
        Upon my beaux and ladies shoulders?
                (Fergusson, 'Mutual Complaint of Plainstanes
                and Causey', lines 29-32)

(4)   For yet the sun was wading thro' the mist
                (Ramsay, 'The Gentle Shepherd', I. i. 111)

(5)   Nae starns keek throw the azure slit
                (Ramsay, 'Up in the Air', line 11)

(6)   Now morn, with bonny purpie-smiles,
        Kisses the air-cock o' St. Giles
                (Fergusson, 'Auld Reikie, lines 23-4)

(7)   Near what bright burn or chrystal spring
           Did you your winsome whistle hing?
                       (Fergusson, 'Hame Content', lines 111-12)

(8)   Or like the snow falls in the river,
           A moment white—then melts for ever
                       (Burns, 'Tam o' Shanter', lines 61-2)

Nos. (1) and (2) are entirely colloquial, with Ramsay using a stock simile ('white as the lilly') of almost proverbial force, and Burns an obvious but vividly realised domestic comparison: neither example is couched in an artificial style which 'was not the natural language of the poet'. No. (3) is 'makars' verse' of high craftsmanship, carefully constructed to use the contrast between demotic Scots and refined Scots-English in order to highlight the class difference between 'low' tradespeople and 'beaux and ladies'. Nos. (4), (5) and (6) all personify natural features: (4) to render an atmosphere of daytime eeriness, but in an image ('wading') such as a real shepherd might well use, whereas (5) creates a delicate tension between homely 'keeks' and the more recondite 'azure'. The next Fergusson pieces are again 'makars' verse': 'purpie-smiles' is a word-creation and the picture of morn kissing the air-cock is daringly artificial, reminding one of the extravagances of rococo painting, while (7) is a most delicate and conscious adaptation of the artificialities of pastoral to Scottish manners—the native 'bright burn' (?pronounced 'bricht') is balanced against the English and European 'chrystal spring', the shepherd's pipe of tradition has become a 'whistle', the local folk instrument, and 'winsome', so the NED informs us, is in the modern literary language 'from the northern dialect', felt here by Fergusson to be popular Scots. Controlled alliteration and assonance combine to raise this couplet to the level of 'pure poetry'. The hackneyed but magical couplet from 'Tam o' Shanter' calls forth, in me at least, the picture of a single large flake falling into a dark, slow current: I respond as fully to it as to any of the lines quoted by Edwin Muir.

7

Recent writers on the vernacular revival have been much concerned with its deficiencies. A hedonist approach suggests that when judged by the almost forgotten criteria of pure poetry the vernacular revival poets, and especially the greatest of them, Burns, wrote at least as many moving and entrancing lines as their English contemporaries, from Pope to Cowper and Crabbe. Even with a poet of alleged 'unified sensibility' like Donne, it is the single great line that we remember most—'A bracelet of bright hair about the bone', 'Else a great Prince in Prison lies'; and if eighteenth-century Scotland produced no major epic and no great tragedy, neither did eighteenth-century England or France.[30]

It is manifestly perverse to blame the people and their languages for the spirit of the age in Europe. Then again, it is said that the true comparison should be with the greatest achievements of other literatures. It is surely permissible to compare the vernacular poets of the eighteenth century with the English Romantics of the next generation. Now the Romantics excelled in short or medium-length forms, like the Scots; their long poems are generally incomplete; the architectonics and intellectual force of the old epic and the drama were already beginning to pass over into the novel. We react emotionally to individual lines, verse paragraphs and episodes from *The Prelude*, but our response to the whole is largely intellectual; when considering poetic quality, it is to Blake's lyrics that we turn rather than to the prophetic books; Coleridge stands or falls by 'Frost at Midnight', 'The Ancient Mariner', 'Christabel' and the fragment 'Kubla Khan'. On my own purely personal calculus, the general pleasure I receive from the best satires, genre poems, epistles and comic narratives of the vernacular revival—pleasures depending on my response to structure and total meaning—is as satisfying as any I get from English poems of comparable length; and the particular pleasures sparked off by the individual lines and passages quoted in the last section, including those picked out by Edwin Muir, are as intense as those of any other 'pure poetry' to which I respond. More than that, a hedonist approach cannot give.

NOTES

1 T Crawford, *Society and the Lyric*, (Edinburgh, 1979 for 1980), p. 31
2 ibid. p. 155
3 *The Letters of Robert Burns,* ed. J de Lancey Ferguson, (Oxford, 1931), I, p. 246
4 For these terms see T Crawford, *Burns: a study of the poems and songs,* 3rd edn, (Edinburgh, 1978): Introduction, p. [iii]
5 Texts of Burns are from *The Poems and Songs of Robert Burns,* ed. James Kinsley, (Oxford, 1968), with the removal of confusing italics.
6 The word *sentimental* is not used here in a pejorative sense, but as a technical term of literary history, applied to the eighteenth-century cult of sentiment.
7 Ramsay's own note. Unless otherwise stated, quotations from Ramsay and Fergusson are taken from *Poems by Allan Ramsay and Robert Fergusson,* eds A M Kinghorn and Alexander Law, (Edinburgh, 1974).
8 *The Poetry of Robert Burns,* eds W E Henley and T F Henderson, (Edinburgh, 1896), I, 393
9 F B Snyder, *Robert Burns: his mind, his personality and his art,* (Toronto, 1936), p. 85
10 *The Poems of Robert Fergusson,* ed. M P McDiarmid, Scottish Text Society, 2 vols, (Edinburgh, 1954-6), I, pp. 137-63, and F W Freeman, 'The Intellectual Background of the Vernacular Revival before Burns', *Studies in Scottish Literature* 16 (1981), pp. 160-87, and 'The Vernacular Movement' in *A Companion to Scottish Culture,* ed. David Daiches, (London, 1981), pp. 393-6.

11 Helena M Shire, *Song, Dance and Poetry at the Court of Scotland under James VI*, (Cambridge, 1969), pp. 165-73

12 'Habbie Simson', in *Bards and Makars*, eds A J Aitken, M P McDiarmid and Derick S Thomson, (Glasgow, 1977), p. 218

13 See G F Jones, '"Christis Kirk", "Peblis to the Play" and the German Peasant Brawl', PMLA, 68 (1953), pp. 1105-25; J Kinsley, 'The rustic inmates of the hamlet', *A Review of English Literature* 1 (1960), pp. 13-25, and Allan H Maclaine, 'The Christis Kirk Tradition: its evolution in Scots Poetry to Burns', *Studies in Scottish Literature* 2 (1964), pp. 3-18, 111-24, 163-82, 234-50

14 Allan Ramsay's additional Canto III to 'Christis Kirk', lines 133-7, *The Works of Allan Ramsay*, ed. Burns Martin *et al.*, Scottish Text Society, 6 vols, (Edinburgh, 1945-74), I, p. 80

15 David Craig, *Scottish Literature and the Scottish People 1680-1830*, (London, 1960), p. 82 and passim

16 ibid. p. 84

17 Crawford, *Society and the Lyric*, pp. 70-95

18 *Works*, S.T.S. edn, IV, pp. 99-100

19 Gerard Manley Hopkins thought these 'the most strictly beautiful lines' of Burns that he could remember (To Robert Bridges, 22 Oct. 1879).

20 *Works*, S.T.S. edn, I, p. 172

21 *The Poetical Works of Shenstone*, ed. G Gilfillan, (Edinburgh, 1854), pp. 262-72

22 *Letters of George Dempster to Sir Adam Fergusson 1756-1813*, ed. James Fergusson, (London, 1934), p. xix

23 For the style of 'sermons of the heart', see Ann Matheson, 'Theories of Rhetoric in the eighteenth-century Scottish sermon' (unpublished PhD dissertation, University of Edinburgh, 1979), pp. 290-333.

24 'Robert had frequently remarked to me' said Gilbert Burns, 'that he thought there was something peculiarly venerable in the phrase "let us worship God," used by a decent sober head of a family introducing family worship . . . Gilbert was "electrified" by Robert's recitation of the poem: "The fifth and sixth stanzas and the eighteenth, thrilled with peculiar extasy through my soul"' (*The Works of Robert Burns*, ed. James Currie, Liverpool 1800, IV, 384-5).

25 *Poems*, S.T.S. edn, II, 71-4

26 A E Housman, *The Name and Nature of Poetry*, (Cambridge, 1933), pp. 46-7

27 In *Edwin Muir: uncollected Scottish Criticism*, ed. Andrew Noble, (London, 1982), pp. 158, 187

28 *Scottish Literature and the Scottish People*, p. 104

29 'Old Scottish Ballads, Broadsides, etc. 1679-1730', NLS Ry III a 10 (71)

30 Scotland did, however, produce major history (Hume, Robertson), an epic genre, and three major biographers—Boswell in this century, Lockhart and Carlyle in the next.

SIX

At the Foot o' yon Excellin' Brae:
The Language of Scots Folksong

Hamish Henderson

If Platitude should claim a place
Do not denounce his humble face:
His sentiments are well intentioned
He has a place in the larger legend.
                    Patrick Kavanagh

In his foreword to Superintendent John Ord's collection of bothy ballads,[1] Principal Robert A Rait of Glasgow University wrote in April 1930:

We have here the real thing—the songs as actually sung in the bothies of the farms in the north. Their text may be evidence of the invasion of the vernacular by southern influence (though many words conventionally printed in English were, and are, pronounced as Scots), but their substance provides a living picture of Scottish rural life, absolutely sincere and free from any form of affectation.

Open Ord's collection at random, and one finds (for example) the following:

Love's hottest glow is kindled in my breast,
  And, oh, but it beats so sairly
There is none in this world can bring me comfort and rest
  But my handsome ploughman laddie.[2]

And again:

Like midges on a summer's day the French around us lie,
But with our British bayonets we'll make them fight or fly;
We'll make them fight or fly, he says, and drive them out of Spain,
That war may cease and bring us peace, and send us home again.[3]

And again:

And if the thistle it be strong,
I fear 'twill jag thy milk-white hand,
But with my hook I'll cut it down,
When we join yon band o' shearers.[4]

When Principal Rait wrote the above quoted passage, collection of folksong with mechanical appliances—the primitive ancestors of present-day tape recorders—had already been going on for more than two decades, but so firmly was scholarship thirled to the printed or written word that he could not be expected to think of invoking the authority of such mechanically recorded song and speech. One could indeed compile quite a sizeable anthology of similar comments on the language of Scots folksong, as it appears in printed collections. The purpose of the present essay is to demonstrate that a curious 'bilingualism in one language' has been a characteristic of Scots folksong at least since the beginning of the seventeenth century; meaning, in effect, since the arrival on the Lowland scene of that magisterial influence on Scottish hearts and minds, the King James's Bible.

However, important though the advent of the Word of God 'in Inglis tung' undoubtedly was—from the earliest smuggled imports to the momentous appearance of the great Authorised Version itself—it would be quite wrong to attribute the galloping anglicisation of the seventeenth and later centuries to the Bible alone. As Stanley Hyman put it in a masterly essay in 1954:

> The finest Scottish poetry has always been bilingual in a curious fashion. Douglas the translator, Dunbar using Latin refrains, Boyd writing in Scottish and Latin, Burns writing in Scottish and English, are all poets for whom Lowland Scots was one of the world's tongues, not the language in which God and Adam held converse.[5]

To this thought-provoking list he might have added the name of George Buchanan, who was capable of writing prose in trenchant Scots and elegant English as well as poetry in justly eulogised Latin, and who throughout his life was probably thinking off and on in what seems to have been his mother tongue—Gaelic.

And when referring to 'Douglas the translator', Hyman might well have made the point that the Bishop of Dunkeld, if he wrote any of his *Eneados* in Dunkeld, was composing in a language he called 'Scottis' in the middle of a Gaelic-speaking population. (Professor Kenneth Jackson and Fred Macaulay were still able to record Perthshire Gaelic from a native speaker in the Dunkeld area as late as 1952.)

Put simply, this means that Scotland—like Switzerland—is (and always has been) a multi-lingual community, and that the language problems of Scottish poets go back at least as far as the Flyting of Dunbar and Kennedy:

> Thow lufis nane Irische, elf, I understand,
> Bot it suld be all trew Scottis mennis lede[6]

and probably a lot further.

It is by no means strange, therefore, that the literary language of the great makars, which Dunbar called Inglis and Gavin Douglas (on one occasion, at least) Scottis, should exhibit signs of linguistic tension rather more complex than is often assumed. The makars were writing 'Inglis', but they were also

Scotsmen, members of a nation with a fierce precocious national pride: it would not be strange, therefore, if their attitude to their own linguistic medium were in some sense ambivalent. They were not Chaucerians, but they were writing under Chaucer's shadow: like all Scottish poets ever since, they knew they were writing 'over against' another and closely related literature, which they could not have ignored even if they had wished to do so.

In the article already quoted, Hyman had some hard things to say about the 'Lallans' poets of the forties, suggesting that they had not come within a mile of comprehending their own historic linguistic predicament; at the end of the essay he referred, somewhat disdainfully, to 'the quixotic effort to write in an artificial and resurrected literary language requiring a glossary in each volume'. Now and then he took a canny pot-shot at Hugh MacDiarmid's bristling carnaptious redoubt, but he also paid tribute to what was for him MacDiarmid's 'most impressive poem' *The Seamless Garment,* in which he found 'something like Henryson's or Dunbar's perfectly achieved linguistic balance'.[7]

> And as for me in my fricative work
> I ken fu' weel
> Sic an integrity's what I maun hae,
>   Indivisible, real,
> Woven owre close for the point o' a pin
> Onywhere to win in.[8]

Hyman's praise was reserved, however, for 'a folk literature unsurpassed by any in the world, the Scottish popular ballads', and he declared:

> If we seek language that is simple, sensuous, and passionate, a corpus of more than a dozen tragic Scottish ballad texts constitutes almost a classic tradition. I think of "The Wife of Usher's Well", "The Twa Sisters", "Edward", "Clerk Saunders", "Sir Patrick Spens", "Johnie Cock", "Mary Hamilton", "The Bonny Earl of Murray", "Child Maurice", "Young Waters", "The Baron of Brackley", "Lamkin", "The Cruel Mother", "The Twa Corbies", and "The Daemon Lover". Alongside these there is a body of Scottish folk song and rhyme in other forms that adds up to as rich a poetic heritage as any we know.[9]

If prose and poetry in a self-conscious literary Scots came increasingly to seem documentations of a sad case of arrested development, the anonymous ballad-makers continued on their way, knowing little and caring less of the niceties of hyperborean lingo and prosody. They were, in any case, operating in a zone which ignored national and political boundaries. The themes of the great tragic ballads to which Hyman refers are elemental folk motifs—and many of these cross national language boundaries. Take 'Lord Randal' for example. This is the ballad of 'the false true love' who poisons her lover; it has been found in innumerable guises right across Europe, but the identity of the ballad remains remarkably stable—even the exact sequence of stanzas being often the same. Why then have the Scottish versions, from Scott's onwards, received such universal acclaim? (Again, it would be possible to list a whole battery of eulogies.) There are no doubt several feasible answers to this question—one possible one being that the Scots ballad-makers had what has been called a 'fierier imagination' than their English counterparts—but I here put forward the proposition that one of the reasons for the unchallenged excellence of many of our ballad versions resides in the actual nature of the language in which they are couched—in what we may term 'ballad-Scots'.

This, the idiom in which the virtuoso song makers were operating, is a flexible formulaic language which grazes ballad-English along the whole of its length, and yet remains clearly identifiable as a distinct folk-literary lingo. Gavin Greig paid tribute to the 'simple, clear and dignified' language of the older classic ballads found in Aberdeenshire; and the strange 'bilingualism in one language', which greatly extends its range, demonstrably makes it a much suppler instrument than the often rather wooden ballad-English. We have already noticed the importance of the arrival of the King James's Bible, and there can certainly be no doubt that it played a vital part in stabilising ballad-Scots, and facilitating a resourceful creative togetherness: a sort of chemical fusion of two distinct but related ballad languages. In the folk field, as well as in the less agile literary Lallans, Scots may be said to include English and go beyond it.

The tape recordings of Scots classic ballads in the archives of the School of Scottish Studies add a new dimension to the study of the 'muckle sangs' as they existed—and still exist—in oral currency in Scotland. Their importance from both a textual and a musical point of view can hardly be exaggerated. Just as the traditional manner of singing the older modal tunes often defies orthodox musical notation, so numerous linguistic and phonetic points (which in print and in manuscript collections are more often than not hopelessly blurred and fuzzed over) leap out at one from the tape recording with a freshness and immediacy which amount in some cases to positive revelation.

The most striking thing which emerges is that the bilingualism referred to by Stanley Hyman is a reality. The tape recording enables one to look behind and through the records of David Herd and Gavin Greig to what the North-East folk singers actually said and sang.

The Buchan folksinger does not sing in the same way in which he speaks. Or, to put it rather differently (and possibly more accurately), he is liable to speak and sing in at least two and sometimes more ways. But here we can easily run into misunderstandings at several levels. Let me clear the ground by making one or two points about folksong in general which would not, I think, be challenged nowadays except by the most incorrigible of armchair romanticists.

1   The language of the older folksong is never purely 'colloquial'; it is formal, even stylised, bearing much the same relation to the normal speech of the singer that the literary language of Augustan art-poetry (say) bore to the everyday speech of the poets concerned. It is in the great songs, licked into shape like pebbles by the waves of countless tongues, that this sense of formality is most marked.

2   The technique of singing the traditional ballads involves a number of definite linguistic conventions which are still to be heard on the lips of traditional singers from Cornwall to Macduff, and from Co. Cork to Suffolk. (The most characteristic of these is the 'wrenched accent'; when a trochaic dissyllable occurs at the end of a line, the accent is shifted to the last syllable—e.g. 'The King has written a braid lettér.')

As Hodgart puts it in his study *The Ballads*, 'The rhythms of folksong do not always correspond to speech-rhythms: the English language is used almost as if it were French, in that full value may be given to normally unstressed syllables.'[10]

3   The modifications caused in the 'Child' ballads by oral transmission are infinitely various, but they remain amazingly constant in mood, personality and development. Consequently the changes which they undergo when passing from one folksong community to another (I do not refer only to linguistic changes) are of extraordinary ethnological interest.

All this is as true of the English ballad singer as it is of the Scots. A Dorset labourer singing 'Lord Lovel' is singing ballad-English, not Dorset dialect—although there may well be an intrusion of Dorset localisms here and there.

Now move to North-East Scotland, and the situation becomes a good deal more complicated. In Aberdeenshire (the shire, incidentally, which provided Child with no less than a third of his principal texts, and which is still today an astoundingly rich mine of song) the native speech of the ballad singer is a very marked idiosyncratic dialect of Scots, very different in intonation, and to a considerable extent in vocabulary, from the south country Doric. This dialect bears a definite relation (a) to the old (vanished) Metropolitan Scots of the pre-Reformation court; (b) to the English of the King James's Bible which has been since the seventeenth century very much the prestige speech over a great part of Scotland.

When he is singing the classical ballads, the Buchan ballad-singer usually tends instinctively to avoid the characteristic Aberdeenshire localisms—(e.g. 'Fa' for 'wha', 'fit' for 'what' etc.). He employs a clear braid Scots, which turns out on examination to be a 'folk-literary' language of great subtlety and sophistication as well as of massy strength.

> Johnnie rose up on a May morning,
>   Ca'd for water to wash his hands.
> Says, gae lowse to me my twa grey dogs
>   That lie bound in iron chains, chains,
>   That lie bound in iron chains.
>
> When Johnnie's mither she heard o' this
>   Her hands wi' dule she wrang.
> Says, Johnnie, for your venison
>   To the green woods dinna gang, gang
>   To the green woods dinna gang.

> It's we hae plenty o' guid white bread
> And plenty o' guid red wine
> So, Johnnie, for your venison
>   To the green woods dinna gang, gang,
>   To the green woods dinna gang.
>
> But Johnnie has breskit his guid benbow,
> His arrows one by one,
> And he's awa to the gay green woods
>   To pull the dun deer doon, doon,
>   To pull the dun deer doon.[11]

These are the opening verses, as I now sing them, of *Johnnie Cock* (Child 114), the archetypal ballad of the 'bold poacher'. To make my version I drew on those of John Strachan (recorded in 1951) and of Jeannie Robertson (recorded in 1953); I also drew on the version which appears in Gavin Greig's *Last Leaves* (page 93)—it was collected from Alex. Mackay, a butcher in Alford—and which is of course included by Bertrand H. Bronson among the versions of Child 114 in Volume III of *The Traditional Tunes of the Child Ballads*. The tune I use is an amalgam of those mentioned. Before this version 'gelled' I moved across from one text to another, and an inspection of the various versions would show why this process is comparatively easy for anyone familiar with 'ballad-Scots': all the variants concerned are from oral tradition, and have had time to settle into what we may truly call a classic mould. Indeed, when Child called *Johnnie Cock* 'this precious specimen of the unspoiled traditional ballad' he was paying a compliment as much to the language as to the story-line.

The language is obviously that of the native Scots ballad-singer, but there is little that would not be immediately comprehensible to a singer in Durham or in Dorset.

Even closer to ballad-English is the following stanza of a beautiful fragment of 'Sweet William's Ghost' (or, it could be, of 'Clerk Saunders') recorded in Fraserburgh in 1954 from an old illiterate tinker woman who hailed originally from the Perthshire Highlands:

> My mouth it is full of mould, Maggie,
> And my breath it is wonderful strong;
> And if I was to kiss your sweet ruby lips
> Your time would nae be long.[12]

Old Betsy's natural speech was that of her clan, which draws on both Deeside and Perthshire elements, as well as on fragmentary Gaelic and luxuriant travellers' cant; but this verse (which I reproduce exactly as she sang it) has one distinctively Scots locution in it. But it should be noted that that single 'nae' means that the whole verse has to be read and pronounced *more Boreali*, and ca's the ground from under the feet of anyone who tries to read it in refined Suddroun.

If it seems strange that a Scots folksinger who never spoke English in
conversation could nevertheless sing in a lingo so close to ballad-English, one
need only point out—as Gavin Greig pointed out in his *Buchanie* articles
seventy years ago—that the language of distinctively English folksongs like
'The Foggy Dew' presents no difficulty to singers who are familiar with the
metrical psalms and paraphrases.

The swing of the pendulum between ballad-Scots and ballad-English in the
language of the classic ballads is sometimes capricious, but it more often
corresponds to deep instinctive aesthetic patterns. Where the Scots ballad-
singer (following countless singer-ancestors) feels that 'dead' sounds better
than 'deid' in a particular verse of 'The Battle of Harlaw', he comes right out
and sings 'dead'. But if you asked him which he had sung, he would probably
have to sing the verse again to find out.

The same oscillation between Scots and English can be seen in the language
of the Scots folktales recorded on tape from Jeannie Robertson, Belle Stewart,
Duncan Williamson and many others in the thirty years since the foundation of
the School of Scottish Studies. It is interesting to compare the language of these
stories with that of the versions collected and retold by Peter Buchan in *Ancient
Scottish Tales* (1829: first printed 1908 by the Buchan Field Club). Buchan's
tales are somewhat wooden anglicised recensions which reproduce neither the
language nor the flavour of his originals; furthermore, the incidental trappings
bear witness to the florid self-indulgent imagination of the editor (e.g. the
opening of 'The Cruel Stepmother', which is number 706 in the Aarne
Thompson Type Index):

> About the year 800, there lived a rich nobleman in a sequestered place in Scotland,
> where he wished to conceal his name, birth, and parentage, as he had fled from the
> hands of justice to save his life for an action he had been guilty of committing in his
> early years. It was supposed, and not without some good show of reason, that his
> name was Malcolm, brother to Fingal, King of Morven.[13]

Nevertheless, Peter's collection does consist almost entirely of identifiable
international folktales (e.g. Aarne-Thompson numbers 300, 303, 313, 325,
326, 425, 510A, 706, 851 and 955); and it is undoubtedly the first repository
we have—and the only one until this century—of tales circulating in the Scots-
speaking areas of the North-East.

Peter Buchan's version of Aa. Th. 313—'The Girl as Helper in the Hero's
Flight', for which his own name is 'Green Sleeves'—contains the swan-maiden
motif often found throughout the world in variants of this tale (cf. my note to
'The Green Man of Knowledge', Scottish Studies vol. 2, pp. 61–85). This is
how Peter presents the encounter between his hero and the girl who will
eventually assist him to overcome his adversary (her father, the Green Man):

The prince went as directed, and hid himself behind the sloe-thorn hedge, when he saw three of the most beautiful swans come and hover over the river for a little time, at length alighted and threw off their swan-skins, when he snatched up the one with the blue wing. After they had continued for some time in the water, they prepared to proceed directly home; but as the one who had the skin with the blue wing could not find hers, she was at a loss what to do, more particularly as the other two told her they would not wait, but go home without her. On looking wistfully around her, she spied the prince, whom she knew, and asked him if he had her swan-skin. He acknowledged the theft, and said, if she would tell him where Green Sleeves stayed, he would deliver unto her the skin. This she said she durst not venture to do, but upon his immediately giving it up, she would teach him how to discover the place of his retreat if he would follow her directions. He then gave her the skin, and she directed as follows.[14]

Here is the same sequence of events, as recounted by a young traveller called Geordie Stewart in Jeannie Robertson's wee house in Causewayend, Aberdeen in 1954:

. . . He lands at the banks o the river. And now, as the blacksmith telt him to hide hissel, so Jack hides hissel . . . just aside the bridge, and he sees this three lovely maidens comin ower, and they were bonnie lassies. But the littlest one was the slenderest, and the most graceful o the lot, you would have thought, you know? So they come trippin ower the bridge and undress, and into the water. And whenever they touch the water, the two oldest ones turned til a black swan, and they swum fast an away. And this youngest one undresses; and he watches where she pits her clothes, and ye ken what like Jack, I mean a fairm servant, never seen a woman in his life hardly, says, "Lord, this is fine!" They're into the water, and they're away swimming. So he's awa up wi her claes, up every stitch o claes she had, everything, even the very ribbons, and hides them.

So the two oldest ones comes out and dresses, and across the bridge and away. And she's up and doon this side, and she says, "Where are you, Jack?"

He says, "I'm here."

She says, "My clothes, please, Jack."

"Ah na na, I'm nae giein ye nae claes," he says. "I was weel warned aboot ye."

She says, "Jack, please, my clothes. Are you a gentleman?"

"Na na," he says, "I'm just Jack the Feel. I'm nae gentleman."

She says, "What have I to do, Jack?"

He says, "Well," he says. He says, "It's a cruel thing to ask, but," he says, "you must help me across this river on your back."

She says, "Oh Jack, you'd break my slender back."

"Ah," he says, "the old smith's nae feel. Ye're nae sae slender." He says, "Ye'll take me across the river."

She says, "Well Jack, step on my back, but whatever you do, on the peril of my life and your life, don't tell how ye got across."

He says, "Okay."

So he jumps on her back, and she takes him across, an he steps up on the bank.[15]

Another very revealing comparison can be drawn between the stilted high-falutin English of Peter Buchan's recensions, and modern translations into workmanlike 'carpentered Scots' of these same tales (which were taken down—according to Peter—from 'aged Sybils in the North Countrie'). Here is the opening of 'The History of Mr. Greenwood', which is Peter's version of the international 'Bluebeard' tale (Aa. Th. 955):

> In the Western Isles of Scotland there lived a very rich man, of the name of Gregory, who had two beautiful daughters, to whom he was inordinately attached, but being vastly rich, he would not suffer either of them to go for an hour out of his presence without a strong detachment of the inmates of his house accompanying them wherever they went and for the purpose of defending them from violent attacks that might be made upon them, or being carried off by the lawless banditti who at that time infested that part of the country. It happened, however, one day when they were at their usual walk and recreation, a little distance from their house, there came up to them a gentleman with his servant on horseback, who accosted them in a rather familiar way, asking them if those men they saw at a little distance were attendants of theirs? They answered in the affirmative. He also put some other questions to them which they did not choose to answer. One of the ladies then wished to know how he was so impertinent; when he replied that, being much attached to the elder of the two, her beauty being so enchanting, he broke through the rules of good breeding.[16]

In a recent number of *Lallans* there is a version of the tale entitled 'The Storie o Caermoulis' contributed by David Purves. This is a recension of Peter's recension, 'pitten intil his ain Scots' by the translator. The opening goes as follows:

> Ae tyme in the Western Isles, thare bade a walthie man bi name o Gregorie that haed twa braw dochters. He loued thaim baith that weill, he wadna allou thaim ti gang outby the houss athout a strang gaird, for in thae days, the kintrasyde wes thrang wi outlaws an ketterins.
>
> Houanevir, it fell that ae day whan thai warna fer frae the houss, a gentilman an his sairvant rade up ti thaim an spiered at thaim anent the gairds that was staunan tae neirhaund. Says he,
>
> "Ma leddies, is aw yon your men staunan owre thare."
>
> The auldest dochter, whas name wes Mysie, wesna verra weill pleised at this an answered him,
>
> "Ay, thai ir that, but what's that ti you, Sir. A'm thinkan ye ir a wee thing forritsum, sae ye ir. We dinna even ken yeir name."
>
> Says he, "Ma name is Caermoulis, an it's no lyke me ti be forritsum, but A wes that taen up wi yeir bewtie, A juist coudna help addressan ye."[17]

Mr Purves has turned out a solid serviceable piece of work which is certainly a vast improvement on Peter's bleached pallid artefact; nevertheless, the difference in idiom between his 'colloquial-literary' Scots and the language of Scots tales collected from oral tradition is (quite understandably) very marked.

One of the best told tales in the archive of the School of Scottish Studies is 'The Cat and the Hard Cheese', which was recorded in Montrose from Bessie Whyte by Peter Cooke and Linda Headlee in 1975.[18] The first part of this story—printed in *Tocher* in 1976—is the familiar fraternal exodus 'to seek their fortune' which is the lead-in to hundreds of Jack tales. The elder brother is offered the wee bannock with a blessing or the big bannock with a curse, and he chooses wrongly: very shortly his head is on a spike on the tyrant bossman's gates. However, when the younger brother is due to set off on his travels, he chooses rightly (i.e. unselfishly)—'Ach, the wee yin'll dae fine'—and his mother takes him at his word:

> So she baked him this wee bannick an she fried this wee callop tae him, an she tied it up in a hankie, an he's away, an he's hi tae the road an ho tae the road, through sheep's parks and bullocks' parks an all the high an the low mountains o Yarrow, an there was no rest for poor Jeck, till the birds were makin nests in his heid an the stones were makin holes in his feet . . . no rest fir him.

This passage—from 'he's hi tae the road'—is immediately identifiable as a 'run' very similar to the lyrically-intensified stereotyped passages well-known in Gaelic folktales—but it also closely resembles those formulaic passages of conventional rhetoric in the ballads which enable the narrator to 'leap and linger', and thus invigorate and sustain the action. The language of the Lallan folktales, in fact, does quite frequently bear a clear resemblance to ballad-Scots, and is in any event nearly always closer to the oscillating bilingual language of folksong we have been describing than to what has been termed 'punterspeak'. (No disrespect to the punters!).

One more example from the wonder tales: here is Jeannie Robertson's version of this same run, which she employed in several of the Jack tales she used to tell:

> He's hey the road, ho the road, doon the road; the tods ging to their holes, and the wee birdies flee awa hame to their nests—but there's nae rest for Silly Jack.[19]

If I may be allowed a personal reminiscence—when my children were small, Jeannie used to tell them her wonder tales, and I well remember how this verbal magic lodged in their minds, and would be reproduced with Jeannie's own incantatory cadences when the children told the same stories to their friends—and to me.

If the language of Jeannie's folktales was comparatively easy for Edinburgh children to understand and reproduce, even easier was the language of her version of the great ballads. Here is the text of her now world-famous version of 'Son David' (= 'Edward' Child 13):

> 'Oh, what's the blood 'its on your sword,
> My son, David, ho son David?
> What's that blood 'its on your sword?
> Come, promise, tell me true'
>
> 'Oh, that's the blood of my grey meir,
> Hey, lady Mother, ho, lady Mother,
> That's the blood of my grey meir,
> Because it wadnae rule by me.'

'Oh, that blood it is owre clear,
My son David, ho, son David,
That blood it is owre clear,
Come, promise, tell me true.'

'Oh, that's the blood of my greyhound,
Hey, lady Mother, ho, lady Mother,
That's the blood of my greyhound,
Because it wadnae rule by me.'

'Oh, that blood it is owre clear,
My son David, ho, son David,
That blood it is owre clear,
Come, promise, tell me true.'

'Oh, that's the blood of my huntin hawk,
Hey, lady Mother, ho, lady Mother,
That's the blood of my huntin hawk,
Because it wadnae rule by me.'

'Oh, that blood it is owre clear,
My son David, ho, son David,
That blood it is owre clear,
Come, promise, tell me true.'

'For that's the blood of my brother, John,
Hey, lady Mother, ho, lady Mother,
That's the blood of my brother, John
Because he wadnae rule by me.

'Oh, I'm gaun awa in a bottomless boat,
In a bottomless boat, in a bottomless boat,
For I'm gaun awa in a bottomless boat,
An I'll never return again.'

'Oh, whan will you come back again,
My son David, ho son David?
Whan will you come back again?
Come, promise, tell me true.'

'When the sun an the moon meets in yon glen,
Hey, lady Mother, ho, lady Mother,
Whan the sun an the moon meets in yon glen,
For I'll return again.'[20]

Blood—Lady Mother—brother—this is indistinguishable from ballad-English, but 'owre clear' and 'wadnae' perform the same service for 'Son David' that 'nae' did for Betsy Whyte's version of 'Sweet William's Ghost'. In any case, the clear, simple, dignified diction of the great ballads could hardly be more eloquently exemplified.—But listen now to a snatch of Jeannie's conversation, recorded—I have to admit it!—without her knowledge; it's a graphic description (recorded in her house at 21 Causewayend in 1954) of an Aberdeen lad who was a kind of local 'King of the Liars':

> . . . sittin' tellin' people a lot o' lees. But ye had to show your manners: ye had to bear this lees; ay, ye had to listen tae them. I jist gaes aboot the hoose—I jist looks at him like that, I says, God bless us Johnnie—God forgive ye . . . I says, I canna help for tellin', I canna. . . . And still, I kent that he was a guid laddie tae—and he's always made welcome in the hoose when he comes in here. But we ken he's a liar! We ken Johnnie cannae open his mooth withoot tellin' one!
> A voice: Ye can aye get a good laugh at a good lee.
> Jeannie: But still—wanst upon a time—I dinna ken whit like he is noo, but I still think he could sing. Because—he used to come tae oor hoose doon there, and he sung bloody good at that time!
> A voice: Oh, he's a lovely singer.
> Jeannie: Doon there he sung tae hiz often. Many's and many's the night he sung to hiz doon there. Because at nights, Hamish, maybe a fiddle played—the pipes played—Johnnie sung—I sung—maybe some of the rest o them sung, and the nicht passed by. . . .[21]

On the double LP 'The Muckle Sangs' (Tangent TNGM/119/D) a couple of the finest examples of auld-style ballad-Scots in the archive of the School of Scottish Studies can be heard in two incomplete but complementary versions of the classic ballad 'Clyde's Water' (Child 216)—one sung by John Strachan of Crichie, near Fyvie, and the other by Willie Edward of Craigellachie. (For an account of the life and exploits of the farmer-singer John Strachan, see *Tocher* 36/37). The ballad is about a pair of ill-starred lovers, victims of their malignant mothers, who in one way or another wish them ill and bring them to destruction. Willie's mother does not want him to ford the Clyde on horseback, and she curses him when he decides to 'put trust in his ain horse-heels'. Here is John Strachan's 'wey' of the central part of the ballad, which describes the hero crossing the river in spate:

> So he rade o'er hills and rade doon dales
> And doon yon dowie den,
> But the rush that rose in Clyde's water
> Wad have feared a hundred men.
>
> Oh Clyde, ye Clyde, ye rollin Clyde,
> Yer waves are wondrous strong;
> Mak me a wreck as I come back,
> But spare me as I gyang.

Oh Maggie, Maggie, Maggie dear
Oh rise an lat me in,
For my boots are fu of Clyde's water,
An I'm shiverin tae the skin.

My stables are full o horses,
My sheds are fu o hay;
My beds are fu of gentlemen
That winna leave till day.

This is a superb example of the supple and sinewy ballad-language praised and honoured by Gavin Greig. The reader (and listener) readily apprehend how close it lies to ballad-English, and yet what a totally different impression it makes.

When Willie reaches Maggie's bower, the other hostile mother impersonates her daughter, and turns Willie away. Now let us hear Willie Edward, another North-East singer who had the ballad, carrying the story forward at the point where Maggie becomes aware of her mother's fraud:

". . . oh mother dear,
Come rede my drowsy dream.
I dreamt sweet Willie was at my gate:
Nae yin wid lat him in."

" 'S lie still, lie still, my Maggie dear,
Lie still an tak your rest:
Since your true love was at your gates,
'Tis full three quarters past."

But it's Maggie rose, put on her clothes,
An to the Clyde she went:
The first step noo that she took in
It took her tae the knee;
The next step noo that she took in
It took her tae the chin.
In the deepest pot in a' the Clyde
She found her Willie in.

"So you have got a cruel mother
And I have got another
But here we lie in Clyde Water,
Like sister and like brother."

His final verse, written down, is indistinguishable from ballad-English, but—like Betsy Whyte's verse from 'Sweet William's Ghost', already quoted—it *must* (because of the Scots in other stanzas) be pronounced *more Boreali.*

After making this recording I asked Willie where he had got the ballad and his reply was as follows:

WE Oh, gosh man, I'm growin' sae auld . . . it's nae easy mindin' sae faur back, man.

HIS WIFE Your grannie, maybe?

WE Ay, my grannie was a great singer.

HH Was she?

WE Ay, she was good at hummin' awa onywey—and sometimes, when she was ill-natur'd, she sang tee![22]

The equilibrium of ballad-Scots and ballad-English was maintained well into the nineteenth century: the same linguistic and conventional techniques as we have encountered in the classic ballads are to be found in many later songs; indeed, they surface occasionally even in the so-called 'bothy ballads' or farmyard songs. Not long after making the above recording, Willie was singing 'The Bonnie Parks o' Kilty', a narrative love song which is as clearly couched in classic ballad-Scots as any of the older songs in his repertoire:

> He's ta'en her by the middle sma' and gently laid her down,
> Where the apples and the cherries were a' hanging down,
> The lilies and the green grass were growing all around
> Where they lay on the bonnie parks o' Kilty, O.[23]

At this point let us call as expert witness the late P W Joyce, who wrote in his *Old Irish Folk Music and Songs* (Dublin, 1909):

The Anglo-Irish peasant poets wrote in pure English, so far as lay in their power, and so far as their knowledge of the language extended. They hardly ever used the broken-English words of the Anglo-Irish folk dialect, such as *ould, darlint, nothin, I'm kilt* and speechless, *onaisy, wonst* as I *wint* out, *becaze, sthrame,* come *hether, consarnin*, let go your *hoult*, etc. But such words as these were constantly used in conversation, not only by the general run of the people, but by the writers of the songs.

Moreover the composers of Anglo-Irish songs very seldom used Irish words mixed with English, either in correct Gaelic spelling or anglicised: such as *asthore, gon doutha, oyeh,* Katie *eroo, alanna, inagh, angishore,* etc.[24]

Because of the superior status of Scots as a literary language (as compared to Anglo-Irish dialect), and because of the fame of poets like Burns and Robert Fergusson and the Ettrick Shepherd, there is quite a large body of nineteenth-century Scots folksong in passable ballad-Scots. Nevertheless, Gavin Greig was undoubtedly right when he commented (writing on 'Traditional Minstrelsy' in *The Book of Buchan*, Peterhead, 1910):

Remembering the general tendency of lyricism to raise language to a higher plane, we must not expect to find much of the undiluted vernacular in our folksongs. Education has made our peasant bilingual in a way, so that in the use of language he readily becomes barometric.[25]

The date by which this process may be said—give a decade, take a decade—to have been consummated can be placed with tolerable certainty at the beginning of the nineteenth century. In spite of the massive influx of English broadside ballads, the creeping anglicisation of the eighteenth century was temporarily halted, thanks to the momentary stabilisation of Scots as a language for poetry; this was directly due, of course, to the splendid services of Allan Ramsay and Robert Fergusson, and above all to the enormous popularity—I had almost written pop-vogue—of the work of Burns.

(It is by no means unusual for Buchan farming folk who are dab hands at the bothy ballads to be able to recite long screeds of Burns: e.g. 'The Twa Dogs', 'Holy Willie's Prayer', and above all 'Tam o' Shanter'. Where the Ayrshire form of a word is markedly different in pronunciation from the North-East form (e.g. *buit* and *beet*), it is possible to monitor on tape-recordings made at different times a fascinating seismographical fluctuation of locutions—pitching, juddering, settling and finally coming to rest.)

It is essential to remember that many of the songs in ballad-English (or the next best thing) were in fact of English origin—either carried north by word of mouth or (as was certainly often more frequent) in the printed *lingua franca* of the broadsides. This applies even to songs which, judging from their titles alone, might have been thought to have originated in Scotland—e.g. 'Caroline of Edinburgh Town'. Dozens of songs must have been transported along the sea routes from Yarmouth and Scarborough. It is maybe not sufficiently realised that during the eighteenth and nineteenth centuries there was just as big an influx of English songs into Scotland as there was into Ireland. (Some of these, of course, may have boxed the compass, moving to Ireland from Scotland or England, and then returning seaborne to their original starting place.) Here and there one comes across some amusing oddities and eccentricities: e.g. 'an 'usiband both galliant and gay', pickled in aspic in the middle of an Aberdeenshire singer's rendering of 'Villikens and his Dinah'; southern English nasalisations as in 'Caroline of Edinburgh Teown [tɛun]'; and *-ly* pronounced *lie* [lai] as in English sea shanties (ear-ly in the morning) and in Victorian barn-stormers' *Bühnenenglisch*.

Beside these meridional curiosities one can set reminiscences of Scots grammatical forms congealed in song when they have long since died out in colloquial Scots, e.g. *-and* instead of *-an*—or *-in'*—as a present participle. In his version of 'An Auld Man Cam Coortin' Me', Willie MacPhee has the pay-off line:

> Syne I crept back tae my dyand auld man.

And Jessie Murray's present participle in *-an* was very marked when she sang:

> Skippan barfut throw the heather.

Some of the linguistic conventions of tinker ballad-Scots *do* seem to echo earlier Scots language forms, e.g. Jeannie Robertson sang (in 'The Gallowa Hills'):

> Wi heather bells and riveris a'.

Paradoxically, songs in dialect (e.g. the Buchan dialect) become more frequent with the increasing provincialisation of Scotland after the incorporating Union of 1707. Some of these dialect songs are excellent—racy, rich, exuberant—but we may lay down as a general axiom that Scots folksong employing a fairly thick dialect is either very localised or comparatively recent. In Article XII of *Folk-Song of the North-East*, published in 1908, Gavin Greig had this to say about 'Humorous Songs':

Humour is not a strong feature of traditional minstrelsy. Our old ballads are nearly all serious, with a distinct tendency towards the tragic. Now and again in ballad and song we encounter humorous touches, and occasionally meet with a ditty which deals avowedly with the fun of something: but for the comic song pure and simple we must come down to quite recent days. "The Souters' Feast" is about as humorous a folk-song as we have ever come across. The situation and the idea may not be original; but the song as we have it is clearly local, and seems to belong to central Buchan—the Maud district, we should say, judging from one kind of evidence or another. It can be traced back for a couple of generations at least, although it does not appear to be old. In a MS. collection of songs made by Peter Buchan between the years 1825 and 1830 there is one called "The Souters' Feast". Mr. William Walker, Aberdeen, is able to give us the first verse:

> There cam' a Souter out o' Oyne.
> Tum, cerry, avum;
> Ridin' on a muckle preen,
> Sing cidi, uptum, avum.

For the rest of the song we should have to go to Harvard University, U.S., where the MS. is now lodged; but we have reason to know that Peter's version would not make for edification though we had it.[26]

The collection to which Greig refers is *Secret Songs of Silence,* a fascinating collection of bawdry of the *Merry Muses* variety—most of it quite definitely in the non-edificatory category—but the version of 'The Souters' Feast', which is the first song in it, is (curiously enough) not bawdy in the least; it is a bizarre gallimaufry of fantastical-farcical Breughelesque humour. As William Walker's transcript of the first verse is not accurate, I subjoin the text of that, as it appears in the manuscript, plus a few select verses:

> There came a Soutter out o' Ein,
> Tum, tirry, arum
> Riding on a muckle prin,
> Sing—Adli, umpti, arum,
> Adli, umpti, dirimdi,
> Didle, dadle, darum.

> There came a Soutter out o' Fife,
> Tum, tirry, arum;
> Riding on a gully-knife,
> Sing—Adli, umpti, arum &c.

There came Soutters far an' near,
Tum, tirry, arum
Frae Turriff, Fyvie an' New Deer,
Sing—Adli, umpti, arum &c.

And there came Soutters out o' Hell,
Tum, tirry, arum;
Riding on the deil himsell,
Sing—Adli, umpti, arum &c. . . .

The Soutter gaed the sow a kiss,
Tum, tirry, arum;
Grumph! said he, it's for my birse,
Sing—Adli, umpti, arum &c.

O gin ye cou'd wash my sark,
Tum, tirry, arum;
As well as ye can grumph an' hark,
Sing—Adli, umpti, arum &c.

An' Oh gin ye cou'd bake me bannocks,
Tum, tirry, arum;
As well as ye can winch an' wannock,
Sing—Adli, umpti, arum &c.

I declare my dearest life,
Tum, tirry, arum;
There's nane but you shou'd be my wife,
Sing—Adli, umpti, arum &c.[27]

Some of the verses in Greig's version, published in the *Buchanie* in 1908, are in much thicker Buchan dialect than the wavering, composite lingo of the *Secret Songs* version. Here are two late arrivals at the Feast:

An ill-faured skyple cam' frae Crimon'
        Tanteerie orum;
A perfect scunner to the women,
        The eedle and the orum;
A muckle hypal haveless loon,
        Tanteerie orum;
Frae the Fite Steen cam' hoiterin' doon,
        The eedle and the orum.
            Thee-a-noodle, thee-a-num,
            The eedle and the orum.

And when they thocht they a' were come,
Tanteerie orum;
A cripple breet cam' owre frae Drum,
The eedle and the orum;
Ridin' on a cripple mear,
Tanteerie orum;
His apron for his ridin' gear,
The eedle and the orum.
Thee-a-noodle, thee-a-num,
The eedle and the orum.[28]

This, like Peter's version of the same song—though to a greater degree—is clearly more dialect than ballad-Scots. It is blood brother to the robust colloquial Scots of the humorous songs such as 'The Tinklers' Waddin'',[29] written by William Watt (died 1859)—which soon joined the older ballads in the repertoires of folksingers from Buchan to the Border (and beyond). To bring the difference between these varying idioms into focus, let us look at another of the songs in Peter's collection, 'The Whirley Wha':

There was a bridal in our town,
Upon a holy day,
And there was muckle, muckle mirth,
And there was muckle play.

The bells were rung, the auld wives sung,
We to the kirk gied a',
When the bride came hame wi' her silly bridegroom,
To play wi' his whirleywha.

First she turn'd her back to him,
And then she turn'd her wame,
And lang she look'd for kindness,
But kindness there was nane.

She took him in her arms twa'
And hiest him 'gainst the wa',
Says—Ly ye there, ye silly auld diel,
Ye've lost your whirleywha.

What's this my father's dane to me?
He's dane me muckle ill
He's wedded me to a silly auld man,
Sair, sair against my will.

Had I been married to my young man,
Though never a sark ava'
He'd lovingly squeeze me in his arms,
And play'd wi' his whirleywha.

> Now a' the lasses o' our town,
> They bear me muckle envy,
> But gin their case was bad as mine,
> Their cheeks wou'd never dry.

> But I'll dress mysell in ribbons fine,
> Nae body e'er sae braw,
> And hire some bonny young lad o' my ain,
> Tae play wi' his whirleywha.[30]

In a note to the above item, Peter states: 'This song was written by Mary Hay, daughter of one of the Earls of Errol after she was married to General Scott, from whom she eloped for want of ——'. We may be pretty confident, however—as confident as we can ever reasonably be in these things—that the 'wey' of it enshrined in the *Secret Songs* has as truly come into being through oral transmission and recreation as any currently recoverable version of such innocent anonyms as 'The Highland Tinker' or 'The Crab Fish'. Peter has a version of the latter quite different from the dozens already on record (or indeed from any of the versions you can come across in sergeants' mess or saloon bar):

> There was an auld priest's wife
> And she was big wi' lad,
> Falaladidum, faladeraldiri,
> And all that she longed for
> Was a sea crab.
> Sing Fala, &c. . .

> Gude morrow to ye fishers,
> That fishes in the fleed,
> Falala &c.
> Hae ye ony crab fish
> To dee a woman gweed?
> Falala &c.[31]

At their best the older bawdy anonyms, products of a long folk process, exhibit, almost better than the tragic ballads, the linguistic *stuff* of ballad-Scots, for they—unlike, for example, some of the texts provided by Mrs Brown of Falkland—practically never give evidence of pen-and-paper work. Another delicious example—'The Wanton Trooper'—will be found quoted in full in my article 'The Ballad, The Folk and the Oral Tradition'.[32] Also quoted in the same article is 'Slow Men of London', which North-East singers would no doubt have thought of as a 'Scots' song, but which acknowledges its origin no less by virtue of its particular brand of ballad language as by the obvious give-away of the place-name. However, it *has* undoubtedly been sung into its *Secret Songs* shape—unlike (for example) 'The Dyer of Roan' which is an excellent example of arch eighteenth-century English bawdry, quite plainly the product of a single pen and intelligence. Two verses will provide an adequate sample:

> The Abbot as you may believe,
> Had but little to say for himself;
> He knew well what he ought to receive,
> For his being so arrant an elf;
> His clothes he got on with all speed,
> And conducted he was by the dyer,
> To be duckit (as you after may read)
> And be cool'd from his amorous fire.
>
> Quoth the dyer, most reverend father,
> Since I find you're so hot upon wenching,
> I have gather'd my servants together,
> To give you a taste of our drenching.
> Here—Tom, Harry, Roger and Dick!
> Take the Abbot, undress him, and douse him.
> They obey'd in that very same nick,
> To the dye-vat they take him and souse him.[33]

Of course, a singer from Turriff or Strichen would sing the above with the local accent, and an English listener might therefore even find bits of it hard to understand, but it would take a long time for such a composed ditty to get even quarterways naturalised. And yet, as I have hinted above, personal experience in the field suggests that many, if not most, North-East singers (especially in the period when Peter Buchan was collecting) would think of it as a Scots song. In the same—or a similar—way, Hume of Godscroft must have thought—or half-thought—that he was writing in his mother tongue when he asserted (in his preface to *The History of the House of Douglas and Angus*, published in 1644:

For the language it is my mother-tongue, that is, Scottish: and why not, to Scottish-men? Why should I contemne it? I never thought the difference so great, as that by seeking to speak English, I would hazard the imputation of affectation. Every tongue hath [its] own vertue and grace. . . . For my own part, I like our own, and he that writes well in it writes well enough to me. Yet I have yeelded somewhat to the tyrannie of custome and the times, not seeking curiously for words, but taking them as they came to hand. I acknowledge also my fault (if it be a fault) that I ever accounted it a mean study and of no great commendation to learn to write or to speak English and have loved better to bestow my pains on forreigne languages, esteeming it but a dialect of our own, and that (perhaps) more corrupt.[34]

If already in the mid seventeenth century a perfervidly patriotic Scots historian could make a statement so apparently self-contradictory, who will find it strange that three centuries later Aberdeenshire folksingers could and did move from undiluted Buchan Scots (in songs like 'M'Ginty's Meal and Ale'[35] and 'The Wedding of M'Ginnis and his Cross-Eyed Pet'[36]) to the unambiguous English of the broadside ballads without seeming to notice the difference—or else paying it scant attention if they did. Here the role played by broadsides from the South, and by wholesale borrowings from them by printers in Scotland, cannot be overestimated. In the nineteenth century broadsides and chapbooks flooded Scotland in their hundreds of thousands, and in many of these printed sheets songs in one or another form of Scots lay cheek by jowl with songs in English. Taking a lucky dip into my own sizeable collection of chapbooks printed in Glasgow, Stirling and Airdrie I draw out a couple at random; one, embellished with a handsome woodcut of a swan surveying its reflection in the water of a wildwood-fringed loch, is printed in Glasgow 'by and for J. Neil' in 1829. It contains the following songs:

1 'Betsey Baker' (in English), for which the air is given as *Push about the Jorum*, with the added note: 'As sung by Mr. Potts, Theatrical Pavilion, Glasgow'. The text includes one English cant phrase:

> He gammoned her to run away
> And I lost Betsey Baker.

One place-name is mentioned: the hero's mother thinks

> 'twoud ease my mind
> If I came up to London.

2 'Who's Master, or A Fight for the Breeches' (in English), also as sung by the popular Mr Potts. A sempiternal comic theme.

3 'York, You're Wanted' (in English), to the air *Alley Croaker*. The adventures of a Yorkshire lad who travels to London to seek his fortune, and marries a rich maiden lady.

4 'The Emigrant's Farewell' (in English, with light sprinklings of Scots). Tune: *My Guid Lord John*. Three sample stanzas:

> Farewell, ye hills of glorious deeds,
>   And streams renown'd in song—
> Farewell, ye braes and blossom'd meads,
>   Our hearts have lov'd so long.
>
> Farewell, the blythesome broomy knowes,
>   Where thyme and harebells grow—
> Farewell, the hoary, haunted howes
>   O'er hung with birk and sloe. . . .
>
> Our native land—our native vale—
>   A long and last adieu!
> Farewell to bonny Tivotdale,
>   And Scotland's mountains blue!

The second specimen was printed in Glasgow 'for the Bookseller'. It is undated but looks as if it is approximately from the same period. The woodcut is of an Oriental warrier wearing a turban, and carrying a scimitar and a dagger. The songs are:

1   'He Comes from the Wars' (in English). A wounded soldier finds refuge in a cottage, and dreams of his mistress.

2, 3 and 4   Sentimental love lyrics in genteel English.

5   'Father Paul' (in English). A bibulous friar who prays 'To rosy Bacchus god of wine'.

6   'King David was a Soldier' (in English with sprinklings of Scots). Sample stanza:

> A soldier and a bonnie lass
>   Went out together one day,
> With kisses and kind compliments,
>   He unto her did say:
> Love, dare I kiss thy ruby lips,
>   'Twoud make me something bolder,
> Oh no, Oh no, my minnie says,
>   I may na kiss wi' a soldier.

There were, of course, many chapbooks circulating which reprinted songs and poems by Burns, Hogg and Tannahill, and other Scots items—including, very occasionally, folksongs collected from singing or recitation—but the point is that chapbooks like the ones I have described were also there in abundance. Here it is important to recall the often noted fact that simple country folk loved to think of a ballad as 'a true ballad'. In a famous scene in *The Winter's Tale* (Act IV, 4) Shakespeare pokes gentle fun at the credulous shepherdesses Dorcas and Mopsa who believe—or want to believe—all the whoppers Autolycus peddles when he is hawking his ballads:

CLOWN   What hast here? Ballads?

MOPSA   Pray now, buy some. I love a ballad in print, a-life, for then we are sure they are true.

AUTOLYCUS   Here's one to a very doleful tune, how a usurer's wife was brought to bed of twenty money-bags at a burden, and how she longed to eat adders' heads and toads carbonadoed.

MOPSA   Is it true, think you?

AUTOLYCUS   Very true, and but a month old.

DORCAS   Bless me from marrying a usurer!

AUTOLYCUS   Here's the midwife's name to't: one Mistress Taleporter, and five or six honest wives that were present. Why should I carry lies abroad?

His next tale is even taller, but he assures them:

AUTOLYCUS   . . . The ballad is very pitiful, and as true.
DORCAS   Is it true too, think you?
AUTOLYCUS   Five justices' hands at it, and witnesses more than my pack will hold.

One does not need to rub in the obvious point that for the Mopsas and Dorcases of North-East Scotland many of the ballads they saw in print, and might not be able to read—for the reverence for print was in part at least a legacy of illiteracy—were not only 'true' but true *in English*. Thus on the 'folk' level the message of the King James's Bible was powerfully reinforced by Grub Street printers and their like all over the island; it must have been a relief to many when the good news sank in that entertainment as well as salvation was available by courtesy of the English language.

And what, in this same period, were the 'crambo-clink' poets—the local bards who aspired to appear in print, with their work proudly displayed under such titles as *Rustic Rhymes, Sangs and Sonnets*—making of the language situation they had inherited? Gavin Greig was later to take an interest in their work, and two exercise books exist containing the texts of articles on 'Bards of Buchan'.[37] In the second of these Greig devotes five pages to Peter Still, whom he dubs 'the typical Buchan bard'. The potted biography which Greig supplies might indeed serve as a prototype of the life-struggle of dozens of similar versifiers.

> He was born in the parish of Fraserburgh, where his father had a small farm, on the 1st January, 1814. He himself took to farm service, got married before he was out of his teens, and by-and-by became a day labourer, taking a turn at such jobs as came his way—casting peats or breaking stones. He suffered all his life from ill-health, but ever bore manfully up. Latterly he took the Blackhouse Toll Bar, where he died in 1848, at the early age of thirty-four.[38]

The first poem of his discussed in the article is a blurred sub-Burnsian look-alike entitled 'The Cottar's Sunday'. The concluding stanza of this poem (which is about half as long again as Burns's, according to Greig) may be taken as fairly representative of a wide tract of similar effusions:

> Lang may the sound of heartfelt praise & prayer
> From Caledonian cottages arise;
> An' lang may Sion's holy heavenly lays
> Be sweetly warbled to the listening skies;
> In this fair Scotia's richest treasure lies,—
> Lang may she guard the gem wi' holy zeal;
> An' may she ne'er her toil-worn sons despise;
> Her fame an' honour rest upon their weal,—
> They of her glory are, an' aye will be, the seal.[39]

One has the impression that Greig was leaning over backwards in this article to be kind to these worthy local bards. He even goes so far as to say, referring to another poem of Peter Still's called 'Jeannie's Lament', that 'it sounds a more intense note than had yet been heard from the Buchan lyre'. Here is one stanza from that poem:

> I never thocht to thole the waes
> It's been my lot to dree;
> I never thocht to sigh sae sad
> Whan first I sighed for thee.
> I thocht your heart was like mine ain,
> As true as true could be;
> I couldna think there was a stain
> In ane sae dear to me.[40]

Compare with this almost any one of the scores of passionate love songs in the Aberdeenshire folk tradition which Greig himself put on record, and one cannot fail to be struck by the extraordinary contrast between the slack, insipid and nerveless lucubrations of the poetasters who wrote with an eye to print, and the verve, spunk and genuine poetry of the anonyms, whether these are celebrating triumphant sexuality, emitting belly laughs at the spectacle of the comedy of sex, or lamenting the tragedy of lost love. Listen, for example, to a version of 'The False Lover Won Back' which Greig himself printed in his column in the *Buchanie:*

> As I went up yon high, high hill,
> And down in yonder glen,
> And the very spot where my love lies,
> And the sun goes never down;
> And the sun goes never down, bonnie love,
> And the sun goes never down;
> The very spot where my love lies,
> And the sun goes never down.

> *Chorus*
> Oh, love me once again, bonnie love,
> Oh, love me once again;
> Isn't sair for me that I like you,
> And you nae me again;
> And you nae me again, bonnie love,
> And you nae me again.

> Oh, fan will ye be hame, bonnie love,
> Oh, fan will ye be hame?
> When the heather hills are nine times brunt,
> And a' grown green again;
> And a' grown green again, bonnie love,
> And a' grown green again.

Oh, that's owre lang to bide awa',
Oh, that's owre lang frae hame,
Owre lang for the babe that's nae yet born
 For to be wantin' a name;
For to be wantin', etc.

The first toon that he came to
He bought her hose and sheen,
And he bade her rue and turn back noo,
 Nae mair to follow him.

The next toon that he came to
He bought her a wedding ring,
And he bade her rue and turn back noo,
 Nae mair to follow him.

He's mounted on a milk white steed,
 And he's helped Maggie on;
Says, It's love for love that I like best,
 Bonnie love ye shall be mine.[41]

When one speaks of anonyms, of course, one must bear in mind that at many stages of the folk process individual minds—and sometimes, quite clearly, powerful ingenious individual minds—have set their seal on new variants. Sometimes a craftsman-poet, endowed with 'a nice judicious ear' (to quote Burns) and immersed in the musical and linguistic traditions handed down to him, must have composed song-poems in the time-honoured prescriptive idiom which were already halfway towards becoming folksongs.

Is one making too big a jump to postulate the existence, at more than one level of society, and at many if not most periods of our history, of makars who foreswore print, and consciously embraced the aesthetic prejudices and the prosodic and musical techniques of an essentially non-literate song poetry? The version of 'Edward' (= 'Son David', Child 13) which Lord Hailes sent to Bishop Percy for inclusion in his *Reliques* might possibly come into this category. Be that as it may, we must surely, on the evidence, make a distinction between the poet who operated with a hopeful eye to print—and the fame (and money) which might accrue from published works—and those who spontaneously and for preference entrusted their wares to the discerning minds and deft mobile tongues of the traditional singers of Buchan and beyond.

Quite a number of such poets will, of course, have been highly literate people, but—as Alan Lomax has pointed out[42]—one of the principal distinguishing characteristics of the Scottish folksong tradition is the part played in it by bookish individuals. The paradox is not as great as it might at first appear. 'Of the making of books there is no end.' One of the reasons for the excellence of our ballad tradition is without doubt the literate Scot's wilful and purposive suspension of literacy.

That this predilection for making direct oral contact with a receptive community has been continued right up to our own day is attested by the popularity of the work of such virtuoso music-makars as Adam McNaughtan, Andy Hunter, Eric Bogle and Ewan MacColl. The work of these accomplished poets—and I am not using the word lightly—is naturally much better known to visitors to folk clubs than to the readers of poetry magazines. And if it is objected that this is a 'forced' development due mainly to the efforts of those connected with the current Folksong Revival, we may counter by claiming that the tradition as it exists today is in large part the heritage of many similar revivals in the past: for example, those which we associate with the names of Gavin Greig, Robert Burns and Allan Ramsay. It is an honourable list, and one that Scotland can be proud of.

To be sure, this phenomenon is by no means exclusively Scottish. Modern Spanish poetry—and particularly the work of Federico Garcia Lorca—exhibits many striking parallels. J L Gili has written of Lorca:

A word or a phrase heard would one day appear in a poem, without his being aware of it. It was all part of his spontaneous approach to his art. Guillermo de Torre, speaking of Lorca's assimilation and subsequent re-creation of Andalusian folk-songs, says: 'He sings them, he dreams them, he discovers them again—in a word, he turns them into poetry.' In this same connection, his brother Francisco says: 'During an excursion to the Sierra Nevada, the mule driver who was leading sang to himself:

> Y yo que me la llevé al río
> creyendo que era mozuela,
> pero tenio marido

(And I took here to the river believing her a maid, but she had a husband.)

Sometime later, one day when we were speaking of the ballad 'The Faithless Wife', I reminded Federico of the mule driver's song. To my enormous surprise, he had completely forgotten it. He thought the first three lines of the ballad were as much his as the rest of the poem. More than that, I thought I could tell that he did not like my insistence, for he continued to believe that I was mistaken'.[43]

It is fitting, then, to conclude with some pertinent lines from Lorca's poem *Balada de la Placeta* (Ballad of the Little Square):

LOS NIÑOS
¿ Qué sientes en tu boca
roja y sedienta?

YO
El sabor de los huesos
de mi gran calavera.

LOS NIÑOS
Bebe el agua tranquila
de la canción añeja.
¡Arroyo claro,
fuente serena!
¿ Por qué te vas tan lejos
de la plazuela?

YO
¡Voy en busca de magos
y de princesas!

LOS NIÑOS
¿Quién te enseñó el camino
de los poetas?

YO
La fuente y el arroyo
de la canción añeja.

The Children: What do you feel in your mouth scarlet and thirsting?
Myself: The taste of the bones of my big skull!
The Children: Drink the tranquil water of the antique song.
    Clear stream, serene fountain! Why do you go so far from the little square?
Myself: I go in search of magicians and princesses!
The Children: Who showed you the path of the poets?
Myself: The fountain and the stream of the antique song.[44]

NOTES

1 John Ord, *The Bothy Songs and Ballads of Aberdeen, Banff and Moray, Angus and the Mearns*, (Paisley, 1930)
2 Ord, op. cit., p. 111, ('The Green Woods o' Airlie')
3 Ord, op. cit., p. 315, ('Nairn River Banks')
4 Ord, op. cit., p. 267, ('The Gallant Shearers')
5 Stanley Hyman, 'The Language of Scottish Poetry', *The Kenyon Review*, (Gambier, Ohio: Winter 1954), p. 35
6 *The Poems of William Dunbar*, ed. W. MacKay MacKenzie, (Edinburgh 1932), p. 14
7 Hyman, op. cit., p. 36
8 Hugh MacDiarmid, *The Complete Poems, Vol. I*, (London 1978), p. 314
9 Hyman, op. cit., p. 26
10 M J C Hodgart, *The Ballads*, (London 1950), p. 57

11   For John Strachan's and Jeannie Robertson's versions, see Bertrand Harris Bronson, *The Traditional Tunes of the Child Ballads*, (Princeton, New Jersey 1966), Vol. III p. 9

12   Bronson, Vol. IV, (1972), Addenda, p. 473. It is curious that a parallel stanza (No. xx) in the version of 'Clerk Saunders' in Scott's *Minstrelsy* has likewise one single Scots locution:

> My mouth it is full cold, Margaret,
> It has the smell, now, of the ground
> And if I kiss thy comely mouth,
> Thy days of life will not be lang.

This might have been thought to be merely the whim of a sophisticated man of letters, were it not for the tape-recorded evidence (SSS Archives, SA1952/42. B29) of a non-literate tinker woman.

Incidentally, when Jean Ritchie re-recorded Betsy's beautiful fragment a year later in my company (copy tape 1953/2 in my possession) the text was identical.

13   Peter Buchan, *Ancient Scottish Tales*, (1829: printed Peterhead 1908), p. 25

14   Peter Buchan, op. cit., pp. 41–42

15   Ed. Alan Bruford, *The Green Man of Knowledge*, (Aberdeen 1982), pp. 17–18

16   Peter Buchan, op. cit., p. 21

17   *Lallans*, No. **18**, (Edinburgh, Whitsunday 1982). David Purves informs me that when he was a child he heard the name Caermoulis from an uncle of his who lived in Selkirk. Caermoulis was a sort of bogie-man figure.

According to Dr Katharine M Briggs (*The Fairies in Tradition and Literature*, (London 1967), p. 37), 'Killmoulis is the mill spirit in the Scottish Lowlands. He is a grotesque creature, with an enormous nose and no mouth, though he is said to be very fond of pork. He bewails any misfortune coming to the mill, but for all that he is fond of mischievous pranks, and can only be controlled by direct invocation from the miller. Occasionally in an emergency he will leave his corner to thrash grain or to fetch a midwife, but as a rule he is more of a nuisance than a help.

18   *Tocher* **23**, pp. 266–273 and *Tocher* 24, pp. 320–3. The 'run' quoted will be found in A. Bruford, *The Green Man of Knowledge*, op. cit., p. 44.

19   Quoted in *Chapbook*, Scotland's Folk Song Magazine, ed. Arthur Argo, (Aberdeen 1965). Vol. 2, No. 5, p. 3

20   'Son David' (= 'Edward', Child 13). SSS Tape Archive SA1960/3. B2. A recording of Jeannie singing this ballad will be found on the LP *Heather and Glen*. Tradition Records, New York, TLP 1047. Side 1, Band 8. For discussions of 'Son David', see Herschel Gower and James Porter, 'Jeannie Robertson: the Child Ballads', in *Scottish Studies* **14** (1970), pp. 41–42, and James Porter, 'Jeannie Robertson's ''My Son David'', A Conceptual Performance Model', in *Journal of American Folklore* 89 (1976), pp. 7–26.

For Jeannie's own comments on the ballad, see Herschel Gower, 'Jeannie Robertson: Portrait of a Traditional Singer', in *Scottish Studies* **12** (1968), pp. 113–126, on p. 125.

21   SSS Tape Archive SX1955/4 A4. (Example Tape: 'The Language of Scots Folksong')

22   *The Muckle Sangs*, Double LP on the Tangent Label, London, TNGM 119/D, Side 4, Band 1

23   Cf. Ord, op. cit., p. 113
24   P. W. Joyce, *Old Irish Folk Music and Songs*, (Dublin 1909), p. 242
25   Gavin Greig, article on 'The Traditional Minstrelsy of Buchan' in *The Book of Buchan*, ed. J. F. Tocher, (Peterhead 1910), p. 233
26   Gavin Greig, *Folk-Song of the North-East*, (Hatboro, Pennsylvania 1963), Article xii
27   *Secret Songs of Silence* by Sir Oliver Orpheus, Bart. of Eldridge Hall [Peter Buchan]. MS Volume in Harvard University Child Memorial Library (25241. 9). The verses from 'The Soutter's Feast' are on pages 1, 2 and 3.
28   Gavin Greig, FSNE, Article xii
29   Robert Ford, *Vagabond Songs and Ballads of Scotland*, (Paisley 1904) (one volume edition), pp. 1–4
30   *Secret Songs of Silence*, p. 80
31   *Secret Songs of Silence*, p. 22
32   Ed. Edward J. Cowan, *The People's Past*, (Edinburgh 1980), pp. 79–81
33   *Secret Songs of Silence*, p. 121
34   Quoted in David Reid, *The Party-Coloured Mind*, (Edinburgh 1982), p. 1
35   Gavin Greig, *Folk-Song of the North-East*, Article cxxxvi
36   G. Greig, FSNE, Article cxxxiv (under title "Sheelicks")
37   G. Greig, *The Bards of Buchan*. Two MS notebooks, the second in possession of the present writer. (Dr William Donaldson informs me that Gavin's notes on these minor North-East poets were published intermittently in a defunct weekly *The Peterhead Sentinel* in 1913–14.)
38   Greig, *Bards of Buchan* II, p. 26
39   Greig, *Bards of Buchan* II, p. 29
40   Greig, *Bards of Buchan* II, p. 30
41   Greig, FSNE, Article xciii (*A* Version)
42   Alan Lomax, Sleeve-note for *World Library of Folk and Primitive Music*, Vol. VI (Scotland), Columbia Masterworks L.P. KL-209
43   *Lorca*, Introduced and edited by J. L. Gili (Penguin Poets), Harmondsworth 1960, Introduction, pp. xiv-xv
44   *Lorca*, pp. 2–3

The title of this paper ('At the Foot o' yon Excellin' Brae') is a line from 'Courtin' Amang the Kye', as sung by the late Willie Mathieson, Dudwick, Ellon. Willie learned it from his second wife. The text appears in the first of his MS songbooks (p. 102); copies of these are in the archives of the School of Scottish Studies. The School also has tape-recorded versions sung by Charlie Reid, Longside and John Adams, Glenlivet.

Gavin Greig printed a version ('Cauries and Kye') in his column in the *Buchan Observer* (FSNE, Article vi).

SEVEN

Scots in Dialogue: Some uses and implications

J Derrick McClure

From the fountainhead of the Waverley Novels, writers of fiction have drawn inspiration for the use of Scots in dialogue. Walter Scott, if not strictly the first then certainly the greatest exponent of the practice, demonstrated brilliantly the resources of Scots—its enormous vocabulary, its wealth of idiomatic expressions, its vast fund of proverbial lore, its peculiar aptness for rhetoric, for argument and for backchat—and from the period of his novels to the present, works in which characters are represented as speaking Scots have abounded in Scottish literature. Yet the wide range of implications inherent in this literary usage have not often been examined. The constantly changing sociolinguistic situation in Scotland, the confused and ambivalent attitudes of the Scottish populace towards Scots, the strange elusiveness even of the concept of Scots, make the choice of Scots or English as a language of dialogue a matter of much greater complexity than is at first apparent.

The simplest approach is to draw an unmistakeable contrast between literary English and a highly differentiated Scots, to assign each to a specific character or set of characters, and to maintain the distinction with complete consistency: to treat Scots and English, at least in the fictional context, as simple alternatives. In plays by twentieth-century dramatists set in relatively remote periods, examples of this can readily be found. For stage performances, producers would naturally accentuate the linguistic polarisation suggested by the printed text by ensuring that the English parts were played by actors with pronounced English accents. Thus in Robert McLellan's play *Jamie the Saxt*, the speech of the Englishman Sir Robert Bowes is consistently and emphatically distinct from that of most of the other characters. So it would have been in historic fact; for Scots in the 1590s was still an autonomous national language, used for both speech and writing by the King as by his subjects: indeed, it is doubtful whether James VI and the English ambassador could in reality have conversed, if each kept to his own language, as easily as they appear to do in the drama. Sydney Goodsir Smith in *The Wallace* employs the same device. In this play, unlike McLellan's, it is not an accurate reflection of the linguistic facts of the period: in the unlikely event that Robert Bruce ever defied Edward I as he does at the climax of Smith's play their exchange would not have been conducted in any Anglo-Saxon tongue; and, more fundamentally, the dialects which would eventually give rise to the Scots and English languages were as yet far less mutually distinct than the literary Scots and English used by Smith. Geographically and socially the linguistic situation in Edward I's England was intricate enough; in Robert I's Scotland still more so: if the international conflict had any linguistic aspect at all, it was in no way comparable to the struggle between Scots and English of the eighteenth century and later. However, surely no one would dispute the view that Smith's *symbolic* use of the two speech forms, each with strong nationalist overtones and consequent power to arouse partisan emotions, is a perfectly legitimate dramatic device.

McLellan and Smith, however, are writing in the sociolinguistic context of the mid twentieth century, when written Scots (in ironic contrast to the spoken forms) enjoys a flourishing existence as a largely autonomous, well-developed and highly distinctive language, with an extensive and consciously national and nationalistic literary tradition. For certain genres in recent and contemporary writing, Scots and English are equally acceptable and viable alternatives. This fact can be used to evoke a period when the same was true of the spoken languages; or the opposition of Scots to English can be used to symbolise the conflict between the nations. But the situation exploited by McLellan and Smith, though real enough, is of course factitious. The Scots of their plays is essentially a literary form. In itself (grammatically and lexically) it is decidely unlike any dialect of Scots actually spoken in contemporary Scotland; and its status as a vehicle for literature is equally, or even more, unlike the status of spoken Scots in contemporary Scottish society. The playwrights have cleared the ground for themselves, so to speak, by assuming that Scots can confront English on the same terms as could, say, Spanish; and so it can, but only this kind of Scots—the artificially developed literary language—and only in certain kinds of writing.

In the Waverley Novels and many subsequent works, account is taken of the fact that the actual situation of Scots is far more complex and less clear-cut than this. Scots by the nineteenth century had come to be associated with the lower classes of society: the use of it in a character's speech could therefore serve as a convenient indicator of his social position.[1] The pretence that it was about to disappear had been fashionable for several decades; and it was in fact true that, since the use of English was gradually percolating down the social scale, differences between the speech of the older and the younger generations were visible[2]: the suggestion of conflict between parents and children, or more generally of long-term changes in Scottish society itself, could therefore be suggested by contrasting the Scots speech of older characters with the English of younger ones.[3] It was also true that since English was a learned language for

many Scotsmen it was associated with a greater degree of formality or intellect-
uality in discourse: it was the public language of a consciously-assumed
persona, whereas Scots was the language of intimacy, domesticity, free
expression of feelings. The most subtle literary exploitation of this distinction is
to be found in the novels of John Galt,[4] and later George MacDonald explored
the implications of the conscious switching from Scots to English which by then
could readily occur in the speech of individual Scots[5]. Nor was (or is) the
phenomenon of language-shifting in reality always a simple matter of using
either Scots or English: the nearness of relationship between the tongues, and
the existence of a large common core of lexical and grammatical features,
ensured that when the two languages came to be spoken in the same country
and by the same people a mixed dialect would arise, tending towards sometimes a Scots and sometimes an English pole depending on the immediate
circumstances of the speaker.[6] This too can manifest itself in the literary
representation of the speech of Scottish characters. The large set of features
shared by both languages can itself lead to a misconception: some writers,
particularly in the present century, have seemingly assumed—erroneously, of
course—that no word which a monolingual Englishman would understand can
be accepted as Scots; and have therefore written in a language more obviously
unlike English, on the lexical level at least, than (probably) any form of spoken
Scots has ever been in reality.[7] Clearly, since the use of Scots in actual life can
be affected by so many factors, there can be no question of assuming that its
appearance in fiction is always for the simple purpose of verisimilitude. A few
of the possible uses of Scots in dialogue will be discussed in what follows, with
particular reference to three novels in which the dialogue is all or virtually all in
Scots, and three in which it is partly in Scots and partly in English.

In a work containing dialogue entirely in Scots, and in a Scots which is
notably consistent, idiosyncratic, and lexically distinctive, the impression given
is inherently unlikely to be one of simple realism. Certainly, throughout the
eighteenth and nineteenth centuries, and still today, it was and is possible to
find Scots-speaking individuals and communities; but not, or not nearly so
readily, monolingually Scots-speaking. The presence of the English language
has been a social and cultural fact of Scottish life since the introduction of the
Geneva Bible; and a writer who ignores this—who in a novel with a nineteenth-
or twentieth-century setting implies that the community depicted is as
uniformly Scots-speaking as in the time of the Makars—is giving at best a
highly selective, at worst a radically false, impression of the society he is
portraying. J M Barrie's *A Window in Thrums* is a notable example of this.[8]
Beyond question, the dialect of Kirriemuir is presented with exceptional skill,
in the limited sense that Barrie very convincingly suggests the pronunciation,
vocabulary, and idiom of this particular area. Of the many distinctively Scots
words which appear in the book, several belong principally or exclusively to
dialects of Angus or at any rate of the East: some examples are *bervie* (a smoked

haddock: from the place-name Inverbervie in the Mearns), *clink* ('in a clink'—in an instant), *dottle* (senile), *pirlie* (earthenware money-box), *silvendy* (safe), *sacket* (rascal). *Stocky* meaning 'chap' or 'fellow' is fairly general, but its application to women is peculiar to Angus: in this book, lamentably, it refers by implication to Queen Mary in a passage which seems designed to present pathetic ignorance as a source of amusement (Chapter 9). The authentic ring of idiomatic Scots sounds in such expressions as 'Him at's mither mairit on Sam'l Duthie's wife's brither' (p. 12), 'Was ye speirin' had I seen . . . ' (p. 13), 'Am [I'm] no nane sure but what am a humorist too' (p. 41), 'Me an' my man comes frae Tilliedrum' (p. 213), and many other unobtrusive turns of phrase. However, though the dialect is in itself perfectly realistic, the sociolinguistic situation implied is scarcely so. With only a few minor exceptions, the many dialogue passages in the book are couched wholly in this unadulterated Angus tongue. There is no suggestion of differences between the speech of one generation and the next: the dialect of Leeby and Jamie (even in spite of the latter's residence in London) is identical to that of their parents. Notwithstanding the remarkable degree of social stratification in the Thrums community and the delicate but pervasive set of external signs by which social distinctions are indicated—the presentation of which is one of the real achievements of the book—there is no trace of social differentiation in the dialect: the 'hopelessly plebeian' Tibbie Birse expresses herself in precisely the same idiom as the family on whose door she does not knock (Chapter 7). At times, hints are given that the linguistic competence of the McQumphas and their acquaintance extends beyond the pristine Angus dialect. The minister's wife, 'a grand lady from Edinburgh' and emphatically an outsider to the Thrums community, speaks English (Chapter 14). So too does the narrator when his words are quoted directly; though his speech occasionally shows the influence of the local idiom (e.g. 'Who did Tibbie get?': p. 22), and it is therefore not out of character that a considerable number of Scots words—*brig, brae, burn, callant, cruizey, dambrod, feikiness, flesher, peerie, redd, roup, sugarelly,* and others—should appear in the narrative. Interestingly, on two occasions a character is described as adopting an 'Englishy' voice for a special social event: Jess when about to receive guests (p. 25) and Leeby when visiting the manse (p. 123); and when the half-witted Johnny assumes the unaccustomed role of messenger conveying a polite request, his speech ('delivered as instructed') assumes a tone of strained formality: 'Mistress Tully's compliments to her, and would she kindly lend the christenin' robe, an' also the tea-tray, if the same be na needed?' (p. 97). Even more suggestive is the fact that on the very few occasions when a character uses a non-Scots form, the result, given the immediate circumstances of the discourse, could sometimes be interpreted realistically: consider, for instance, Jess's 'I wouldna wonder, no, really I would *not* wonder' (p. 16), and her quotation of Hendry's '*Not one soul* in Thrums 'll daur say that to me but yersel, Jess' (p. 55): giving their words the authoritative tone of the literary language?; or Hendry's 'I mind when I had the headache, hoo a *small* steak . . . ' (p. 29), spoken when attempting to prescribe for the sick Jess: elevating his speech to the register expected of a doctor? However, these departures from the dialectal norm of the book are extremely scarce; and their effect is less to show that Barrie is, after all, aware that other registers would have been available to his characters than to emphasise by contrast the remarkable rigidity of their normal speech patterns. That the conversation of their real-life counterparts would have been as monolithic as this can no more be accepted as literal fact than that the maunderings of Tammas Haggart would (as we are asked to believe) have been accepted in Kirriemuir as pearls of wit and wisdom.

Yet the literary function of Thrums speech is clear. Barrie is portraying the idealised fantasy of a childhood-like world: a tiny, closed, static community, long since consigned to oblivion. The dialect, in its uniformity and high degree of differentiation from Standard English, emphasises the isolation of the community: isolation from everything, in fact, that exists on a wider or more general scale than the individual or the family. In this world, poverty and sorrow, though certainly present, raise no philosophical problems: they are not discussed, because nothing more need be said than that they are the will of God, but simply endured with passive courage. There are no social changes that have to be pondered or scrutinised, no political or religious controversies in which the characters are required to adopt and justify an individual viewpoint. In fact, life for the Thrums populace presents no intellectual challenge whatever. Leeby's keen powers of observation are applied to itemising the imperfections of the minister's furniture; Jess's gift for deduction to arguing from the size of a milk-jug to the identity of a visitor. The use of language, therefore, is virtually restricted to its simplest function of conveying factual information; and for this there is no need for any linguistic facility beyond that learned at the mother's knee. Not only is there practically no sign of the bilingualism which in reality would certainly have existed in Barrie's Kirriemuir, but the Scots speech is itself banal: the rhetorical brilliance of the Scots-speaking characters in the Waverley Novels is entirely lacking; for what is there in the lives of the Thrums people to inspire it? Of course, this community is a monstrous fabrication: the Scottish third estate, by common agreement and ready observation a notably articulate, perceptive and argumentative people, are presented as a set of virtual morons. Barrie's use of dialect admirably serves his purpose; but his purpose is not to present the actual social and sociolinguistic facts of Scottish life.

In a curious and somewhat paradoxical way, Barrie's linguistic practice can be seen as, in intention at least, a handsome tribute to his mother tongue. The manifest care with which he reproduces the idiom in its most conservative form unmistakably reveals a genuine affection for it: he has evidently thought it worthy of being written with a high degree of linguistic integrity, even if his

idea of linguistic integrity is somewhat naive. His practice contrasts strikingly
with that of, say, S R Crockett in *The Raiders*, where the unmotivated
switching between Scots and English in the dialogue seems to betray a
somewhat cavalier attitude to Scots on the author's part. (As one example:
'Even thus has my life been, Paitrick. I have been most of my time but a great
gull diving for herring on an east-windy day. Whiles I hae gotten a bit flounder
for my pains, and whiles a rive o' drooned whalp, but o' the rale herrin'—desperate few, man, desperate few.' (Chapter 2).) And by putting his Thrums
dialect into the mouths of characters who are intended to evoke the reader's
respect and affection he by implication categorises it as a language fit for saints.
In *The House with the Green Shutters*, the iconoclastic George Douglas Brown
pointedly suggests the corrupt nature of the society depicted by the language of
the characters, which is idiosyncratic and far from being a philologist's model
of the Ochiltree dialect: the vulgar pomposity of Provost Connal, the prim and
spiteful acidulousness of Deacon Allardyce, the ineffectual sentimentality of
Johnny Coe, are most effectively suggested by orthographic devices which
depart strikingly from the conventions of written Scots.[9] But it is in keeping
with Barrie's attitude to his characters that their dialect should appear in a state
of prelapsarian purity.

   Nonetheless, this association of the language which Burns and Scott had
used for great literature with as grossly misleading a picture of Scottish society
as the Thrums populace in this novel cannot be regarded as other than
deplorable. A comparison with another local dialect novel which—be it
noted—had appeared nearly twenty years earlier, William Alexander's *Johnny
Gibb of Gushetneuk*, demonstrates the falsity of Barrie's assumptions.[10] The
two books have several obvious features in common. Large tracts of both consist
of dialogue passages in broad Scots. Alexander, in fact, is more uncomprom-
ising than Barrie in this respect: his Garioch speech is still less immediately
accessible to readers of standard English than the Kirriemuir dialect of Barrie's
novel; the Scots words that appear in the narrative sections of *Johnny Gibb* are
both more frequent and (in many cases) less generally known than those in
Thrums: in the first chapter alone we find *toon, doon, stane*; *arles, burnie,
dook, drows, fee* (i.e. hire), *forebreist, gatefarrin', hirple, knablick, loan,
lowse, loon, muck, neep, nervish, sea-ware, threep*, and the phrases *gae doon
throu, far fae stoot, rape-thackit, fite-heidit, sair een, scabbit faces and sic like,
a stoot young folla*[11]; and whereas Barrie feels himself obliged to prepare the
reader for what is to follow by a chapter-long apologia, Alexander hits his
audience at the very outset of the book with half a page of dialogue beginning:

   "Heely, heely, Tam, ye glaiket stirk—ye hinna on the hin shelvin' o' the cairt. Fat
   hae ye been haiverin at, min? That cauff saik'll be tint owre the back door afore we
   win a mile fae hame. See't yer belly-ban' be ticht aneuch noo. . . . "

Two further shared features, both related to the choice of language, are that the principal characters in each book belong to the lower ranks of society—manual workers and peasants; and that each has a historical setting: the action of *Thrums* takes place vaguely in the early nineteenth century, that of *Johnny Gibb* begins at 4.30 a.m. on a day in late June 1839. However, a fundamental difference is that whereas Barrie's novel is set in an imaginary community as remote from the actual social developments of nineteenth-century Scotland as his Never Land, Alexander's is a genuine documentary novel. Only the characters are fictitious (one might even suggest that only their names are fictitious, for it is surely a permissible assumption that some of them are drawn pretty closely from life): the social and religious issues which occupy so important a place in the book are authentic fact. This is not irrelevant in discussing the different attitudes to the Scots language implicit in the two novels. Alexander wrote: 'As the dialect in which the various personages in the story naturally utter themselves is one of great force and expressiveness, some pains were taken to render it accurately, both as to idiom and orthographical form'[12]; and Barrie has clearly acted on the same principle. But whereas Barrie attributes Scots speech to fabricated characters who use it to discuss only trivia, Alexander employs it in drawing highly realistic portraits of energetic, intelligent, and well-informed men (and women) who use it to grapple with matters affecting the whole substance of their lives.

The density of Alexander's dialect is authentic: Aberdeenshire's reputation as the home of several of the most (to outsiders) opaque speech forms in Scotland is of long standing; and since even today the North-East is linguistically one of the most conservative areas in the country, it is reasonable to assume that the same was true a century ago. Alexander Mackie in his introduction to the 1908 edition of *Johnny Gibb* writes: 'The dialect will not yet die awhile, but there is little doubt that under a compulsory English education its purity and breadth of vocabulary are *already* on the wane' [italics mine]; but in other parts of Scotland a gradual loss of the most distinctively Scottish features of the dialects had been observed decades earlier. (It is noteworthy that some hints are given in the book that the Scots of the rising generation is becoming less distinctive than that of their elders: Mrs Birse, who despite her social pretensions never modifies her dialect (except when ironically parodying Dawvid Hadden's affectations: 'There's people that k-no's their richts' (p. 252) is finally faced with a defiant daughter saying, 'No, mother, I'll do nothing o' the kin'' (p. 266)). And Alexander shows conclusively that such a dialect need not be restricted in its use to discussion of personal and domestic matters. The first few chapters of *Johnny Gibb* give few hints of the momentous issues shortly to be raised: some sharp comments from Johnny on the ruling class and its representatives—

"The tae half o' oor lairds is owre the lugs in a bag o' debt. I wud hae them roupit oot at the door, and set to some eesefu trade." (p. 15) provide the only suggestion that this is a novel of somewhat wider scope than a typical Kailyard product. But when in Chapter 4 the Scots-speaking Johnny challenges the English-speaking minister on a Scripture-based argument, and bests him, it is evident that we are in a very different world from that of Thrums.

> "Weel, sir," replied Johnny, "ye made a hantle o' the poo'ers that be, an' the duty o' absolute subjection to them. Noo, sir, lat me tell ye that the Apos'le never inten'et to set up either the laird or the minaister as ane o' the poo'ers ordeen't to bear rowle owre's i' the fashion that ye seem't to approve so muckle o' . . . " (p. 28)

Though vocabulary items which are unique to Scots are not frequent, this is unequivocal north-eastern dialect. The orthography is clearly intended to suggest a very striking difference between Johnny's speech and that of the minister (the latter, though he would probably not speak the dialect, would in reality have a pronounced local accent; but his dialogue as written is standard English): Alexander even attempts, unnecessarily, to exaggerate the difference by using non-standard spellings for words of which Johnny's pronunciation and the minister's would be identical (*Apos'le, bizness*). Only in the quotation 'servant of all', at the end of this speech, does a strictly English (in the exclusive sense) form appear. And the effect of the speech is not only to reveal something of Johnny Gibb's character, but to demonstrate that a speaker or writer of Scots can, without sacrificing the integrity of his language, discuss in a serious and credible way matters of political and philosophical import. This is still more effectively shown a few chapters later, when Johnny, Maister Saun'ers and Donald M'Craw discuss a (historical) dispute in the parish of Marnoch and its wide-ranging implications. (That Donald's 'Celtic'—not further specified—origins should be indicated in his speech only by an inconsistent tendency to pronounce the definite article as *ta* is not as false as a modern reader might assume: Gaelic-Scots bilingualism was to be found in western Aberdeenshire until well within living memory. At the time of writing the last speaker of Braemar Gaelic is still alive, and her non-Gaelic speech is pure Buchan.[13]) Though the three men share a common commitment to the principle of non-intervention, their attitudes are subtly differentiated by their language. Blind old Donald, less able than the others to take an active part in Kirk politics, is the most prone to appeal to Scripture and to adopt the phrasing of Presbyterian pulpit eloquence (or are his 'Alas! alas!' (p. 41) and 'Wae, wae to ta men that forder sic unsanctifiet wark' (p. 42) meant rather to suggest the tone of a Gaelic lament?): 'An' has the airm o' ta secular poo'er raelly been streetch't oot to touch ta ark o' ta Kirk's spiritooal independence?' (p. 41)—'Praise to Him that rules ta hearts o' men that we hae faithfu' witnesses i' the lan'!' (p. 42)—' 'I will overturn, overturn, overturn,' saith ta prophet' (p. 43). Maister Saun'ers, most directly concerned with the particular case under discussion, shows his indignation by rhetorical questions and hyperbolical phrasing: 'Whaur's[14] the richts o' conscience there, I wud like to ken?' (p. 40)—'It's aneuch to gar ane's bleed boil to think o' 't' (p. 41)—'I'll gie the lugs fae my heid gin they dinna gae on noo, neck-or-naethin, to cairry oot this sattlement' (p. 42). Johnny, who is only just coming to realise the full extent of the threatened conflict, appeals to facts as he sees them: 'Lat yer Presbytery be fat they like, the Assembly'll never thole sic ongaens' (p. 41)—'They winna daur to disobey the Assembly' (p. 42). In this dialogue the phrasing is homely ('There's ower mony o' them tarr't wi' the same stick,' Johnny observes: p. 42); the rhetoric, if forceful enough, scarcely merits comparison with, say, that of the Covenanters in *Old Mortality*; and the dialect is as completely 'provincial' as it could be; yet the intensity of the men's convictions and the strength of their personalities, as revealed in their speeches, transcend the undistinguished setting of the conversation—a blind pensioner's lodging-house in a small seaside resort—and leave the reader with the impression that Johnny Gibb and his friends are indeed of the stuff of which Covenanters were made.

For Barrie, Scots is in some sense a museum piece; and his intention, it is not too fanciful to suggest, is to embalm the tongue: to preserve it for posterity in the hushed atmosphere of the tomb of a beloved ancestor. For Alexander, it is as vital as the Garioch peasant community. The outstanding feature of *Johnny Gibb* is not his skill in suggesting the sounds and cadences of the Garioch tongue, but his underlying confidence in its resources. The lack of attention paid to his novel in its own time and later, except in its home area, not only is a sad reflection on the taste of the Scottish reading public: it has entailed the loss of what might have been one of the most enlivening and enriching influences on dialect literature.

Still another attitude to Scots is manifested in a more recent novel, which though even more purely local in its reputation than *Johnny Gibb* is linguistically interesting enough to merit discussion here: W P Milne's *Eppie Elrick*.[15] Here the author's intention was evidently to resurrect the Buchan dialect: to reconstruct it in a form pre-dating any considerable English influence whatever beyond the presence of the Bible and (for some) the Catechism, and to demonstrate the full potential of this by using it as extensively as possible. The language of the book suggests that Milne has collected a vast amount of data from the most conservative forms of the Buchan tongue available to him, and by extrapolating from this derived a systematically codified language, consistent in its grammar and orthography and representing a hypothetical 'pure' form of the dialect at the peak of its independent development. The historical setting for the novel is a patent excuse for the presence of this reconstructed dialect. (Whether the universal Buchan speech of 1715 would have differed from the most conservative forms to be heard, or remembered, in 1956 in any other respect than in being less affected by standard English influence is a question with which Milne does not concern himself, tacitly assuming a negative answer.) And unquestionably, the author proves that his

dialect is a possible medium for narrative. The Scots passages occupy pages-
long tracts of the book: indeed, with the exception of John Service's *The Life
and Recollections of Dr Duguid* (an undistinguished effort in the tradition of
John Galt's memoir novels, interesting only for its rich store of Ayrshire dialect
words), *Eppie Elrick* is the nearest thing in the present writer's knowledge to a
full-length novel entirely in broad Scots.

From a purely linguistic point of view, the handling of the dialect is nothing
less than masterly. Even to write a work on this scale in a dialect with no
tradition of prose literature is a considerable achievement; and the representation of the tongue is wholly convincing. Idiomatic phrases abound: Milne
yields nothing to Barrie or Alexander in his ability to evoke an extremely
distinctive speech-form, nor in his refusal to make any concession whatever to
readers unaccustomed to it. 'A wis 'e weers o' forgettin you a'thegidder' (p. 1),
'A'm dootin 'e caal's been some muckle for ye' (p. 5), 'Sit in aboot tae the fire
noo, Mains, ur we get 'e pottitch riggit tae the rodd' (p. 15), 'Dyang awa
. . . an' nae deave ma an' me i' the heid hurry' (p. 24), 'See tae [i.e. look at]
that flan o' reek' (p. 26), 'Ye easy ken fat's adee fin 'ey yoke tee wi the
backdracht' (p. 28), 'Fat like a day o't hae ye hid oot by?' (p. 37), 'A pat it 'at
rodd like ye ken' (p. 44), 'A hinna wull 'at ye're dyaan tae draa me neist' (p.
59), 'Saa A niver sic a mengie o' wranglesome breets' (p. 145), 'A cudna bit be
on taal somebody' (p. 195): the startling grammatical divergence between this
dialect and the standard literary language is evident throughout the book. Most
of Milne's nonce orthographic forms are readily comprehensible, but even an
experienced reader may require an instant's reflection before recognising in
kiss, wumma, hivvn or *yaafu* the equivalents of *because, with me, haven't* and
awful. And through this highly idiosyncratic medium, Milne presents, for
those willing to make the requisite effort, a very absorbing account of the first
Jacobite rising.

The tone of the book is established, neatly enough if not very subtly, in the
first few lines: the use of a Scots adjective (douce) and a very local-sounding
place-name (Ugiehaach) evoke the parochial atmosphere, and the reference to
Queen Anne and the Biblical tag 'it came to pass' emphasise the chronological
remoteness of the setting. The carefully if somewhat laboriously presented
picture of social life in the Buchan ferm touns of the early eighteenth century is
interesting and realistic; and the attempt to show the rising from the point of
view of the cannon fodder—peasants not greatly interested in the political
issues involved, nor in the practical question of who should sit on a distant
throne, but obliged willingly or otherwise to endure danger and very inglorious
discomfort when summoned, is both laudable in itself and convincingly
achieved. Ominously Barrie-esque humours occasionally appear in the
portrayal of the characters, as when Eppie, who is stated to be and indeed
clearly emerges as an intelligent woman, draws from the story of Solomon's
judgement the moral that infants should not sleep with their mothers; but

these are rare, and on the whole the characterisation is lifelike, if scarcely as lively as in *Johnny Gibb*. (The arresting combination of the macabre and the pathetic in the figure of Katie Tulloch is a particularly fine achievement.)

Yet a puzzling feature in the writing becomes increasingly conspicuous as the book progresses: an astonishing disparity between Milne's linguistic skill and his ability to provide a satisfactory fictional context for the demonstration of it. That he should wish to add interest to the dialogue by including many proverbs and aphorisms of local currency is justifiable on both literary and documentary grounds; but his technique of introducing them at times shows a singular paucity of imagination, as in the following passage:

> If he did not leave a clean and tidy plate, she would say, "Laadie, ye're leavin a plett like a swine's troch."
>
> Again, if he asked a bigger helping than he could manage, he would be told, "A doot yer ee's muckler nur yer wime," or he would be stimulated to finish his plate by the somewhat cryptic injunction, "Teem yer plett, man. The thing 'at's i' yer wime's nae i' yer testamint."
>
> On the other hand, if he did appear to be eating more than was good for him, she would mildly remonstrate,
>
> "Crater, ye've seerly tint 'e boddom o' yer wime" (pp. 58-9)

Aphorisms are sometimes presented with a quasi-disclaimer such as 'The nearer even, the mair beggars, as the aal-farran folk eest tae say' (p. 194): could there be a fictional setting in which such a practice was less necessary or appropriate than in this novel? Worse, the excuses for the lengthy passages in Scots are transparent and, if the criterion of naturalism is applied, often woefully unconvincing. Eppie, we are told in the second sentence of the novel, 'like most people who live alone, . . . was prone to speak aloud to herself and to argue out the plans and motives for her actions' (p. 1); and this leads to a chapter of which about a third consists of Eppie's quoted words, addressed to the foundling infant, the cat, or herself. Later (Chapter 7), we are asked to accept a ten-page monologue in which Eppie recounts in full detail, with verbatim reports of conversations, the story *which she supposedly heard in the first instance from her cousin Tammas* of the Laird's reception of the Pretender's envoy, and (Chapter 22) the autobiography of Katie Tulloch as narrated to her dog ('Foo sorra am A tellin you a' this? Ye ken't as well as A dee masel': p. 208); to say nothing of many shorter passages of monologue and dialogue in which characters—some of whom play no part whatever in the novel, appearing only to tell their stories—recount events in the broad Buchan dialect.

That Milne was unaware of the gross literary weakness of this device is beyond credence; but to condemn him for resorting to it enforces a confrontation with the fact that the alternative would have been to abandon all pretence of a narrative framework in English and write the novel entirely in Scots. And this final step was clearly regarded by Milne as too radical. The entrenched tradition that Scots prose must be supposedly spoken by an identifiable character could not be defied outright, though it is stretched far beyond the limits of credibility. Indeed, one wonders whether Milne is not subjecting it to a subtle form of criticism, almost a *reductio ad absurdum*. Scots *can* be used for narrative prose, and he proves this by simply doing it; but if readers must have the placebo of a fictional Scots-speaking narrator, he will give them that too, even at the cost of drastically weakening the structure of his novel. Milne's pride in his linguistic heritage has resulted in what might be seen as a pretty devastating attack on the assumptions governing its literary use—assumptions which have unnecessarily constricted its development. Whether or not this was Milne's intention, the impression finally given by his book is that it is first and foremost an essay in Scots writing, only secondarily a novel. Writers of greater artistry have generally been able to find a more satisfactory balance between the two aspects of their work.

A substantially monolingual cast of characters in a novel must, if literal credibility is the aim, either be drawn from a relatively restricted social compass or be set in a historical period pre-dating the pervasive anglicisation of the upper social and educational classes. Barrie, Alexander and Milne, with different purposes and to very different effects, meet one or the other of these conditions. (In *Eppie Elrick,* the lairds and leddies who make brief appearances in the book speak as broad a Scots as the peasantry: cf. Eppie's conversation with Leddy Mairjorie of Tillymachar Castle in Chapter 22.) Fictional settings wider in their social range or more recent in their chronological period may be expected to entail a set of characters who are less linguistically consistent: some may speak Scots and some English, or individual characters may vary more or less erratically in their speech. The purpose in representing such a linguistic situation, however, need no more be simple realism than in the case of a novel with dialogue entirely in Scots; and the author's attitude to the Scots tongue may be clearly revealed by his linguistic practice.

A desire for linguistic accuracy on the social and historical level need not conflict, for example, with a desire to exploit the expressive resources of the Scots tongue. The Scots-speaking characters in the Waverley Novels generally belong to one or another of the social classes in which their real-life counterparts would indeed have spoken Scots; but many of them show a superb gift of eloquence which would perhaps not be so often encountered outwith literature. A notable later example of a novel in which each character's language is very convincingly chosen to give some social or personal information about that character, but in which Scots is also employed for impressive poetic effects, is R L Stevenson's *Weir of Hermiston*.[16]

Kirstie and her relations, of rugged Border stock, draw on the rich mine of their ancestral speech. Lord Hermiston also speaks Scots; but in his portrayal the use of the vernacular is not an indicator of social class and only incidentally of place of birth, but of character: he is a man without pretensions to refinement, forcefully contrasted in speech as in personality with his gentle aristocratic colleague Lord Glenalmond. For this reason, his speech is strongly differentiated from that of the Elliotts: with far greater frequency than in their dialogue the author departs from Scots and English orthographic conventions to indicate his pronunciation (*haangit, caapital, noansense, poalitics, Goad*); and his eloquence, powerful though it is, does not draw on lyrical imagery but on irony, Biblical rhetoric, and the blunt vigour of a homely vocabulary:

> "You're all for honesty, it seems; you couldn't even steik your mouth on the public street. What for should I steik mines upon the bench, the King's officer, bearing the sword, a dreid to evil-doers, as I was from the beginning, and as I will be to the end! Mair than enough of it! Heedious! I never gave twa thoughts to heediousness, I have no call to be bonny" (p. 72).

Archie normally speaks English: that he shares the speech habits not of his father but of Lord Glenalmond, in whose dialogue, 'He's getting a big lad' (p. 39) is one of very few Scots forms, is of course part of Stevenson's method of depicting his relationship with the two older men. However, it is entirely realistic that Archie's English should be evidently a language acquired during the course of his education—in his childhood he is heard speaking in something closer to the language of his parents ('No, I cannae see it. . . . And I'll tell you what, mamma, I don't think you and me's justifeed in staying with him': p. 24)—and that Kirstie's magnificent appeal should move him to the extent of evoking a reply in the mother tongue which she uses: 'Ay, but Kirstie, my woman, you're asking me ower much at last. . . . Ye're asking what nae man can grant ye, what only the Lord of heaven can grant ye if He see fit'' (p. 252).

Still more delicate and sensitive is Stevenson's treatment of Christina's language. In her first meeting with Archie, her attempt to cover her agitation by demonstrating the refinement of 'a well-behaved young lady who had been to Glasgow' (p. 156) is indicated in part by a dearth of Scots forms in her speech. 'My aunt and my sister-in-law doesna agree very well. Not that I have much ado with it. But still when I'm stopping in the house, if I was to be visiting my aunt, it would not look considerate-like' (pp. 168–9): the negative suffix *-na* and the use of *does* with a plural subject, *much ado, if I was to be visiting . . .* , and *considerate-like* are observable as Scots grammatical features; but the phonology and vocabulary, as far as we can see, are of standard English. Archie's sympathetic, 'I am sorry' evokes a response with just a suggestion of increased Scotsness (for diminished reserve): 'I whiles think myself it's a great peety'; but when he, as if claiming too much ground on the strength of this, replies with an overt compliment, her immediate retreat is marked by a virtual disappearance of obviously Scots features: except for one *wouldna*, her next two speeches contain none. Finally, a confidence arising from her having directed the conversation onto her home territory—the topic of dress—is suggested by a neatly-ordered speech from which Scots forms have vanished entirely (unless we count 'terrible conspicuous'). English (of course, it would be Scottish English: her entire dialogue would be spoken in a Border—or perhaps Border varying with Glasgow—*accent*) as the language of reserve, Scots as that of intimacy: the subtly developing relationship is beautifully suggested by the linguistic modulations. Later, in their last recorded conversation, her chaos of emotion is reflected in a language which oscillates from one pole to another of the Scots-to-English continuum, from the desperate dignity of 'I'll be wishing you good evening, Mr Weir' to the fury of 'Gang to your ain freends and deave them!' (p. 264). In striking contrast to the inconsistency of her language with Archie, Christina in her easy and trusting relationship with her brother Dand speaks as unabashed Scots as he does himself: 'Will ye no gie's a kiss, Dand? . . . I aye likit ye fine' (p. 181). The bilingualism of Lowland Scotland furnishes Stevenson with a means of character drawing which he utilises in an expert fashion.

In the case of Kirstie's speeches during her 'nocturnal visit' (Chapter 8) to Archie, her eloquence is, likewise, perfectly in character. At more than one point earlier in the novel, tribute has been paid to her conversational skill: 'She was a brave narrator' (p. 112): 'She told this tale like one inspired' (p. 122). In the context of the novel, too, this scene contributes most poignantly to our appreciation of Kirstie's tragedy. This aspect of her dialogue, however, is much less to the purpose than the poetic splendour of the passage. At all levels of language—the compelling rhythm of 'Ye'll have to look in the gurly face o'm, where it's ill to look, and vain to look for mercy' (p. 246), the vivid sensual images presented singly ('Ye mind me o' a bonny ship pitten oot into the black and gowsty seas' (p. 246)) or in cumulative sequence ('the bonny simmer days, the lang miles o' the bluid-red heather, the cryin' o' the whaups, and the lad and the lassie that was trysted' (p. 248), the startling collocations in 'Do ye no think that I mind how the hilly sweetness ran about my hairt?' (p. 249); and in the imaginative force of 'The world and the folks in't are nae mair than clouds to the puir lassie, and heevin nae mair than windle-straes, if she can but pleesure him!' (p. 249), or—best of all—the reflective passage beginning 'Folk have dee'd sinsyne and been buried . . . ' (p. 248)—the master-hand of Stevenson the poet is evident. And though Scots is his medium, the poetic quality of the passage is derived largely from factors which operate independently of the presence of Scots words and sounds: one notices in passing that in a particularly memorable line, 'But this yin had a tongue to wile the birds frae the lift and the bees frae the foxglove bells' (p. 248), there are few forms that are peculiarly Scots. A language scholar like Milne may produce work which is admirable as a technical exercise; but the finest literary monuments to the Scots language have been created by writers who combine a thorough knowledge of the structures of the language with the imagination and craftsmanship of poets.

The fact that Scots came in the course of the eighteenth century to be used

less by the upper classes and more exclusively by the lower led to the sociolinguistic situation ably depicted by such novelists as Scott and Stevenson. It also
led to an inculcated presupposition among the social élite that Scots was at best
passé and at worst vulgar. This has had the regrettable result that the literary
use of the language can be an easy means of inviting a patronising or
contemptuous attitude to a speaker. Characteristically, and to his immense
credit, Walter Scott is never guilty of this. Many of his Scots-speaking characters
have foibles that arouse our amusement, and some are disreputable enough;
but in no case is a character marked for the reader's disapproval by the mere
fact of his using Scots speech. Such an attitude is illustrated all too clearly by a
work dating from early in the history of the Scottish novel: Susan Ferrier's
Marriage.[17]

A number of different forms of Scots can be observed in this novel. Sir
Sampson Maclaughlan and his formidable Lady (an admirably presented
character) employ servants whose idiolects, with their pervasive *tas* and *hurs,*
suggest a parody of quasi-Highland speech rather than any attempt at realism:
the same character in the space of two pages (pp. 103–4) produces 'Hur [you]
may see Lochmarlie hursel [himself]', 'Hurs [they're] aw awa tull ta Sandy
Mor's', 'Hurs [she's] i' ta teach tap', and 'Hur's [he's] helpin' ta leddie i' ta
teach tap'. The old Laird of Glenfern speaks a Scots which varies somewhat in
density: variations for some of which naturalistic reasons could be suggested.
His first recorded words, addressed to his impossible daughter-in-law, are
'What! not frightened for our Highland hills, my leddy? Come, cheer
up—trust me, ye'll find as warm hearts among them, as ony ye hae left in your
fine English policies' (p. 13). This speech could have contained several more
Scots forms than it actually does (*no feart, Hieland, hairts, amang*), and this
may conceivably represent an attempt at party manners for the beautiful and
elegant Englishwoman. After better acquaintance, he expresses his opinion of
her, and her husband, in a denser Scots: 'A bonny bargain, indeed, the [*sic*:
should be *that*?] canna stand the pipes. . . . She's no the wife for a
Heelandman. Confoonded blather, indeed! [Harry has just referred to the
pipes as a 'confounded bladder'] By my faith, ye're no blate!' (p. 26). In a
speech addressed to his other son Archie, he states his personal position in Scots
but resorts to English to deliver a command motivated by a consideration for
social propriety: 'Troth, but I'll hae aneugh to do, if I am to stand up for a' my
friends' wives. . . . But, however, Archie, you are to blame: Leddy
Maclaughlan is a very decent woman; at least, as far as I ken, though she is a
little free in the gab; and, out of respect for my auld friend Sir Sampson, it is
my desire that you should remain here to receive him, and that you trait baith
him and his Leddy discreetly' (p. 32). As his irritation with his daughter-in-law
increases, so does the density of his Scots in talking of her:

"What was the meaning o' a' that skirling and squeeling I heard a while ago? By my
faith, there's nae beating this din! Thae beasts o' your wife's are aneugh to drive a

body oot o' their judgment. But she maun gie up thae maggots when she becomes a farmer's wife. She maun get stirks and stots to make pets o', if she maun hae four-fitted favourites; but to my mind, it wad set her better to be carrying a wise-like wean in her arms, than trailing aboot wi' thae confoonded dougs an' paurits.'' (p. 66)

Harry's maiden aunts, with their pathetic pretensions to elegance, appropriately enough speak in a more anglicised style than their brother, though some Scots forms intrude: 'There are some excellent family broth making below, and I'll desire Tibby to bring a few' (p. 16), 'Only look at thae young lambs . . . see what pickters of health they are!' (p. 24), 'I'm afraid your Ladyship will frighten our stirks and stots with your finery' (p. 36), 'I am sure, Donald, that was na' like you!' (p. 52). One may presume that these 'lapses' are intended by the author to suggest their inability to rise completely above the essential vulgarity of their natures. A fourth style is visible in what modern readers will surely find the most entertaining scene in the novel, the reminiscences of old Lady Macshake, 'born at a time when Scotland was very different from what it is now. Female education was little attended to, even in families of the highest rank. . . ' (p. 221). Here a very idiomatic and lexically dense Scots is used, which even contains some eye-dialect forms (*Ingland, wunder, cummin, vaalu*). With her cataracts of clauses, her gift for sarcasm 'Are ye come to spend your honest faither's siller, ere he's weel cauld in his grave, puir man': p. 213), irony ('A bonny impruvement or ens no, to see tyleyors and sclaters leavin', whar I mind Jewks an' Yerls': p. 215), and insult ('I wonder what ye're aw made o'. . . . A wheen puir feckless windlestraes': p. 214), and her vivid imagination—

''. . . an' as sune as ilk ane had eatin their fill, they aw flew till the sweeties, an' fought, an' strave, an' wrastled for them, leddies an' gentlemen an' aw; for the brag was, wha could pocket maist; an' whiles they wad hae the claith aff the table, an' aw thing i' the middle i' the floor, an' the chyres upside doon.'' (p. 218)

—this remarkable dame might almost be a preliminary sketch for Galt's matchless Leddy of Grippy.

Ferrier's skill in writing Scots and differentiating between registers within it is by no means inconsiderable; but her attitude to the language is unmistakable. Authorial comments abound: Glenfern is described as having 'something the air of a gentleman, in spite of the inelegance of his dress, his rough manner, and provincial accent' (p. 12); and his outburst quoted above as 'this elegant address' (p. 66). The generous and clear-sighted Lady Douglas expresses a judgment on him and his sisters which is clearly that of the author: 'No doubt, they are often tiresome and ridiculous; but they are always kind and well-meaning' (p. 72). An ironic tone is sometimes audible in the authorial explanations of words, e.g. 'that ornament to a gentleman's farm-yard, and a cottager's front door, ycleped, in the language of the country, a *midden*' (p. 29), or the footnote to the word *beast* as applied by Miss Girzy to a cooked herring: 'In Scotland, every thing that flies and swims, ranks in the bestial tribe' (p. 30). Besides the rough-mannered old Laird and his silly sisters, Scots is associated with inept servants ('. . . the fire's a' ta'en up, ye see . . . there's parritch makin for oor supper; and there's patatees boiling for the beasts; and—': p. 25), discourteous landlords ('The horses were baith oot, an' the ludgin' a' tane up, an' mair tu': p. 199), and petty thieves ('O deed, Sir, it's no' my fault! . . . ye canna lift the bouk o' a prin, but they're a' upon ye': p. 210): a Scots tongue is something which automatically gives a bad impression. Certainly there can be no misconstruing Ferrier's purpose as a naive jest obtained by setting Scottish manners against the assumed norm of English: if the world of Glenfern and his sisters (not to mention Rev. Duncan McDrone, Miss Macgowk and Lady Girnachgowl) is not very attractive, it is certainly no less so—some might think, a good deal more so—than that of Lady Juliana and her brother (not to mention Miss Patty McPry, Dr Redgill and Admiral Yellow-chops). Indeed, the social commentary which the novel contains is very harsh indeed: the characters presented for our unstinted admiration, Lady Douglas and her adopted daughter Mary, are specifically people in whom exceptional personal qualities are able to triumph, at the cost of considerable sorrow, over the disadvantages inflicted on them by their social circumstances. But it is rather unpleasantly clear from Ferrier's use of Scots that her attitude to the language is infected with the presupposition that it is inherently an inferior form of speech.

Much more delicate and more revealing is the use made of the contrast between Scots and English in James Hogg's *The Private Memoirs and Confessions of a Justified Sinner*.[18] Hogg's Scots, at its best, far excels Ferrier's for subtlety and variety: the finest passage of Scots writing in *Marriage*, the dialogue of Mrs MacShake, is slapstick compared to, for example, the superb rhetoric of Samuel Scrape's tale (pp. 197–203); and the implications of the choice of language are much less facile and more wide-ranging.

In many of the book's Scots passages, undoubtedly, Hogg like Stevenson is simply exulting—not too strong a word—in the expressive power of Scots and his own skill in handling the medium. The cross-examination of Bessy Gillies, for example, provides a fine illustration of the natural aptitude of Scots-speakers for vigorous repartee. Her mistress, she states, was 'dung doitrified' (p. 65) and 'made a great deal o' grumphing an' groaning' (p. 66); and the house was 'in a hoad-road' (p. 66). The question whether she was at home when the robbery took place elicits a very emphatic denial:

"Was I at hame, say ye? Na, faith-ye, lad! An I had been at hame, there had been mair to dee. I wad hae raised sic a yelloch!" (p. 65),

and she recollects countering with equal emphasis her mistress's charge that she had left the door open: 'The ne'er o' that I did, . . . or may my shakel bane never turn another key' (p. 66). If the reader is amused at her misunderstanding of 'particulars' and 'ruined and undone', he cannot fail to admire the readiness of her response to what she thinks has been said. Elsewhere in the book, the vocabulary and idioms of Scots impart added pungency to the thinly-disguised home-truths of John Barnet ('Hout na, sir, it's only bad folks that think sae. They find ma bits o' gibes come hame to their hearts wi' a kind o' yerk, an' that gars them wince': p. 104), the cunning of Samuel Scrape ('A Cameronian's principles never came atween him an' his purse, nor sanna in the present case; for as I canna bide to make you out a leear, I'll thank you for my wages': p. 195), and the brutality of Johnny Dods ('Come out, ye vile rag-of-a-muffin, or I gar ye come out wi' mair shame and disgrace, an' fewer haill banes in your body': p. 216). Best of all is the opening section of the tale of Robin Ruthven as narrated by Samuel Scrape (pp. 197–99), in which the resources not only of Scots words and phrases but of a profusion of traditional rhetorical figures—alliteration ('Ye silly, sauchless Cameronian cuif!'), inversion ('. . . an' a proud deil he is'), catalogues ('For a' their prayers an' their praises, their aumuses, an' their penances, their whinings, their howlings, their rantings, an' their ravings, here they come at last!'), hyperbole ('. . . that reards and prays till the very howlets learn his preambles'), metaphor ('. . . o'er weel wrappit up in the warm flannens o' faith, an' clouted wi' the dirty duds o' repentance')—combine to produce one of the most memorable verbal cantrips in all Hogg's works.

Besides his use of Scots for sheer literary effect, Hogg, like others of Scott's successors, uses language choice to imply social ordering; often, predictably and not unrealistically, associating Scots with the lower orders of society. A question of the English-speaking Lady Dalcastle to her maid is answered with 'O dear, mem, how can I ken?' (p. 11). The jailer's first few speeches—why he should later assume English is far from clear—are in a forceful Scots containing (for no reason that is ever explained) some north-eastern forms (*fat, fa, foo*): 'Fat the deil are ye yoolling an' praying that gate for, man?' (p. 149). Johnny Dods and his wife, despite the contrast in their dispositions, share a uniformly Scots idiom, as do Tam Douglas and his household. The most striking extended passages of Scots dialogue in the novel are assigned to Bessy Gillies, John Barnet and Samuel Scrape, all members of the servant class. By contrast, the well-bred Arabella Logan does not speak Scots; even the not-so-well-bred Laird of Dalcastle has few Scots forms, and his son George has none. The principal exception is Baillie Orde, the father of Lady Dalcastle, who in his brief appearance near the beginning of the novel (p. 9) uses at least a few Scots forms (*an', wi', sae, ane, aince, guidit, lounder*): but he is an elderly man, and the contrast between his speech and that of his daughter could be seen as a realistic indication of changing sociolinguistic habits.

The conventions of exploiting the poetic resources of Scots and using the Scots-English contrast to indicate character or social circumstances are well-established, though Hogg applies them skilfully. More peculiar to this novel is the use of language contrasts as a counter in the moral debate at the centre of the book. Very roughly, the characters speak in one of three registers: Scots, an English close to the standard literary language of Hogg's period, and an archaic and *recherché* English pervaded with Latinate vocabulary and with echoes of the Authorised Version of the Scriptures.[19] Of these three registers—the mother tongue, a learned language with which most Scots were at least passively familiar, and the professional tool of a highly-trained group—the clearest contrast is between the first and the last. The Biblical register is associated with the Wringhims and Gil-Martin: not with the clergy as a class, for Mr Blanchard's warning to Robert is conspicuously not a sample of florid pulpit eloquence but a forceful and lucid piece of reasoning couched in a language far closer to common speech than that of his interlocutor; but specifically with the representatives of Calvinism in its perverted and destructive form. (In Samuel Scrape's tale, the section describing the disguised Devil and his sermon is related not in Scots but in this exalted English.) And in the novel, the most powerful and vigorous expressions of antipathy to the Wringhims and their works are put into the mouths of Scots-speaking characters. The confrontations of John Barnet with the senior Wringhim and of Samuel Scrape with his *protégé*, in which the servants with their homely and realistic Scots easily defeat the masters with their pulpit English, form two of the most impressive scenes in the book; and Johnny Dods's immediate hostility to the Sinner, and Tam Douglas's terror of him, are forcibly expressed in their blunt peasant dialects. If the Sinner is anything, he is a *wretch* in the original sense of the word: an exile, a man cut off from the rest of humanity. This alienation is indicated by the gulf between his language and that of the people who execrate him: theirs is the mother tongue. A further subtlety is added to Hogg's presentation of the conflict by a striking and somewhat unexpected feature of the book: the Scots-speaking characters do not on the whole emerge as a particularly attractive bunch. Though we may respect John Barnet, few of us could actually *like* him; and of Samuel Scrape, Johnny Dods and Tam Douglas it would be hard to find anything really complimentary to say. What they share, however, is a mistrust of and revulsion from the Wringhims. (The likeable Bessy Gillies, who never comes into direct contact with them, is irrelevant to the present point.) Even 'James Hogg' cuts no very gracious or courteous figure; but what he is doing by his brusque dismissal of the Editor's curiosity is, precisely, declining further association with the entire Wringhim affair. Surely it is a tenable view that in the Scots voices of Samuel Scrape and the others can be heard the earthy common-sensible realism which, without the benefit of education or refinement, recognises instinctively the presence of evil and shies away from it at once. Rude, short-tempered, ignorant and pusillanimous these men may be; but their human failings are a thousand miles away from the devilry of the Wringhims and their creed.

Scots is a language of which the expressive power remains great, though its literary development has been erratic and unsystematised because of the peculiar history of the spoken form. This is well-known; and the superb achievements of the greatest of Scots writers have often been remarked upon. The mere fact of writing in a tongue other than the official standard, however, implies some conscious decision on the part of the author; and his possible motivation, and the mode in which it emerges in his work, has been investigated much less extensively. Even this brief discussion of certain individual texts has served, it is hoped, to illustrate some of the varying attitudes to the language which its literary use may imply.

NOTES

1 Cf. Graham Tulloch, *The Language of Walter Scott*, (London, 1980), chapter 8
2 Cf. I K Williamson, 'Lowland Scots in Education: An Historical Survey (Part 1)', *Scottish Language* 1, (1982), pp. 54-77
3 For a discussion of this in one novel, see J D McClure, 'The language of *The Entail*', *Scottish Literary Journal*, 8:1 (May 1981), pp. 30-51)
4 Cf. J D McClure, 'Scots and English in *Annals of the Parish* and *The Provost*', in *John Galt 1779-1979*, ed. C A Whatley, (Edinburgh, 1979), pp. 195-210
5 Cf. Roderic McGillis, 'The abyss of the mother tongue', *Seven: an Anglo-American Literary Review*, 2 (1981), pp. 44-56.
6 For a comprehensive examination of this, see A J Aitken, 'Scottish speech: a historical view', *Languages of Scotland*, eds A J Aitken and T McArthur, (Edinburgh, 1979), pp. 85-118.
7 Cf. Caroline Macafee, 'Nationalism and the Scottish Renaissance now', *English World-Wide*, 2:1 (1981), pp. 29-38.
8 References are to the Hodder and Stoughton edition of 1894
9 Cf. J D McClure, 'Dialect in *The House with the Green Shutters*', *Studies in Scottish Literature* 9, (1971-2), pp. 148-63
10 References are to the Towie Barclay Castle edition of 1979, which is a facsimile of the 1884 edition.
11 Incidentally, the obtrusive and irritating inverted commas which mark these words and phrases in later editions of the book, including the recent reprint, do not appear with the same frequency in the earliest texts.
12 In the preface to the 1880 edition
13 Cf. David Clement, 'Highland English', *Scottish Literary Journal*, Supplement 12, (Summer 1980), pp. 13-18.
14 This is a pure error in the 1884 text. The 1880 edition has the authentic North-Eastern form *faur's*.
15 References are to the P Scrogie (Peterhead) edition of 1956.
16 References are to the Chatto and Windus edition of 1896.
17 References are to the Oxford English Novels edition of 1971.
18 References are to the Oxford Paperback edition of 1970.
19 Cf. Iain Campbell, 'Author and audience in Hogg's *Confessions of a Justified Sinner*', *Scottish Literary News*, 2:4 (June 1972), pp. 66-76.

EIGHT

An Awkward Squad: Some Scots Poets from Stevenson to Spence

Kenneth Buthlay

What verse in Scots might be thought to have led up to the modern revival known, embarrassingly to some, as the 'Scottish Renaissance'? The products of the 'Renaissance' which above all else gave it credibility in this respect, the best Scots poems of Hugh MacDiarmid, were so unlikely and arrived at by such a peculiarly individual process, that they might seem to have no antecedents—an impression fostered by his account of his experience as being like 'a religious conversion' when he suddenly began writing in a medium 'to which up till then I had never given a thought'. Yet he showed at times a degree of familiarity with some of the work by his recent predecessors in Scots verse which one would not expect from the generally low opinion he expressed of it in print. And among the many projected books or pamphlets he never got around to producing there was one he mentioned in conversation with apparent enthusiasm, which was to have been devoted to their attitudes towards the poetic use of Scots.

This would certainly have included Stevenson, despite MacDiarmid's scanty interest in his work in other respects, because Stevenson in his Scots verse came to represent for him a stand by the individual artist against the movement which concentrated on the delimitation and conservation of local dialectal usage, on the grounds that he must find his own intuitive way to some sort of literary language that would work for his purposes, however mixed and impure it might appear to the linguistic specialists of the time. Nevertheless, it was a stand which was more impressive in principle than in practice.

Stevenson thought of his writing of Scots verse very much in terms of the eighteenth-century vernacular revival, as is indicated by his signing himself 'Robert Ramsay Fergusson Stevenson' in a letter in which he tells Henry James about his collection, *Underwoods* (1887). Mention of his having written in Scots sets off in him a humorous defence-mechanism—'my native speech, that very dark oracular medium'—and he is inclined to take over from the Burns of the verse epistles that deprecating attitude towards what he writes as being, not

poetry, not even respectable verse, but just crambo-clink: 'I rhyme for fun.'
Hence Stevenson's tendency to stick to the standard Habbie or so-called Burns
stanza, amplifying the whirr of the familiar machinery with plenty of feminine
rhymes, and contented if, having rolled up his sleeves to show the reader what a
guileless buddie he is, his sleight of hand can still slip a few touches of pathos
past his guard.

   Along with his undoubted affection for the language he feels the need, when
writing Scots verse, to adopt a humorously deprecable persona, somewhat as his
Scots prose exchanges with Charles Baxter involved comic role-playing with the
characters of the disreputable elder 'Thomson', and his crony 'Johnstone'.
Indeed, he places the poem called 'The Scotsman's Return from Abroad'
specifically in the context of 'a letter from Mr Thomson to Mr Johnstone'. This
is one of his strongest pieces, and one of the few that contrive to end effectively,
in this case with the returned exile's heartfelt appreciation of the minister's
sermon:

> O what a gale was on my speerit
> To hear the p'ints o' doctrine clearit,
> And a' the horrors o' damnation
> Set furth wi' faithfü' ministration!
> Nae shauchlin' testimony here—
> We were a' damned, an' that was clear.
> I owned, wi' gratitude an' wonder,
> He was a pleisure to sit under.[1]

The breaking, and braking, of his tetrameter couplets with the switch from
feminine to masculine rhyme and the metrically awkward line—

> We were a' damned, an' that was clear—

this is timed to perfection. The pity is that the craftsmanship, and the persis-
tence needed to sustain it, are less in evidence in his Scots poems than in his
English (or Scots-English) ones, a handful of which used to be staple anthology
pieces, and still should be, for they are excellent poems of their kind. The
author of 'Blows the wind today', 'I will make you brooches', and 'Requiem'
was a considerable poet.

   Yet Stevenson tended to regard the writing of poems as limbering-up
exercises *de courte haleine*, often in convalescence, and his efforts in Scots are
not amongst the more strenuous of these. Their derivative nature and narrow
range testify to that, as does a hint of posturing along with the genuine
sentiment in his Note to *Underwoods*, where he plays the part of Burns playing
his part of the 'simple Bard' in the Preface to the Kilmarnock volume:

   . . . I would love to have my hour as a native Maker, and be read by my own country-
   folk in our own dying language: an ambition surely rather of the heart than of the
   head, so restricted as it is in prospect of endurance, so parochial in bounds of space.

When in his Scots poems he echoes Burns at the height of his powers—the great satiric Burns of 'Holy Willie's Prayer'—the reality of Stevenson's declared ambition to become a 'native Maker' is abruptly brought home to the reader. In 'A Lowden Sabbath Morn', which suggests a hangover from the spiritual fare of 'The Cotter's Saturday Night', he dares to apply a touch of that satire to Scottish religious bigotry, only to add an apologetic note explaining that of course his own local ministers of the gospel were most admirable specimens of Christian virtue. And he has second thoughts about the earthiness which use of the vernacular encouraged in him, changing the line 'An' winter turned his icy bum' in the manuscript of one of his poems to 'birds may bigg in winter's lum'.[2] But these timidities do not matter much in themselves: it is the quality of the verse that lets us down, the failure to press home the point by concentrating the resources which, as the writer shows from time to time, he does undoubtedly possess.

One feels that, for Stevenson, to write verse in Scots is still to some extent a linguistic exercise, so that it strikes one as not just a joke when he says:

> No' bein' fit to write in Greek,
> I wrote in Lallan.

Scots as a 'beuk-language' is something that has to be learned almost like a dead, classical language. And although the spoken tongue is not quite dead yet, it is not difficult for him, in 'The Maker to Posterity', to project himself into a time when it will be utterly so:

> Few spak it than, an' noo there's nane.
> My puir auld sangs lie a' their lane,
> Their sense, that aince was braw an' plain,
>   Tint a'thegether,
> Like runes upon a standin' stane
>   Amang the heather.[3]

(Incidentally, could the author of 'The Eemis Stane' have had these 'runes' at the back of his mind when he wrote that poem?)

Stevenson is very aware of technical problems with written forms due to the lack of an adequate Scots orthography. He would welcome normalisation in that respect, but has the creative writer's resistance to the norms of the dialectologist which would tend to preserve a local consistency by constricting the resources at his disposal. 'Among our new dialecticians', he says in his Note to *Underwoods*,

> the local habitat of every dialect is given to the square mile. I could not emulate this nicety if I desired; for I simply wrote my Scots as well as I was able, not caring if it hailed from Lauderdale or Angus, from the Mearns or Galloway; if I had ever heard a good word, I used it without shame; and when Scots was lacking, or the rhyme jibbed, I was glad (like my betters) to fall back on English.

But of course this practice was not confined to Scots words he had *heard*: it applied likewise to what he had *read* in his eighteenth-century predecessors. And although Stevenson does not say so, the practice of the so-called 'Ayrshire ploughman', Burns, was actually similar to his own.

Sir George Douglas thought in 1893 that Stevenson and James Logie Robertson might be the heralds of a new Scots revival. Scots for him was a peasant dialect, and he said of these two writers:

> They employ the language of the peasant in the manner of the scholar, and they are the first, I believe, who have so employed it. Of course there have been men of letters, men of learning, before now who have used the dialect; but when they did so they had no aim but to speak as like peasants as they could. With Mr. Robertson and Mr. Stevenson, especially the former, the aim . . . is wholly different. They are "stylists" in the language of the unlettered. Their classic elegance, their *curiosa felicitas*, keeps step with their command of, with their erudition in the Doric. Is this yet another augury that our native tongue is soon to be ranked among the dead ones? If it be, it is the only happy augury of that sad consummation of which I have ever heard; for in this case death carries within it the germ of a new life. And it is to Mr. Robertson and Mr. Stevenson, and to the followers—for I think there will be followers—in the movement which they have inaugurated, that we must look for a revival of poetry written in the Scottish dialect.[4]

This seems to imply that, once Scots is well and truly dead, it will happily no longer be identified as the dialect of unlettered peasants. If it is then resurrected for poetic purposes, it should prove to be socially and academically more respectable, as is foreshadowed by what Douglas considers to be the elegant 'erudition' of Stevenson's and more especially Robertson's usage. But then Douglas, whose reputation as an authority on Scots language and literature is a fair indication of the ignorance of such matters fostered by the Scottish educational system in which his contemporaries took such pride, admired Robertson as a stylist whose Scots differed altogether from 'the slovenly dialect of Ramsay, the haphazard dialect of Fergusson, and the uncritical dialect of Burns'. (The likes of Henryson and Dunbar presumably 'had no aim but to speak as like peasants as they could'.)

Whatever one makes of this, it will certainly not convey an accurate idea of what Robertson's procedure actually was. Douglas would lead one to think that this learned gentleman shunned anything reminiscent of the 'peasant', whereas in fact he deliberately adopted a 'peasant' persona and wrote in Scots under the name of a supposed shepherd of the Ochils, 'Hugh Haliburton'. Everything Robertson said in his preface and notes to Haliburton's poems in *Horace in Homespun* (1886) was intended to assure readers that they dealt with 'flesh and blood realities, moving about among the Ochils at the present moment' and that their language was the every-day speech of this shepherd:

> The dialect employed by the Author . . . is that variety of the Scottish language which is still in vigorous use among the regular inhabitants of the Ochils. It is the

Author's mother-tongue and every-day speech. Into this speech words and phrases, which are commonly regarded as peculiar to other districts of the country, may have been imported—in a perfectly natural way.[5]

The latter we are to suppose had occurred by the migration of shepherds from these other districts. And another influence, since this peasant is not unlettered, would be his reading of such as Burns, Scott, and Wilson, who have 'enriched and, to a great extent, assimilated the various Scottish dialects'. Passages that appear to be in English, we are told, are really in the 'Sabbath Scotch' which 'an unusually elevated or serious train of thought in the mind of a Scottish peasant seems to demand'.

It is true that many of the poems have in fact been adapted from or suggested by Horace, but the result is very much 'Horace in Homespun', and the point of view taken by the writer is that of the Ochil shepherd, 'Hughie', who would be as unlikely to read a Latin poet as he would Baudelaire. The 'bit of Latin at the beginning' of Hughie's poems is supposed to have been added later by his 'editor', Robertson, who 'sees in Hughie's experience of life among the hills of Scotland a remarkable correspondence to that of Horace, twenty centuries ago, in ancient Rome'.[6]

By writing Scots poems based to a greater or lesser degree on texts and themes in Horace, Robertson is of course following one of the trails laid down by Ramsay. Like Stevenson, he looks back to the eighteenth-century revival and sticks to its well-worn tracks. But—much as he would consciously deplore anything of the sort—there is no escaping the implicit condescension in his adoption of the role of Hughie: condescension which is brought out embarrassingly in his attitude in the Preface to *Horace in Homespun* towards the very qualities with which he himself has supplied his *alter ego*.

As to the quality of his writing, he rarely rises above the routine competence in versifying which was sufficient to attract a wide readership for his poems when they appeared in the newspapers; but when he does so his work still deserves some respect. For example, compare with Ramsay's most successful adaptation of Horace, 'Look up to Pentland's towring taps', Robertson's version, which begins as follows:

> Fra whaur ye hing, my cauldrife frien',
>   Your blue neb owre the lowe,
> A snawy nichtcap may be seen
>   Upon Benarty's pow;
> An' snaw upon the auld gean stump,
>   Whas' frostit branches hang
> Oot-owre the dyke abune the pump
>   That's gane clean aff the fang.
> The pump that half the toun's folk ser'd,
>   It winna gie a jaw,
> An' rouch, I ken, sall be your beard
>   Until there comes a thaw![7]

Although he felt the need to adopt his simple shepherd persona when he wrote in Scots, Robertson was well aware that in the past it had been the speech of all classes:

> The cottar spak' it in his yaird,
> An' on his rigs the gawcie laird.

By appeal to the past also he had no doubt it was no mere dialect but a language, and when in his long 'Lament for the Language',[8] written before he adopted the role of Hughie, he celebrates his literary predecessors, he goes back beyond Scott and Hogg and the eighteenth-century trio to Lyndsay, Dunbar and Barbour. But it is all too characteristic of Robertson that, in the act of claiming that the language which is dying in contemporary speech lives on in the literature, he sinks to a level of verse that undermines the literary values he is asserting:

> Though from the lips, of speech the portal,
> It lives in Literature immortal.

He is rather more convincing, at least to someone who agrees with him precisely about the Scots shibboleths, when he insists in schoolmasterly fashion on the psychological value of the native sound-system:

> . . . Ilka letter gat its due
> The first page o' the Carritch* thro',
> An' ne'er a lisp was tolerated,
> An' 'lock' for 'loch' like Sawtan hated,
> An' aye the 'r', tho' crank awee,
> Gaed birlin' aff the mooth-ruif free.

However, as its original title indicates, this poem is a long lament for the *decadence* of the language, the loss of 'oor nationality, oor name,/Oor patriotic love for hame', and the destruction of traditional rural society by the growth of industrialised towns with their spider web of new-fangled telegraph wires and railways. Robertson's view of his Scots literary inheritance, as of religion, manners and customs, was often nostalgic and defeatist: 'the guid auld times are a' gaun by.'

His more combative side emerged in his prose when he protested vigorously against 'the effacement of national distinctions by the imposition of a uniformity of ideas, taste and character' on a Scotland which was becoming a species of English province, castigating the wilful neglect of a literature which had been graced by William Dunbar ('of no less vigour and versatility', in his view, than Burns), and told the Scottish universities that they should attend to the cultural needs of their country 'by founding a Chair or at least establishing a few lectureships for Scottish literature'.[9] But that was only a century ago.

---

* *Carritch*—the Shorter Catechism, usually printed with the alphabet on the first page, in the interests of a Godly Scottish education.

Robertson wrote essays on Ramsay and Fergusson (whose 'Farmer's Ingle' he championed *vis-à-vis* 'The Cotter's Saturday Night'), and edited Ramsay, Thomson, Burns and Scott. But the best he could do for the great, shamefully neglected Dunbar was 'a Selection from the Poems of an Old Makar adapted for Modern Readers',[10] which painfully sums up his predicament in the Scotland of his time.

The Dunbar of 'The Tua Mariit Wemen and the Wedo' is of course silently censored out of existence, and at the other end of the scale Robertson tends to turn the makar's higher flights not into modern Scots but into something very close to standard English. For example, his version of 'The Thrissill and the Rois' soon resorts to a staple English poetic diction of Nineties vintage, into which a Scots word is very occasionally inserted, sometimes just for the sake of a rhyme. There is, however, one point at which Robertson feels a need to Scotticise Dunbar. Confronted with the line,

> And lat no small beist suffir skaith na skornis,

he with infallible couthiness elects to change 'small' to 'wee'. It's a great wee word, 'wee', as Tom Leonard has assured us: 'and Scottish/it makes you proud'. And that way lies a Wee Willie Dunbar.

On the other hand, when Robertson is faced with the beautifully poised poem, 'Sweit Rois of Vertew', we get a Rabbie B. Dunbar. Funking, not surprisingly, the challenge of finding a modern equivalent to that elegant simplicity, he turns the poem into a pseudo-Burnsian song, with a plethora of Ohs and Os. Thus

> Sweit rois of vertew and of gentilnes,
> Delytsum lyllie of everie lustynes,

becomes

> Thy glance, thy grace, thy winsome face,
> And a' the charms about thee, O.

It is as hard to imagine what this is supposed to do for Dunbar as it is to see the point of the operation Robertson performs on the religious poem which begins:

> Done is a battell on the dragon blak;
> Our campioun Chryst confoundit hes his force.

What is the linguistic difficulty of the original which the reader has to be spared at the cost of Dunbar's powerfully effective alliterating stops, so that the above becomes:

> The fight is ended with the dragon black,
> Christ stands victorious in the deadly stour?

Or take the splendid victory of rhythm and rhyme over syntax in Dunbar's line,

> The signe triumphall rasit is of the croce.

What excuse is there for libbing this of all its singularity, unless to reduce it to the level of some latter-day hymn book, with

> High shines the cross in this triumphant hour?

In his approach to Dunbar, Robertson seems to have taken a leaf out of Ramsay's *Ever Green*. His attitude is that he can do pretty well anything he likes with Dunbar's text in 'adapting' it for his modern readers—a presumption which is hard to accept from a scholarly man of letters in 1895, whatever excuses may be found for Ramsay's bad example. True, Robertson never reaches the sublime vulgarity with which Ramsay has Dunbar plugging his book for him in 'Lament for the Makaris'—

> Then sall we flourish Evir Grene . . .
> *Timor mortis non turbat me.*
> 'Quod Dunbar.'

But he does things like turning Dunbar's 'New Year's Gift to the King' into a gratuitous effusion 'To an Editor' ending with the rubric, 'Quod Hugh Haliburton, on 31st December 1892'. His worst sin is to have deluded himself into thinking that he could substitute his own rather shabby technical effects for the brilliance of 'the greatest European "makar" between Chaucer and Spenser'.[11] But in his own way he was undoubtedly pointing 'Back to Dunbar': a slogan MacDiarmid was to adopt and spell out more pointedly as: 'Dunbar—Not Burns!'.

The 'Hugh Haliburton' poems collected in *Horace in Homespun* achieved a great popular success; and MacDiarmid certainly read them, and was much impressed by Mrs Robertson's report that farmers eagerly awaited the appearance of what they called 'Hughies' in the *Scotsman* and that at least one upland bothy had its walls papered with the poems as they were cut out of the newspaper. His own preference, however, was for another writer whose poems appeared in that period and who also manifested what begins to look like a peculiarly Scottish compulsion by using a pseudonym: James B Brown ('J. B. Selkirk'). Brown was a competent versifier in English and the author of an earnest little work called *Ethics and Aesthetics of Modern Poetry*. He wrote only a handful of poems in Scots, and one suspects that Border loyalties played some part in MacDiarmid's feeling for these.

Perhaps there is another link between the two men in the fact that Brown turned instinctively to Scots when confronted by the emotional crisis of a death in his family. But he is one of these writers who felt obliged to adopt a Scots persona on a lower social and cultural level than their own. This takes the form of a humble emigrant who writes verse letters to Tammas, his friend back in Ettrick.

The theme in Brown's verse that may have most attracted MacDiarmid is his deep feeling for the compulsive rhythms of a Border burn, which 'canna rin without a turn':

> I see't this moment, plain as day,
> As it comes bickerin' o'er the brae,
> Atween the clumps o' purple heather,
> Glistenin' in the summer weather,
> Syne divin' in below the grun',
> Where, hidden frae the sicht and sun,
> It gibbers like a deed man's ghost
> That clamours for the licht it's lost,
> Till oot again the loupin' limmer
> Comes dancin' doon through shine and shimmer
> At headlang pace, till wi' a jaw
> It jumps the rocky waterfa' . . .
> While on the brink the blue harebell
> Keeks o'er to see its bonnie sel',
> And sittin' chirpin' a' its lane
> A water-waggy on a stane.[12]

John Buchan (another self-confessed 'nympholept' who ever since his boyhood forays amongst the burns of Tweeddale translated 'every land with which I was connected into the speech of its rivers') picked out that passage to represent Brown in his excellent anthology *The Northern Muse* (1924), which was very well known to MacDiarmid, and it may be rather more than a coincidence that some of the latter's best Scots poems, looking back in the early thirties to his Langholm boyhood, developed similar motifs in his own splendid celebration of Border water music.

Before that, in *A Drunk Man Looks at the Thistle*, MacDiarmid had echoed some lines in Brown's poem 'Selkirk After Flodden':

> . . . A' the lads they used to meet
> By Ettrick braes or Yarrow
> Lyin' thrammelt head and feet
> In Brankstone's deadly barrow!
> O Flodden Field![13]

And in the previous year he had used the passage as a touchstone for genuine Scots poetry as distinct from the mere verse which, he said, was all a writer of Buchan dialect like Charles Murray could aspire to:

> That rises infinitely above Mr Murray's compass. Compare it with any passage in *Hamewith* or *In the Country Places*; the difference . . . is a measure of the difference between Scottish poetry and Scottish verse—between the power of the Doric and the merely prosaic, if vigorous and diverting, uses to which Mr Murray puts an inferior form of it. For his particular dialect is perhaps the poorest of them all and certainly the least capable of being used to genuine poetic purpose.[14]

To this R L Cassie retorted by declaring that the whole passage quoted from Brown was not Scots, on the grounds that ' "thrammelt" is the only strong Scots word used' in it, and 'the thought was evidently formulated in English'.

He then proceeded to render it in the dialect he (and of course Murray) favoured, what he called northern (strictly north-eastern) Scots.

Cassie was convinced that the writer of Scots should concentrate on the features which distinguish it from standard English, the admixture of which with the native tongue he deplored, and for him the great merit of the north-eastern Scots dialect lay in the fact that it was most clearly differentiated from the imposed English norm—'nearly as divergent from standard English as the modern Scandinavian languages are from one another'. MacDiarmid, however, tended (at least when it suited his argument) towards the position adopted in theory by Allan Ramsay: that Scots *included* English, which Scots-speakers acquired as a school language. And in any case his Border ear was offended by the 'intractabilities of uncouthness' he said it encountered in the speech of the North-East and its 'clipping devitalising pronunciation with its transmutations of ''wh'' into ''f'' and so on'.[15]

Perhaps north-eastern loyalties play their part in my conviction that personal feuds are accountable for MacDiarmid's view of the Aberdonians as a sub-human species, which might be thought a trifle harsh:

> . . . less than human as to my een
> The people are in Aberdeen.

It is at any rate the case that his attitude towards Charles Murray's dialect is as jaundiced a specimen of linguistic prejudice as any he himself complained of:

> Anything further from the conceivable norm—anything more corrupt—it would be difficult to find in any dialect of any tongue. . . . He has done nothing to repurify a dialect which he found in a corrupt state and to put it to nobler and higher uses.

What lies behind this is, first of all, MacDiarmid's antagonism towards the use for poetic purposes of regional dialects as distinct from a 'generalised' Scots considered as a national literary language; and secondly, his prejudice against the Buchan dialect in particular as being furthest removed from the Lothian on which established literary usage was based, not to mention his own regional dialect—by his own criteria, of course, also 'debased'—which was so different from Buchan that the latter seemed to him like a foreign tongue. He had at any rate a valid point when he noted that a writer of Buchan dialect had a very small literature behind him, and that the use of a generalised Scots was the likeliest way of resisting the tendency towards fragmentation and constriction of range.

There was just one poem by Murray in his uncouth dialect for which MacDiarmid had a good word: 'The Whistle'. Although even this he declared to be not poetry but 'versified prose and of a passéist order at that', he nevertheless considered that 'it will live in Scottish literature'. But there is another poem, very different from Murray's staple products of exiled nostalgia for the rural Aberdeenshire of his youth, which suggests ironically that of all the poets who had recently preceded him in Scots it was Murray who in this instance came closest to MacDiarmid's cast of mind and prefigured some of the imagery of his own Scots poems. This is 'Gin I Was God', which appeared in Murray's collection *In the Country Places* (1920) and was included by MacDiarmid in his anthology of contemporary Scottish poetry *Northern Numbers*, Second Series, 1921:

> Gin I was God, sittin' up there abeen,
> Weariet nae doot noo a' my darg was deen,
> Deaved wi' the harps an' hymns oonendin' ringin',
> Tired o' the flockin' angels hairse wi' singin',
> To some clood-edge I'd daunder furth an', feth,
> Look ower an' watch hoo things were gyaun aneth.
> Syne, gin I saw hoo men I'd made mysel'
> Had startit in to pooshan, sheet an' fell,
> To reive an' rape, an' fairly mak' a hell
> O' my braw birlin' Earth,—a hale week's wark—
> I'd cast my coat again, rowe up my sark,
> An', or they'd time to lench a second ark,
> Tak' back my word an' sen' anither spate,
> Droon oot the hale hypothec, dicht the sklate,
> Own my mistak', an', aince I'd cleared the brod,
> Start a'thing ower again, gin I was God.

Ostensibly dismissing Murray ('the Whistle') and Violet Jacob ('Tam i' the Kirk') as one-poem writers, MacDiarmid in 1925 proposed as 'the greatest contemporary Scottish poet' a man approaching seventy who if known at all to his readers was known primarily as a sculptor, Pittendrigh Macgillivray. He based the case for Macgillivray's pre-eminence as a poet on the following, quoted from an article he had written a couple of years before:

> His verse has the traditional dourness and undemonstrativeness of the Scot. A deliberate plainness, that subtle choice of the prosaic which in sum-effect can be so startling and distinctive, a Spartan aesthetic, lift these verses into a category of their own as undoubtedly the most authentic expressions of certain well-known but seldom-articulated aspects of the Scottish genius since the days of the Old Makars. . . . Austere and uncompromising, his work resembles the mountains of Scotland: grey, gaunt, cold, fog-bound—it is only on intimate approach that their marvellous colouring may be appreciated or their wealth of unobtrusive flowers discovered.[16]

What these flowers are, in terms of Macgillivray's poetry, one never learns; and indeed MacDiarmid managed to write a lengthy piece in *Contemporary Scottish Studies* in praise of his candidate for the Scottish laureateship without naming one of his poems or quoting one line of his verse, while in his earlier article it is only the sinister image of crows and worms in 'Kirkyaird Geordie' that one can detect exerting a specific attraction on him.

So which of Macgillivray's other poems could he have admired? Surely few enough of the poems in *Pro Patria* (1915), all in English, with 'use o' England whaur the U.K.'s meent' and jingoist jingles running the gamut from the Boer to the Great War. The level of the verse is never very high, sometimes very low, and one can hardly envisage MacDiarmid swallowing Macgillivray's version of war, a matter of which the former had some recent experience. The Murray of 'Dockens Afore His Peers', a satire of an exemption tribunal, would have been much more to the point.

That leaves only one other published collection by Macgillivray, *Bog-Myrtle and Peat Reek* (1922). Presumably we must rule out the section in this book written in his native Aberdeenshire dialect, though curiously enough MacDiarmid never reproached *him* for using the same corrupt dialect he condemned with reference to Murray. As his sub-title makes clear—*Verses Mainly in the North and South Country Dialects of Scotland*—Macgillivray saw himself here as a *dialect* poet, and though he could write in at least two dialects to suit the part of the country he had in mind, these were kept carefully distinct: no 'synthetic Scots' for him. Also, although MacDiarmid tried to link him with the Auld Makars, his book was very much in the vernacular tradition established in the eighteenth century. This is clear from the traditional spread of subject-matter (including sentimental Jacobitism), the stanza-forms and basic stylistic features, the typographical devices, and even the quality of the paper used in its production. Its eighteenth-century provenance is further emphasised in the author's Notes when he refers to

> the century of Ramsay, "Tullochgorum", Fergusson and Burns, the fountain-heads, one may say, of the Scots Vernacular and the character of verse still in vogue—

a vogue which surely he himself subscribes to as one of those who 'follow the traditions of these masters'. The scope of an ambition confined well within traditional limits is suggested accurately enough by his own interpretation of his title:

> "Bog-myrtle" is for the simple sweetness of our native life, and "Peat Reek" for its homely character and pungency of wit.

But MacDiarmid indicated what may have been Macgillivray's special virtue to him—his austerity as an antidote to the excesses of the Kailyard—when he claimed, rather too confidently I think, that 'he is incapable of facile sentiment of any kind'. And there is another element that one can see as appealing particularly to him. After the genteel emasculation of so much post-Burnsian verse, it is refreshing to find Macgillivray returning to the frankness of an older attitude towards sexual matters.

Many of his poems were obviously written with a tune, often a folk tune, in mind; and this procedure involves a simple mode of language with the skill of the writer being displayed in musical repetitions of short colloquial phrases and rhythmical patterns. It is difficult to see why these song-based lyrics or the 'occasional' poems which accompany them should be associated with the Auld Makars (represented, for MacDiarmid, above all by the sophisticated Dunbar) rather than with the vernacular revival that goes back little further than Ramsay. And the level of technical accomplishment they exhibit is likely to recall Ramsay more often than Burns, the 'Saint Robert' of one of the poems.

Macgillivray is not being unduly modest when, in the Epilogue to the book, he describes his poems as 'rhymin' games and ploys'. These are the occasional diversions of an aging artist (none of them written before he was forty) whose real work was his sculpture. Probably his best poem is 'Mercy o' Gode', which appeared in MacDiarmid's *Scottish Chapbook* in 1923. Although he follows the procedure of adopting the persona in Scots of a shepherd or farm worker, the resonance of the poem goes well beyond the range which this familiar ploy would lead one to expect. It depicts two old Beckettian tramps who are spending the night in a graveyard and passing the time before sleep by arguing about the purposes of God and Man. One is a believer whose religion has gone sour, the other a confirmed atheist, and we never discover which (if either) won the argument. Macgillivray seems for a moment to be stuck with a platitudinous comment by his rustic observer, but recovers to end on an effective note of irony:

> But as nicht drave on I had needs tak' the road,
> Fell gled o' ma dog—
> The love o' a dog:
> An' tho' nane wad hae me that day at the fair,
> I raither't the hill for a houff than in there,
> 'Neth a table-stane, on a deid man's lair—
> A deid man's lair—
> Mercy o' Gode.

From the *Scottish Chapbook* this poem found its way into *Modern Scottish Poetry* (1946), thus claiming Macgillivray for the modern 'Scottish Renaissance' movement. Of his other two poems in that anthology, 'Glances' is an embarrassingly coy, traditional piece, and 'Abasshyd' is an exercise in archaic diction, a weird mixture in which the non-Scots features overpower the Scots ones, though the contest was hardly worth the effort involved. The editor of the anthology does not indicate where 'Abasshyd' came from, but I have noticed that it also appeared in W H Hamilton's *Holyrood* (1929), where it is declared to be 'XVth Century English'.

A more interesting linguistic experiment by Macgillivray in something like Older Scots appeared in the *Evergreen*, the periodical in which Patrick Geddes announced a short-lived 'Scots Renascence' in 1895. This poem seems to have been a by-product of the interest in things medieval fostered by the Celtic movement in Scotland. I have never seen it in print elsewhere, and it seems to me worth preserving as at any rate a curious artefact:

Ane Playnt of Luve

O hart, My hart! that gyves na rest,
Bot wyth luve madness dois dismaie;
For all thingis ellis, ye haif na zeste,
Nor thocht; bot luve may drive awaye.
            Deir hart, be still,
            And stay this ill,
        Thi passioun sall me slay!

O hart, My hart! haif mercie nowe,
On me thi mastir, Sorrow's selfe:
Fra hir that will na luve allowe,
Desyre na moir the horded pelf.
            Deir hart, in pane
            Quhy wilt remane?—
        Haif mercie on thi selfe!

O hart, My hart! tho' sche be fair,
As moon bemys quhyte, or starris that schyn—
Tho' all hir partis haif na compare,
It makis nocht, gif hir hart disdeyne.
            Deir harte, gyve ease,
            Fra luve release
        Of ane that is nocht myne.
                    QUOD
                    PITTENDRIGH.

It would appear that Macgillivray very soon turned his back on such experiments, since anything of that sort is proscribed by the principle he said he followed in writing the poems collected in *Bog-Myrtle and Peat Reek,* the earliest of which is dated 1896. In point of fact it was the principle rather than the poems that MacDiarmid got to grips with, and—ironically enough, in view of his commendation of the result—he flatly rejected it. Macgillivray said in his Preface:

I have used the North and South dialects of our Scottish Vernacular in so far only as I have a living knowledge of their words, idiom and accent; and I have done nothing in the way of making a curious mosaic of *"auld-farran"'* and obsolete words, such as no Scot of any period or district ever spoke. There is, I believe, a modulation of tone and accent resulting from the habitual sequence of vowels used in the idiom of each district. These factors of tone and accent, shaped through generations by subtle feelings and sympathies, produce for the native the harmonious music of his Mother tongue. To assemble obsolete words from periods remote and from dialects of districts apart and strange to each other in idiom and in the pronunciation of the same words, may produce a kind of literary language of Scots for the scholarly appreciation of those who have no intimacy with the voice of any of our dialects; but the result, although often witty enough, and obviously truly sympathetic in intention, can never, I think, touch the heart like a true native diction from any one of the quarters.

'So far as Scotland is concerned, that remains to be seen', said MacDiarmid, writing as C M Grieve and avoiding any reference to his own Scots poems. The literary history of other countries, he claimed, drove him to a contrary conclusion in thorough disagreement with Macgillivray:

> I see no reason why an artificially and quite arbitrarily contrived "generalised" Scots should not yet become an effective medium just as the Norwegian *landsmaal* has done. Dr. Macgillivray's view is the conventional one of our vernacular revivalists or conservators; but a new nationalistic spirit is abroad and is elsewhere achieving—as it may yet even in Scotland—miracles unimaginable to an older generation.[17]

Some of our linguistic experts may raise more than an eyebrow at what might seem MacDiarmid's 'naive' confidence in the exemplar of *landsmaal* (Nynorsk) in rebuilding a national language that for centuries had been discarded for literary purposes; but amongst the authorities he had behind him was that kenspeckle linguistic expert of the day, Professor W A Craigie, who was then gathering materials for what was to become the *Dictionary of the Older Scottish Tongue*. In a lecture to the Vernacular Circle of the London Burns Club in 1921, available to MacDiarmid in print from 1924, Craigie had said:

> If anyone doubts the possibility of recreating a literary tongue, capable of expressing all the necessary ideas which must occur in dealing with literature, history, science, and even philosophy, I will direct him to what has been written in the new Norwegian tongue within the past twenty years. He will there find the triumphant refutation of all that the sceptics allege against the mere possibility of such a language.[18]

There is no question of Macgillivray's remarks in his Preface having been directed at MacDiarmid's poems in 'synthetic Scots', as is alleged by C M Cammell.[19] The Preface is precisely dated 17 December 1921, and the first of MacDiarmid's Scots poems appeared in September 1922. Influenced by the recent intensive development of dialect studies, Macgillivray was adopting a stance which was becoming common among enthusiasts for 'the Vernacular', from which it was adjudged that a writer of Scots ought to use only the living speech of a dialect known to him at first hand. To anyone blinkered enough to apply that criterion with linguistic exactitude to literary products, there was certainly no shortage of targets for Macgillivray's remarks.

Among the more recent examples may have been the experiments of Lewis Spence, to whose use of 'Middle Scots' Cammell concedes that Macgillivray was not sympathetic. I am not sure how far one can rely on Spence's dating of these, or of the extent to which his friend Macgillivray may have been familiar with them at the time. Possibly it was around 1910 that Spence wrote the first of his 'Middle Scots' sonnets, one of which appears in his little broadsheet, *The Phoenix and other Poems* (1923), and a total of four in the slim volume of his *Collected Poems* (1953). But his various statements about such matters are not consistent, and there can be little doubt that the centring of critical attention on MacDiarmid caused Spence in later life to inflate the importance to himself and others of these early experiments, which in 1929 he was very ready to discount as the products of 'a merely antiquarian exercise'. By 1954 he was writing in the following vein:

> When I returned to Edinburgh in 1909 it was with a very definite object in view—the restoration of the Scottish language from its depressed and indeed chaotic condition to a state of modern literacy. . . . Middle Scots literature . . . appealed to me as the only trustworthy basis on which the rehabilitation of the Scottish tongue could well be essayed. My main intention was to modernize that phase of Scots in such a manner as would make it serviceable for use at the present time in prose and verse by following the analogous process by which Chaucerian English had developed into modern English, this being indeed the simplest and most efficacious means to my hand.
>
> The process, indeed, occupied many years of labour in my spare time. By the late twenties I had completed perhaps half of my task when Mr. MacDiarmid (who had applauded my endeavours and was fully knowledgeable concerning them) ventured upon his scheme for the formation of a generalised Scots drawn from all the known phases and dialects of that tongue and which he described as "Synthetic Scots".[20]

Confidence in the accuracy of this is not encouraged by the recollection that 'The Watergaw', which Spence regarded as MacDiarmid's masterpiece in 'Synthetic Scots', appeared in 1922, not 'the late twenties'. But in any case the notion of Spence's single-handedly, and in his spare time, undertaking the development of the Scots language through a process which would parallel the development of Chaucerian into modern English is quite as mind-boggling as anything dreamed up by the rival MacDiarmid propaganda machine.

In 1929, aged fifty-five and with the bulk of his published verse behind him, he made this judgment of the work in Scots of MacDiarmid and himself:

> Speaking frankly, neither has been successful, nor has one or other made any impression worth alluding to save among a very narrow circle, although both contain the germs of possible improvement. This is probably due to the fact that both were too sweeping in method, the results, indeed, proving almost of the nature of burlesque in some extreme cases. Although the intention in both instances was of the best, in practice it was so abused as to eventuate in oddity and even absurdity at times.[21]

He then condemned MacDiarmid for 'ruthlessly trawling the pages of the Scots dictionary for words and expressions of fantastic, droll and whimsical sound and appearance' in a work which he called *A Drunk Scotsman Looks at the Thistle*. A laboured process of this sort did not accord with the instant composition which 'inspiration so clamantly requires', and furthermore MacDiarmid was deficient in Scots grammar. Passing on to his own work in Scots, Spence concluded that

> the tendency was to overdo the archaic in verbiage, and the result was frankly disastrous. It had, too, a hybrid form, such as might have been expected from a mingling of the Chaucerian with the speech of modern Cockaigne—a ludicrous and

piebald appearance; and worst of all, no one understood the bulk of it save its creator alone, though ardent spirits were not wanting who professed to comprehend it. Cool reflection revealed it as the result of an over-hasty enthusiasm of questionable utility and more than questionable taste.

Although he then dismissed them as products of 'a merely antiquarian exercise', Spence's sonnets in an approximation to Middle Scots include what is probably his finest work, 'Portrait of Mary Stuart, Holyrood' and 'The Queen's Bath-House, Holyrood'. While from a linguistic point of view they would have to be categorised as pastiche (like so much else that is worth reading in modern Scots), their language harmonises with their subject-matter to the extent that the poet sounds convincingly like a highly talented successor to James VI's 'Castalian band'. The poems are in essence courtly conceits, elegantly phrased, and animated by the Romantic fervour with which Spence responded to the associations of the tragic queen. The choice of the sonnet form, with its historical links with an apprentice period in the literary development of the modern languages, might be said to reinforce the impression of a formal exercise, but the craftsmanship is of a very high order—on a par with the technical excellence of William Drummond in English—and in my view is its own justification.

Portrait of Mary Stuart, Holyrood

Wauken be nicht, and bydand on some boon,
Glaumour of saul, or spirituall grace,
I haf seen sancts and angells in the face,
And like a fere of seraphy the moon;
But in nae mirk nor sun-apparelled noon,
Nor pleasaunce of the planets in their place,
Of luve devine haf seen sae pure a trace
As in yon shadow of the Scottis croun.

Die not, O rose, dispitefull of hir mouth,
Nor be ye lillies waeful at hir snaw;
This dim devyce is but hir painted sake,
The mirour of ane star of vivand youth;
That nor hir velvets nor hir balas braw
Can oueradorn, or luve mair luvely make.

Even a much less successful, self-conscious imitation of a Middle Scots poem, 'The Pavone' ('in the quhilk the makar compares Juno's bird with Hope'), displays considerable skill in its execution, and the emphasis thus placed on craftsmanship was certainly desirable in the state of Scots verse as Spence found it. Here he manipulates an elaborate ten-line stanza-form, with hexameters and tetrameters stiff with internal rhymes in counterpoint against the movement of end-rhyming pentameters, and a heavy binding of alliteration. Again, all this artifice may reinforce the initial impression of an ingenious exercise in an antique mode, but, partly because of one's sense of the perilous state of the language itself, one takes Spence's prosodic exercises in Scots much more seriously than anything of the kind he tried in English. The latter never went much further than juggling with pretty phrases in roundels—one of several indications that his taste in English verse was fixated around the Nineties.

His serious interest in the old Scots language, the technical apparatus of its verse-forms and the sonority of its rhetoric, resulted in most of what is valuable in Spence's verse. Without it, one feels he would just have gone on indulging his appetite for the dubious Scottish Romantic fare represented by such favourite words as 'glamourie', 'eldritch', and 'ferlie', speciously excusing himself on the grounds that 'the tradition and tendency of Scots poetry . . . is, and always has been, obdurately romantic'. But Older Scots had its own dangers for him, as may be indicated by these lines, quoted from the most archaic of his sonnets, 'Eidolon':

> Thus beaute in ane rude and angrie warld
> Is richtswa refeit by the wilroun ways
> Of felloun frekes and ouer the barrets harled.
> O harmisay!

O harmisay, indeed! Callooh, callay! Like the correspondent signing himself 'Gavin Dunbar' in the *Scottish Educational Journal* in 1925, one is inclined to prefer Lewis Carroll—who by the way wrote a ballad in very promising Scots called 'The Lang Coortin''. But Gavin Dunbar's own venture into 'Middle Scots' is worth remembering, especially for these lines, which evidently celebrate a goal in the top corner:

> The skuggis of the sichand blonkis
> Gart bismyng bismeiris pingill,
> Til rebaldis rigbanis crynit fast
> Jow-jordan-heidit at the ingle.[22]

I trust this will not be thought merely frivolous. Some of Spence's experiments are so vulnerable to mockery precisely because he took himself too solemnly when he donned his velvet breeks before composing. MacDiarmid could sometimes get away with an even more outlandish garb and posture because his diabolical sense of humour was lurking just around the corner, in the company of such as James Joyce.

Sensibly enough, Spence tried to get beyond the kind of rhetoric employed by the persona of even the most successful of the 'Middle Scots' sonnets to something that could be more directly related to his own personality in his own time. The very spelling of Older Scots made everything he used it for seem heavily antiquated—though one might note in passing that it had the advantage of avoiding the ubiquitous apostrophe of modern Scots orthography, which is misleading in so far as it tends to suggest that Scots is an aberrant form of standard Southern English, and furthermore one that is limited to colloquial styles. However, with the old spelling comes a heavy obligation to preserve propriety by using only the more venerable stylistic devices.

Spence's response to the problem of how to make use of his genuine feeling for Older Scots without getting trapped in an antiquated persona took the form of 'essays in verse couched in the novel amalgam of old and new which the writer labelled "gentlemen's Scots", to distinguish it from the peasant and urban varieties'. It was about these experiments that he felt most pessimistic in 1929, concluding that:

> So deficient is the vocabulary of modern Scots in terms suitable for the higher or more classical forms of poetry (though serviceable enough for the purest form of rural or ballad verse) that too large an infusion of Middle Scots words had perforce to be introduced.[23]

But if he wrote many such poems, very few have survived in print. The best of the available specimens in what he called 'gentlemen's Scots' is probably 'The Prows o' Reekie', an effective tribute to Edinburgh which shows that he could in fact handle Scots with the sort of dignity he aimed at without having to load it with an antiquated vocabulary. It is true that he still used old-fashioned stylistic devices for this purpose, but that was also the case with all his poems in English. Another successful example of what he said was 'gentlemen's Scots', though there is scarcely even a weak infusion of the expected Middle Scots words in it, is 'The Gray Etin', the imagery of which is more striking than is usual with him. Auld Reikie is seen first as a dragon raxing out 'to drink her mornin' frae the sea' and then as a cheese swarming with human maggots indifferent to what the poet would like to think is his prophetic voice. Both these poems appeared in *The Phoenix* in 1923.

It is difficult now to credit that Spence, with a small handful of such poems, was at one time regarded (at least in some Edinburgh circles), not only as the champion of 'gentlemen's Scots' against the uncouth clytach or haggersnash of MacDiarmid, but as a poet whose achievements rivalled the latter's. Present-day attitudes towards the idea of a 'gentleman' are irrelevant here and must be discounted, but one may doubt if that was ever the right word for what Spence wanted. It was really an educated man's language that he felt was called for, and if education in Scotland had anything to be proud of it was after all a democratic virtue to which it might stake its claim. The trouble was that Scots education was (and very largely still is) an education in the non-use of Scots.

In 1925, before they quarrelled and became increasingly antagonistic, MacDiarmid put on record his admiration for some of Spence's work in Scots, especially the craftmanship of 'Portrait of Mary Stuart, Holyrood', which he compared very favourably with Mark Alexander Boyd's fine sonnet, 'Cupid and Venus'. Indeed, he declared that Spence was 'the first Scot for five hundred years to write "pure poetry" in the vernacular'[24]—a considerable advance on

Spence's compliment to him: 'no poetry for a century and a half has reflected so much of the authentic Scotland as the poems in Mr. MacDiarmid's recent book *Sangschaw*'.[25] MacDiarmid admired technical skill in the handling of 'word-music and sound-suggestiveness' by the older poet, just as he admired it in a traditional lyric like 'Mary's Song' by Marion Angus—a first-rate poem, in my opinion, now undervalued simply because its genre is out of fashion with critics. It is all too easy to overlook the unobtrusive effect which a consistently good ear for rhythm had in the work of Angus and (to some extent) Violet Jacob, by way of helping to dislodge Scots verse from its Kailyard rut. MacDiarmid did not miss such things. But to sum up the matter of his early relationship with Spence, a parting word may be quoted from Spence himself, writing in the *Scottish Literary Journal* of 6 August 1926:

> I certainly admire much of Mr Grieve's work, but to associate my own efforts, literary and propagandist, with his, is fair to neither of us. In a recent leading article, the *Glasgow Herald* comparing my work with that of Mr Grieve, remarked: 'They are poles apart in language and subject matter. . . . Mr MacDiarmid (Mr Grieve) draws his vocabulary from Scots anywhere and of any time: Mr Spence derives from the old "Makaris".' That puts the matter in a nutshell. Mr Grieve is engaged in an effort to popularise "synthetic" Scots, while my own predilections and propaganda strive towards a literary revival of the old Court Scots, which it is not intended should displace, but supplement, the current Doric, providing Scottish poets with a more polished literary instrument. And may I say here that so far from "defying accepted canons of art", I am a strict adherent to accepted forms in verse, and have frequently been adversely criticised for my conservative attitude in this regard.

In some other regards too, no doubt. But perhaps the crucial difference between these two writers was MacDiarmid's eager awareness of, and adaptability towards, much of the literary and intellectual milieu of *contemporary* Europe, in which he was convinced Scots verse must take a forward-looking stance if it was to 'revive' in any sense he thought worthwhile.

NOTES

1 *Collected Poems,* edited by Janet Adam Smith, second edition, (London, 1971), p. 170
2 *Collected Poems*, pp. 149, 488
3 *Collected Poems*, p. 145
4 'Introductory Notes', *Contemporary Scottish Verse,* (London, 1893), p. xiv
5 Note to Glossary, Hugh Haliburton, *Horace in Homespun,* (Edinburgh, 1886), p. 97
6 Preface, *Horace in Homespun*, p. vii
7 *Horace in Homespun*, p. 58
8 *'For Puir Auld Scotland's Sake'*, (Edinburgh, 1887), pp. 164-80. The poem was originally entitled 'On the Decadence of the Scots Language, Manners, and Customs', in *Poems,* (Dundee, 1878)

9   'A Plea for Scottish Literature at the Universities', in 'For Puir Auld Scotland's Sake', pp. 156-63
10 Dunbar, (London, 1895)
11 James Kinsley, Preface, The Poems of William Dunbar, (Oxford, 1979), p. vi
12 'The Last Epistle to Tammas', Poems, (Edinburgh, 1905), pp. 28-9
13 Poems, p. 57. In A Drunk Man, 'Brankstone' becomes 'Branksome'. (David Murison has reported pointing this out to MacDiarmid, who received the information with great equanimity.)
14 'Charles Murray', Scottish Educational Journal, 10 July 1925. Reprinted in Contemporary Scottish Studies, enlarged edition, (Edinburgh, 1976), p. 7
15 Contemporary Scottish Studies, (1976 edn), p. 16
16 'Pittendrigh Macgillivray, II—As Poet', Scottish Nation, 16 Oct. 1923, p. 10
17 Contemporary Scottish Studies, (1976), p. 68
18 The Scottish Tongue, (London, 1924), p. 45
19 Heart of Scotland, (London, 1956), p. 113
20 'Poets at Loggerheads', Scotland's Magazine, 50, no. 8 (August 1954), 33-5
21 'Scots Poetry To-day', Nineteenth Century and After, 106 (1929), 253-68
22 Contemporary Scottish Studies, (1976), p. 68
23 'Scots Poetry To-day', p. 257
24 Contemporary Scottish Studies, (1976), p. 62
25 'The Scottish Literary Renaissance', Nineteenth Century and After, 100, (1926), 123-33, p. 127

NINE

Mid Twentieth Century Drama in Lowland Scots

†John Thomas Low

with particular reference to six plays

Robert McLellan *Jamie the Saxt*   *The Flooers o Edinburgh*
Robert Kemp *Let Wives Tak Tent*   *The Laird o Grippy*
Alexander Reid *The Lass wi the Muckle Mou*   *The Warld's Wonder*

A group of important plays, written in the mid twentieth century by Scottish authors in English, Scots-English, or entirely in Lowland Scots, may be said to constitute a body of classics of the Scottish theatre. Many of them have their roots in history, legend, aspects of Scottish society; some are adaptations of literary works; others present dramatic portraits of types or great figures from the past. Indeed, from some of these, it looked at one time as if Scotland, in a national theatre not yet created, might have built up its own Age of Kings or Great Historical Personages sequence, stimulated not so much by the Shakespeare Age of Kings sequence at Stratford as by the Guthrie-Kemp production of Sir David Lyndsay's mediaeval morality play *The Three Estates* at the Edinburgh International Festival in 1948. Such a sequence could have begun with Sydney Goodsir Smith's *The Wallace* (1960) and Robert Kemp's *King of Scots* (1951), diversified with James Bridie's *John Knox* (1947) and Robert Kemp's *Master John Knox* (1960), and culminated with Robert McLellan's *Jamie the Saxt* (1937) and Stewart Conn's *The Burning* (1971). As in the Stratford sequence, the chronological order of events and presentation would not have reflected that of the composition of the works.

A much larger, if less grand, sequence could be made up of Scottish classic plays based on literature, legend, aspects of social history. The nucleus, to a considerable extent illustrated by the programmes presented at the Gateway Theatre, Edinburgh, 1953–65,[1] would include James Bridie's *The Queen's Comedy* (1950) out of material from the *Iliad*, R J B Sellar's *The World my Parish* (1954) out of Galt's *Annals of the Parish* and *Weir of Hermiston* (1958) out of R L Stevenson's unfinished novel, Alexander Reid's *The Lass wi the Muckle Mou* (1950) out of Border history and legend, *The Warld's Wonder* (1953) out of Border wizardry and legendry, and *Voyage Ashore* (1956) out of the legend of Odysseus' return, Robert Kemp's *Rob Roy* (1959) out of Scott, *The Daft Days* (1957) out of Neil Munro, and *The Scientific Singers* (or *A Nest of Singing Birds*) (1955) on an eighteenth-century Aberdeen college and kirk musical controversy. This sequence would be enriched by the addition of Robert Kemp's adaptations of two Molière plays *Let Wives Tak Tent* (1948) and *The Laird o Grippy* (1955), and Robert McLellan's three comedies of manners on Scottish eighteenth-century topics—*The Flooers o Edinburgh* (1954) on anglicisation, *Torwatletie* (1946) on religious and political conflicts, and *The Hypocrite* (1967) on Scottish puritanism. For a sequence of dramatic portraits or studies of Scottish types—doctors, ministers, schoolmasters—we should have to draw on such Bridie masterpieces as *The Anatomist* (1930), *A Sleeping Clergyman* (1933), *Mr. Bolfry* (1943), and *Mr. Gillie* (1950).

Enough has been said, I hope, to establish that there *is* a corpus of Scottish classic plays; which could be further exemplified by such one-act pieces of worth as James Scotland's *Baptie's Lass* and *The Daurk Assize*, John S McCabe's *The Friars of Berwick*, George Waddell's *Kirkpatrick's Gowd*, Alexander Scott's *Untrue Thomas*, Robert McLellan's *The Changeling* and *Jeddart Justice*, and James Bridie's *The Pardoner's Tale* and *The Amazed Evangelist*.

This survey is, however, particularly concerned with plays which use the Lowland Scots tongue as the main linguistic medium. This means that I must exclude a number of works in the corpus, some of them mentioned above, and also the major works of our leading mid twentieth century dramatist Bridie himself; although I am aware that he reveals great skill in using Scots in parts of many of his major plays, particularly *The Sunlight Sonata, The Anatomist, Mr. Bolfry,* and *The Baikie Charivari*.[2]

Since the Guthrie-Kemp revival of *The Three Estates* in the late forties, indeed since the earlier days of the Glasgow Citizens' (and the MSU years at Rutherglen)[3] and particularly since the demise of the Gateway Theatre in the mid sixties, there have not been many opportunities to hear plays written entirely in Scots. Scottish repertory companies in recent years have been gey sweir to tackle classic Scottish plays in English or Scots-English,[4] let alone in Lowland Scots. The neglect of Bridie is the obvious example. Artistic directors may feel they have sound reasons for this: they may believe that their audiences have neither an interest in nor a knowledge of the cultural and linguistic patterns reflected in these plays; and it is true that the pressures of mass culture from TV and other media may be 'educating' Scottish audiences out of their own culture. This can only be regretted and deplored.

However, there are signs of a change. There have been occasional revivals of important Scottish plays and even of classic Scottish works in Lowland

Scots—more often, it is true, by talented amateur groups than by professional companies. For the purpose of this survey, I have decided to concentrate on certain works entirely in Lowland Scots by three dramatists of the mid century who seem to me to have an outstanding knowledge of the language and great skill in handling it dramatically—Robert McLellan, Robert Kemp, and Alexander Reid. I must stress that this is a personal choice necessarily restricted for the purpose in hand.[5]

In recent years I have been fortunate enough to see again productions of three of the six plays I have selected for detailed study—*Jamie the Saxt* by Robert McLellan, *The Lass wi the Muckle Mou* by Alexander Reid, and *Let Wives Tak Tent* by Robert Kemp. The other three—McLellan's *The Flooers o Edinburgh*, Reid's *The Warld's Wonder*, and Kemp's *The Laird o Grippy*—I have not seen on the stage since the brave days of the Gateway; so that memories of these are less clear-cut. In treating these six texts from the mid twentieth century as dramatic scores, and in placing the emphasis on their vocal and aural impact, I shall be trying to assess the power and the achievement, and perhaps also for the future the potential, of Lowland Scots as a linguistic medium for the stage.

Robert McLellan   *Jamie the Saxt   The Flooers o Edinburgh*

Jamie the Saxt was first performed at the Lyric Theatre, Glasgow, by the Curtain Theatre Company, in April 1937, with J D G Macrae as His Grace King James. It was revived in 1956, by which time J D G Macrae had become Duncan Macrae, something of a legend in his own time. It was revived again in the spring of 1982 by the Scottish Theatre Company, who presented it at Kirkcaldy, Stirling, Inverness, Glasgow, but not Edinburgh. It was the most successful of the company's productions to date.

The action of the First Act takes place in February 1591, in Bailie Nicoll Edward's house in Niddry's Wynd, in a room used as a retreat by King James at a time of great unrest. Out of the opening conversation between Mistress Edward and Bailie Morison comes an impression of the disorder and damage caused by the Earl of Bothwell's opposition to the King and a reminder of the King's obsession with the evil of witchcraft. The charm of Jamie's Danish Queen is indicated in the flash of a reference to Logie's flattery: 'He say I hae a guid Scots tongue in my heid afore lang.' The dialogue between Atholl and Logie touches more serious matters—Bothwell's witchcraft, Chancellor Maitland's scheming and greed, the King's traffic with the Papists and his need for 'siller frae England'.

The first high moment is the entry of King Jamie with Bailie Edward and Lord Spynie: he has just come from hunting and is tired and hungry. Here is the man who is destined to succeed Elizabeth and preside over two kingdoms, and the first words McLellan gives him are, 'God, I'm wabbit'. It is an effective linguistic touch used dramatically to reduce the illustrious to human proportions.

The central event behind this first act is the murder of the Bonnie Earl o Moray at Donibristle near Aberdour by the Earl of Huntly. In an early scene, the Huntly plot and the dangerous situation developing for Moray are summarised dramatically in the dialogue between the Queen and Ochiltree:

THE QUEEN   My Lord, at Dunibrissel? What is wrang?

OCHILTREE   Yer Grace, Huntly left the Toun this mornin wi mair nor a hunder o his men, to mak for the Leith races. He didna gang near them! He crossed the Firth at the Queen's Ferry and rade for Dunibrissel! And the Bonnie Earl's there wi haurdly a man.

The sharp division between the plotters of the murder, including the King and Maitland, on the one hand, and those who would defend Moray on the other, is dramatically underscored:

THE KING   . . . Jock, hou mony are there i' the Toun the nou?

MAITLAND   Errol's here, wi Hume and Angus.

THE KING   . . . Then tell them to staun bye the Toun Gaird gin ony try to force the ports! Lennox, Ochiltree and Atholl, ye'll gang til yer ludgings and bide there till ye hae leave to move.

OCHILTREE   Yer Grace, ye'll regret this! . . . It's nae threat to yersell, but if Huntly kills the Bonnie Earl I winna rest till I hae split his croun!

In the concluding dialogue of the First Act, Jamie, as a student of George Buchanan, demonstrates to Sir Robert Bowes, the English Ambassador, his acquaintance with rhetoric and the Socratic method; but later in that dialogue he also reveals himself, in his dealings with Elizabeth of England, both as a shrewd politician and as a hard-up Scot. Justifying his relations with the Papists as a means of destroying Bothwell, he proposes to Sir Robert:

THE KING   Gin oor dear sister were to mak us anither praisent o some siller, sae that we could fit oot a weill furnisht body o men to bring the blaggard to the gallows, something micht be done aboot the ither maitter then!

SIR ROBERT   Your Majesty, the question of money was raised in my dispatch. . . . The Queen my mistress hath instructed me to say, your Majesty, that until her wishes concerning the Papists are regarded, she can make no further grant to your exchequer.

THE KING   The Deil tak her for an auld miser!

The Second Act, set in 'the Kingis chalmer in the palace of Halyroudhous', July 1593, builds up quickly to the confrontation between Jamie in *déshabille* and Bothwell with sword drawn; but when the Lords Lennox, Ochiltree and Atholl appear, an act of submission is put on:

BOTHWELL   (*dropping elaborately on his knees*)   Maist Gracious Sovereign . . . We submit oorsells maist humbly to yer royal mercy.

THE KING   Ye leears, ye're cheyngin yer tune because the Lords are here. What are ye daein in my chalmer at aa?

The drama outside—the mob clamouring for a sight of the royal couple—
impinges on the drama inside—Jamie being allowed by Bothwell to put on his
breeks. This is no portrait of a heroic king: Jamie in *déshabille* is at the mercy of
Bothwell and in the presence of a growing band of nobles turning against him.
He is forced to show himself at the winnock; but it is the Queen who is given
the warmer burst of cheering. On Bothwell's orders Jamie dismisses the crowd:
'Ye can dae nae guid makin a steer ablow the winnock'; and the drama now
concentrates on the argument between the Kirk as represented by the priest
Bruce and the King as personified in James VI, Jamie showing his intellectual
mettle, Bruce making his points for the Kirk. McLellan tests here the validity
and virility of Scots in disputative prose:

> THE KING   . . . Ye're in the horns o a dilemma! Gin the Kirk suld be independent
> o the Temporal Pooer it daesna need acts o attainder. Gin it daes it canna be
> independent o the Temporal Pooer! Ye're flummoxed, I tell ye!
> BRUCE   Whan the Temporal Pooer interferes wi the weilfare o the Kirk it's for the
> Kirk to interfere wi it. Ye hae favoured the warst enemies o the Kirk and o
> Scotland baith, and gin ye winna cheynge yer coorse it maun be cheynged for ye.

In a more pompous style that illustrates the leisurely flourish of which Scots is
capable, Sir James Melville lectures the King on his duties: 'The foremaist o a
prince's aims, yer Grace, suld be the advancement o the true releegion, for gin
we neglect God we canna prosper.' The real drama of the conflict between
Jamie and Bothwell comes when Colville presents the document granting
pardon to Bothwell and insisting that Jamie rid himself of the faction of
Maitland, Glamis and the Humes; but McLellan adds touches to show the
working of Jamie's cunning: 'The suner the folk are pacified the better. They
maun believe I'm reconciled to the blaggard. . . .' The tailpiece to this Second
Act—Jamie's meeting with Morton's young daughter—has a quiet comedy
that sharpens the satire on the character of the King. Not realising she is in his
presence, the lassie sums up what she has heard:

> THE GIRL   That he's faur frae braw, and weirs the maist horrid auld claes. And he's a
> gey glutton, and sweirs and drinks ower muckle.

At the beginning of the Third Act, in the opening dialogue in the King's
chalmer between the King and this same young lassie now completely in his
confidence, the emphasis is not on any sexual relationship but on the King's
cowardice and superstition as he contemplates a nocturnal flight: 'It'll be gey
frichtsome crossin that kirkyaird in the daurk.' The Queen's suspicions and
jealousy of this girl are turned to good account by Sir James Melville when he
proves to the King that the jealous outburst is a proof of her fidelity to Jamie:

> MELVILLE   . . . whan her Grace fand Morton's dochter in your chalmer here she was
> gey upset. . . . Noo think, yer Grace. Wad she hae felt like that gin she hadna
> kent ye were the faither o her bairn?

In Jamie's final confrontation with Bothwell, it looks for a time as if Bothwell has the upper hand, being able to flourish the intercepted letters in which Jamie has written for help from the notorious Lords Hume and Huntly. McLellan's Scots handles the legal and learned dialogue with great spirit here: Jamie argues elaborately; Bothwell answers more briefly: but the passage ends in a short burst of colloquial Scots:

THE KING And wha are ye to demand loyalty? Ye mebbe haena been foun guilty, but ye arena an anointit King. I'm gaun to Falkland, I tell ye, and ye hae nae richt to stop me!

BOTHWELL I hae a richt to stop ye till ye hae signed oor agreement! I was to be paurdont for treason gin I was acquitit o witchcraft.

The intrigue and manoeuvring are given a new twist when Lennox enters and turns the tables against his own group by siding with Jamie, making it clear that he will play no Bolingbroke–Richard II game with Bothwell against the King.

I staun whaur I stude aye. I didna bring ye in to usurp royal authority.

The break-up of the alliance amongst the Lords is further developed in the argument between Bothwell on the one hand, playing for his own advantage, and Lennox, Ochiltree and Morton on the other, which ends in a sword scuffle. With the entry of Sir Robert Bowes, however, comes a complete change of atmosphere. After chiding the King for allowing disorder and laxity (and drawing from him spirited objections) he turns to Bothwell in a confrontation in which Bothwell, as intriguer and secret ally of Elizabeth, is completely routed:

Very weill, Sir Robert. We dinna daur offend her Majesty o England.

The final act tends to be overloaded with intrigue; but the main lines are discernible: retribution is overtaking Bothwell and the tide now flows in favour of Jamie. At first unable (and not very willing) to finance the raid against the Papists, he gradually comes into possession of facts through messages and letters in code that prove Bothwell's desertion to the Papists, the duplicity in his relationship with the Kirk, and his alliance with England. Bruce uses an eloquent pulpit Scots in cursing Maitland; and the curse has its comic effect in bringing on the Chancellor's pains. Triumph and vindication come for Jamie at the dramatic moment of Colville's revelation that Bothwell has 'jeynt the Papist lords for Spanish gowd':

THE KING I wad paurdon the Deil himsell for that news! . . . I can haurdly tak it in. To think o't! . . . My warst enemy destroyed by his ain folly! Aa my troubles washt awa by ae turn o the tide! Man, Jock, it's lauchable . . . .

Now the King is determined on the raid against the Papists; and the final entry of Sir Robert Bowes gives rise to the most powerful sequence in the whole act and play. Jamie's taunting of Sir Robert and his plotting has a certain Scots rhetoric:

> THE KING   . . . Aye, Sir Robert. . . . Ye may weill gowp like a frichtent fish. Ye're a proved plotter, a briber o traitors, a hirer o murderers! Whan I think hou ye hae leived amang us, respectit by gentle and simple in the Toun, treatit like a lord at Coort, honoured wi my ain freindship and invitit often to my very table, I tak a haill-hairtit scunner at human nature!

Moreover, the highly significant (for Jamie himself) difference between the Scottish Kirk and the English Church *and* a shrewd impression of Her Majesty o England as a politician emerge here in Jamie's sermon to the English Ambassador:

> The Protestant Kirk! It's a Presbyterian Kirk! They winna acknowledge their Sovereign as their speeritual heid! They elect men o their ain to tak the place o my bishops in the Three Estates! I woner what the Queen yer mistress wad dae, if the preachers o her ain Kirk in England denied her authority! Wad she show nae ill-will? I ken she wad, for by God, there's nae sovereign in Christendom hauf sae shair o Divine Richt as Her Majesty o England.

Sir Robert is able to weather the storm, however, for he has 'the best caird in the pack', as Maitland observes: he plays on Jamie's hopes of the English succession.

Jamie, left alone with his Chancellor at the end of the play, reveals his satisfaction in the coming accomplishment of all his ambitions and a sense of destiny that has its undoubted dramatic power: 'Bothwell on the scaffold, the Papists houndit doun, the Kirk in my pooer . . . and then, in the end, the dream o my life come true.' As a reaction to Jamie's high-flown outburst, the comic spirit reasserts itself near the end. Maitland remarks drily: 'But the auld bitch isna deid yet'; and the King ripostes: 'Jock, here's to the day. May the mowdies sune tickle her taes.'

The Flooers o Edinburgh, presented in the 1954-5 and 1957-8 seasons at the Gateway, has qualities of comic and linguistic power with underlying serious social criticism that puts it on a level with *Jamie the Saxt*. It is an appropriate play to deal with in a volume such as this, for it shows in dramatic action the forces in eighteenth-century Scotland that were making for the demise of Lowland Scots as a socially acceptable language. Set in the period following the Forty-five Jacobite Rising, it reflects the social changes in Scottish society brought about by the events of 1603, 1707, 1715 and 1745. Lady Athelstane, Girzie Carmichael, daughter of a man killed at Culloden, remains steadfastly Scots, still hoping for the return of the forfeited estate of Craigengelt; Sir Charles Gilchrist, Lord Stanebyres, father of the arch-angliciser of the play young Charlie, also remains Scottish in attitude and speech, as does young Kate, Girzie's niece, who is in sharp contrast to her at times reluctant wooer, young Charlie. In Act One we eventually meet three other anglicisers—Scots depressed about their Scottish speech and painfully conscious of their 'uncivilised' background. The Rev. Daniel Dowie has had some success with his long poem in English 'The Tomb'; but, although gratified to hear praise of it from fellow Scots, he is appalled to hear of his mistake in rhyming 'breast' with 'feast'. John Douglas of Baldernock, a member of the Faculty of Advocates, confesses that he is worried about *his* speech: 'doun Sooth I'm no intelligible.' The English 'Hoose o Lords lauched' in his face:

> The English Hoose o Lords is oor Supreme Coort nou, sae we'll hae to talk like Englishmen or gie up pleadin.

The third Scot depressed about his accent and speech is another minister, the Rev. Sandy Lindsay; but he is a Moderate and therefore disapproved of by the Rev. Dr Dowie. He it is who proposes that they should 'tak lessons frae Sheridan the actor'. Ironically, however, it is an Englishman who attempts to redress the balance against Scots. Captain Sidney Simkin, who, aware of the 'gardy-loo' problems and surprised that 'Scotch gentlemen of estate . . . do not . . . spread it (gardy-loo ordure) on their fields' to produce 'excellent crops', admires Scottish dancing, Scottish lassies, and—Scottish speech.

The Second Act is remarkable for the picture it presents of the contrasting speech of father and son—Scots and English, the political graft of the day—the cost of a seat in parliament, and the contempt of a young Scot on the make for traditional methods of farming. The dominating personality of this act, however, turns out to be a Nabob back from India who is just as ambitious politically as young Charles Stanebyres but much more practical. From his conversation with Lady Athelstane we learn that his real name is Auchterleckie and that his 'faither was meenister o Craigengelt at ae time'. The Nabob's conversation with Sidney Simkin builds up to a climax that has strong dramatic irony within its comedy. Telling of his 'twenty-twa' years in East India the Nabob startles the English captain by telling of the 'wide interests and great culture' of some of the Indian princes, their appreciation of music, art, and literature, and their knowledge of Persian and Sanskrit. In a brief sentence in answer to Simkin's unasked question why he himself 'hasna taen the bother to learn to speak English', the Nabob sums up an important theme of the play—the affectation of the Anglo-Scot:

> Weill, Captain, I hae mair sense nor waste my time. Did ye no hear the young birkie we had in here the nou? Whan a Scotsman tries to speak English it's past tholin.

The Nabob has his political philosophy too: he is against the idea of making India a British dependency, and thinks it should be governed by 'its ain princes'. So, in order to propagate his political ideas, he has come home 'to staun for paurliament'. He has come well equipped: he has 'kists fu o gowd' to buy the burghs of Lanerick by bribing 'ilka provost, bailie, deacon and cooncillor'.

The final act (III) demonstrates the tidy structure of the play. In turn each of the Scots who have been learning the English and anglicising themselves returns to report progress or lack of it. Baldernock has to admit to Lady Athelstane he has 'dune wi the English'. Mockingly, Girzie sums up his vain efforts:

> Efter yammerin and yatterin for months in front o a gless? Efter learnin aa yon lists of Scotticisms? Efter peyin Sheridan aa that siller?

Sandy Lindsay turns up now able to speak English but telling of the dangers to Scotchmen in London:

> . . . it is hardly safe for a Scotchman to appear on the streets, unless, of course, he either remains silent or speaks good English.

Not meaning to, Sandy 'clypes' on Dr Dowie who next appears, speaking a ponderous English under a broad Scottish accent but frequently throwing it off to reveal his pithy Scots. A quarrel flares up between these two, in the course of which Sandy not only accounts for the 'scart' on his cheek—he was hurt in a scuffle in a London street—but reveals that Dr Dowie 'gaed to the theatre', which, as a good Presbyterian, he should not have done. Dowie lingers long enough after Sandy's departure to hear Sidney Simkin, the Englishman, praise Scottish songs, and Girzie remind him that Allan Ramsay wrote in Scots. This is one of the most significant passages of dialogue in the play. Dowie, as a loyal Anglo-Scot, assures Sidney: 'Oor ain dialect is aa richt for a bit sentimental sang, but for the higher purposes of literature it is inadequate', but, as he goes on to stress that Scottish writers—Home, Tamson, Baird, Blacklock, Beattie—'aa write English nou', Lady Athelstane chips in to say pointedly (presumably less than a decade before Burns's birth): 'Mebbe someane else'll write Scots yet.'

Meanwhile Girzie's brother, home after so many years in foreign wars, turns out to have been transformed by English army experience, now regarding the French as his natural foes rather than as his allies. His arrogance almost drives Jock out of Lady Athelstane's service. Lady Athelstane, disillusioned about her brother, and Kate, disillusioned about Simkin (who has admitted he is a married man) turn to their old admirers. Kate persuades Charles to propose in Scots—'Will ye mairry me?'; but she spoils it by herself accepting in artificial (and faulty) English—'Yes, Charles, I shall.' At the end of the play Jock, as the indispensable manservant, has the last word on the Stanebyres-Lady Girzie match:

> Weill, my lord, she's a gey kittle craitur, but if ye eir fin her mair nor ye can haunle, juist come to me.

The play glances at an old Scotland fast disappearing, so that the speech by Lady Athelstane that leads up to Stanebyres' proposal has a strong thematic relevance:

> Ye're a left-ower frae the auld Scotland I belang to mysel. We'll need ane anither in oor auld age, Stanebyres, to keep oorsells in coontenance.

It could indeed be said that in the eighteenth century Lowland Scots lost its
confidence and ceased to be socially acceptable in educated circles; and, as the
play makes clear, many Scots then, as now, were prepared to accept that
Scotland had become a province and that London was now the centre of the
whole island. Yet a revival of the Lowland Scots tongue in literature came in
the second half of the eighteenth century and another in the mid twentieth. So
there we have the paradox of *The Flooers o Edinburgh*: Robert McLellan in the
mid twentieth century writing a play about the demise of Lowland Scots in the
eighteenth century, and using the linguistic medium that seemed then to be
dying.

Robert Kemp[7] *Let Wives Tak Tent   The Laird o Grippy*

Robert Kemp's 'free translation into Scots' of Molière's *L'école des
femmes—Let Wives Tak Tent*—was first produced in 1948, when it ran at both
the Gateway in Edinburgh and the Citizens' in Glasgow, with Duncan Macrae
as Oliphant. It was again performed at the Gateway in the 1961-2 season with
first Duncan Macrae and then Walter Carr in that part. The Scottish Theatre
Company revived it in their opening season in Spring 1981, with Rikki Fulton
in the leading part.

In the First Act we see something of Kemp's method: he keeps closely to the
Molière original in scenes and actions, but transforms the French setting and
atmosphere into Scots in idiom, allusion and background. A good example
occurs in the first scene where the middle-aged Arnolphe is discussing with
Chrysalde plans for marrying his ward Agnès. To Chrysalde's doubts about the
wisdom of marrying a stupid woman, Arnolphe replies with allusions to
Rabelais' legendary characters Pantagruel and Panurge:

> A ce bel argument, à ce discours profond,
> Ce que Pantagruel à Panurge répond:
> Pressez-moi de me joindre à femme autre que sotte,
> Prêchez, patrocinez jusqu'à la Pentecôte;
> Vous serez ébahi, quand vous serez au bout,
> Que vous ne m'aurez rien persuadé du tout.

In his version, Robert Kemp draws on the traditions about the wise Aberdeenshire fool Jamie Fleeman who served the Laird o Udny; and so he makes
Oliphant (Arnolphe) reply to his sceptical friend Gilchrist (Chrysalde): 'to this
learned argument, to this weighty sermon, I reply as Jamie Fleeman did to the
Laird o Udny, "Prig me to wed a wife that's no a fule, and though you preach
and plead till Whitsunday, you'll be dumfounert to see that you've no moved
me an inch!"'

The climax to the First Act comes in the fourth scene where Walter the lover
(Horace in Molière) reveals to Oliphant as a friend, not knowing he is the Laird,

that he is in love with Agnes and that Agnes returns his love. The comedy of
the recognition, the dawning on Oliphant that Walter is wooing Agnes behind
his back, is broader in Scots than in French. Molière's 'Et l'on m'en a parlé
comme d'un ridicule' becomes in the more colloquial and harsher Scots: 'They
speak o him as though he was a donnart sumph'; and later the general French
term 'fou' is translated by the special Scots term 'gype'.

Act Two Scene Five of the play is one of the most celebrated scenes in
Molière, for the comedy and pathos both in its simple straightforward dialogue
and in its more complicated narrative dialogue; and wisely Robert Kemp keeps
close to the Molière text here. Oliphant asks: 'Weel, what news hae ye?'; and
Agnes replies: 'The wee cat's deid.' Oliphant comments: 'A pity . . . but . . .
we're aa mortal.' The pathos of love and the comedy of situation come together
in a passage of dialogue where Agnes with great naïveté (partly assumed?)
describes the visits she has had from her young lover. The dramatist plays on
the idea of the man being wounded by love for the girl and goes further than
Molière in exploiting the idea for comic purposes:

> AGNES   . . . Dumfounert I said, 'Me? I hae woundit somebody?' 'Aye, yestreen
> frae the balcony.' 'Waes me', said I, 'what could hae been the cause o that? Did
> I let something faa on him without kennan?'
> OLIPHANT (*aside*)   Wad to God it had been a causey!

Act Three Scene Two consists of a long speech by Oliphant and readings by
Agnes from a book called 'The Rules o Wedlock'—at first sight not very
promising material dramatically. In Molière's hands, and in the hands of Kemp
following him closely, however, this material is skilfully exploited for satirical
and comic purposes. The French brings out the satire on the bullying male
tersely and drily; the Scots brings it out rather more resonantly and heartily: 'Le
mariage, Agnès, n'est pas un badinage' becomes 'Mairrage, my dear Agnes, is
no lauchan maitter'; and there is a fascinating glimpse of the two languages
coming together through Scots borrowing from French: 'A d'austères devoirs le
rang de femme engage' translates into 'The position o wife cairries wi it certain
dreich devoirs'. The satire resides in the frankly stated case for male chau-
vinism: no rhetoric from Women's Lib can equal the effect in the lines:

> Bien qu'on soit deux moitiés de la société,
> Ces deux moitiés pourtant n'ont point d'égalité:

which is transformed with the directness of Scots into: 'They may be the twa
halfs o creation, but aa the same they're no to be thocht o as equal.'

It is a characteristic of this kind of comedy to follow the long-winded
speeches or moralising with drama. This is illustrated in the Third Act with the
unfolding of the intrigue concerning the love-letter that is dropped with the
chuckiestane from Agnes's window. The long speech of narration unbroken in
the French original Kemp breaks up with three asides by Oliphant: 'What's he
bletheran aboot?', 'Perdition, damnation, abomination', 'I'll drap doun in a

dwam'. The letter from Agnes to Walter is read in all its apparent simplicity and feeling; and an irresistible comic zest arises from the contrast between Oliphant's restrained fury and the exaggerated idealistic love of the young couple as revealed by Agnes's letter and Walter's rapturous comments. Again we note the interpolated asides in the Scots version: 'The sly limmer', 'The double Jezebel'. It is worth noting here again as a feature of Kemp's translation his exploitation of the Scots borrowings from French: 'Did ye e'er see onything mair doucely expressed?' ('Avez-vous jamais vu d'expression de plus douce?')

At the opening of the Fourth Act Oliphant's soliloquy for a time retains for him the sympathy of the audience: 'I was sair fashed, provokit, desperate against her . . . yet never did I see her sae bonnie.' By the end of the speech, however, Oliphant's scorn and vindictiveness have dissipated the sympathy; and so the audience is ready for the comedy-of-errors situation in which the Lawyer, all set to draw up terms for the marriage settlement, answers in legal form the questions and thoughts in Oliphant's continuing soliloquy. The contrast between the intense self-questioning of Oliphant and the practical legal solutions offered by the Lawyer points the comedy here:

OLIPHANT   I love her, and that's at the ruit o aa my care.
LAWYER   If that's the wey o't ye may gie her mair favourable treatment.

The scene in which Gilchrist tries to reason with Oliphant and persuade him to take less extreme measures with Agnes (Act IV Scene 7 in Kemp, Act IV Scene 8 in Molière) is a fair test of how far Scots can be used in prose of rational argument. The language is closer to English, yet the Scots flavour is still there:

GILCHRIST   To conduct oursels weel in difficulties o that kind, as in aathing else, we maunna flee to extremes. Dinna follow the example o sic folk, a thoct *owre* guid-natured, as tak a pride in thae ongauns. . . .

Dramatically, what emerges here is the contrast between the rational Gilchrist and the emotional Oliphant; linguistically, although there are obvious difficulties of vocabulary in setting Scots in abstract argument, Kemp's work here indicates the possibilities and illustrates the adaptability of the language:

GILCHRIST   . . . I wad far rather be what you ken than see mysel weddit to ane o thae guid wives whase tantrums mak quarrels out o naething, these dragons o virtue, chaste she-devils, aye preenan themsels on their meikle wisdom. . . .
Ech sirs, ye maunna sweir, for fear o bein perjured.

The stage direction at the end of Act Four links with the beginning of Act Five: Walter in attempting to climb to Agnes's window is knocked off the ladder and beaten. Oliphant sees all this and is appalled at the violence done to Walter. Then Agnes comes up to rescue her lover and together they 'run off up the Canongate'. There is nothing corresponding to Kemp's detailed stage direction in Molière; but Arnolphe's opening speech in the Fifth Act of the original makes plain what has happened; and the old man's concern for the

young man's safety is obvious in both versions: 'L'ordre était de le battre, et
non de l'assommer'—'I telt ye to gie him a lickin, nae to caa the life oot o
him.' Perhaps the Scots is more vehement.

Robert Kemp's version often resorts to that device already referred to of
breaking up a long speech with asides that indicate rueful comic reactions to
unfolding developments of deception—as here again in Act Five Scene Two:
'Oh, the sleekit jaud', 'Oh, has she joukit me yet?' Irony too is a favourite
device: Walter asks 'You'll really undertak this lichtsome duty for me?' and
Oliphant replies '. . . I'm fair cairrit awa at this chance o servin ye—leeze me
on the Providence that sends me it' (an interesting classical Scots translation of
'Je rends grâces au ciel de ce qu'il me l'envoie'). In all this and in the stage
direction 'He hides his neb in his cloak' (Molière: 'Il s'enveloppe le nez de son
manteau') there is also open burlesque on cloak-and-dagger conventions.

In the last scene, by the careful working out of the artificial, complicated
plot, Agnes proves to be both the bride chosen for Walter by his father and his
own true love. The tale of the secret wedding, the bairn put out to nurse in the
country, and the flight of the father from his native land: these are all part of
the romantic machinery of the plot of classical comedy, as indeed are the final
recognition of the lovers as destined for each other and the exit of Arnolphe/
Oliphant 'tout transporté'—'cairried awa'. The interest for us lies in the way
Lowland Scots can cope with this kind of drama. In the original French the
exiled father is depicted as having achieved the success abroad denied him in
France. None of the universal truth behind this is lost in changing the setting to
Scotland: one could even say that it is if anything made more vivid. There is a
certain artificiality about the Scots used in the formal conclusion to the play:
'By the douce bond o a mutual love, I hae gien my love to this dear lass'; but in
rendering the last two lines of Molière:

> Payer à notre ami ces soins officieux,
> Et rendre grâce au ciel, qui fait tout pour le mieux—

Robert Kemp returns to something of the special idiom of Scots, and in doing
so, fills in the significance of the original: '. . . to pay back our friend for his
eident cares, and to gie thanks to Providence that aye warks for the best.' The
Scots version retains all the dramatic power of the original: the fascination lies
in the skill with which Robert Kemp replaces a tight concise French with a Scots
mostly idiomatic and lively, relapsing occasionally into the artificial and the
pastiche—and even then perhaps justified in so doing by the context.

The Laird o Grippy, an adaptation into Scots of Molière's *L'avare*, was given
its first performance at the Gateway Theatre in 1955, with John Laurie as the
Laird. At the Citizens', Glasgow, in the same year Andrew Keir played the
leading part. On Tuesday, 27 March 1979, the BBC broadcast a TV version
which they called *The Miser*, and in which the word 'tocher' was changed to
'dowry'. Rikki Fulton played the Laird.

In the opening love scene of the play between Elspeth (Elise in Molière) and Hector (Valère) the romantic background of lover's bravery and self-sacrifice is appropriately conveyed in Robert Kemp's traditional Scots. Elspeth recalls how they first met and indicates the situation of love-intrigue: '. . . how ye loupit in the gurly sea to save my life at the risk o your ain, and syne swam wi me to the shore. . . . For my sake . . . ye've chosen to bide here in Embro and . . . taen the place o steward wi my faither.' In realistic style Hector describes the two abiding weaknesses of Elspeth's father, the central figure of the play: 'The miserliness o the Laird o Grippy gangs clean owre the score'; and, on the subject of his love of flattery: '. . . there's nae whigmaleerie sae daft that he winna swallow it, if ye dish it up wi a kitchie o praise.' The scene between Elspeth and her foppish self-centred brother Nigel (Cléante in Molière) introduces the second love affair, that between Nigel and his Mirren, and leads directly into the two main complications of the play—Nigel's need for money (for he is extravagant and Mirren is as 'puir as a kirk moose') and the Laird's desire to marry Mirren himself. But more important than these is Grippy's avarice, his love of gold; and the first intensification comes in the scene where Grippy by himself expresses his worry about the safety of his buried treasure: 'My certes, it's a gey sair trauchle when a man has to hide about his house a muckle lump o siller.' When the family group come together, the idiomatic Scots is heard to great effect, first when Grippy tells his son how he has been censuring Elspeth: 'I was gien your sister her kail through the reek yestreen . . .', but especially when he attacks Nigel's finery and style: '. . . I'm fair scunnert at your ongauns. Ye shairly fancy yoursel the Duke o Buccleugh' (an interesting rendering of 'vous donnez furieusement dans le marquis'). The subject of marriage introduced by Nigel is taken up smartly by the Laird, and leads to the celebrated passage in which Nigel is encouraged to paint an attractive picture of his love Mirren Clatterinshaws at his father's prompting and then is told Grippy himself is to marry her. The portrait of the father as tyrant is further developed when Grippy announces he intends Elspeth to marry Maister Cramond—'. . . a canny man, a man o mense and sense, . . . no a day mair than fifty'. When Hector disguised as the steward enters, there develops an intriguing classical comic situation: appointed judge in the dispute between father and daughter, the true lover in disguise has to flatter and temporise with the old man; and it is in this sequence where Grippy is stressing the most attractive feature—for him—of the proposed marriage between Elspeth and Cramond that the word 'tocher' (that gave the BBC such a problem in 1979) is repeated to great rhythmic and comic effect. To Hector's temporising the Laird repeats again and again—'Withoot a tocher' (more staccato in the French— 'sans dot'). This passage that illustrates so vividly Grippy's greed and tyranny ends abruptly when the Laird hears a dog barking in the distance; and here again the use of a special Scots word adds the comic touch: 'Was yon a dog I heard howfan?'

The Second Act builds up to a first recognition scene—the confrontation between son as young borrower and father as lender taking extortionate interest. In the leading up to this climax there are some noteworthy Scots renderings of the Molière text: 'le plus malgracieux des hommes' becomes 'a carnaptious auld deil' (a fair description of Grippy!); and the terse but neutral phrase 'L'affaire ne se fera point?' becomes more pictorially vivid in Scots: 'Then we're up against a stane wa?' In the actual confrontation, a good-going slanging match sets in, again enriched by colourful Scots lexical items:

> GRIPPY   Dae ye no think shame at your skulduggery that has pushed ye into this
> dreadful wastrie?
> NIGEL   Dae ye no blush to dishonour your birth by jukery-pokery o this kind?

In the Third Act Mistress Frizzell's dialogue with Mirren forms a prologue to the girl's meeting with old Grippy: her feelings are summed up at this point:

> Aye, I can see the Laird o Grippy's no the death a woman wad choose for hersel. By your peely-wally looks I doubt the thocht o that young birkie ye tellt me o has come back. . . .

The high point of the act—the appearance of Grippy in his specs before Mirren—has something of the comic force of Malvolio's appearance before Olivia; and his attempts at gallantry strike the exaggerated note of farce:

> Dinna tak umbrage, my doo, if I come afore ye wi my glesses on my neb . . . but it's wi glesses that we observe the heavenly bodies, and I'se maintain and uphaud that you're a heavenly body, the heavenliest body in aa the clanjamphrey o heavenly bodies.

After the dialogue of *double entendre* in which Mirren befools and beguiles Grippy in Nigel's presence, Nigel takes over from his father as wooer, as if helping his suit; and the climax of comic action is reached when Nigel takes the diamond ring off Grippy's fingers and uses the moment of confusion to persuade Mirren to accept it:

> Miss Mirren, my father's in a rage wi me, and it's aa your wyte. . . . Ye'll mak him tak the apoplexy. For God's sake, madame, dinna conter him ony mair.

In the Fourth Act the comedy of conflict and cross purposes that develops between father and son is appropriately given a local Scottish setting: the father tells the son: 'I have settled on a decent widow woman at Dalkeith, and I'll yoke ye tae her.' The end of the act is marked by the stealing of Grippy's box: Bodkin tells Nigel he has 'nabbit the treasure-kist'; and the final soliloquy presents the pathetic figure of Grippy bemoaning its loss. From memories of seeing the play in French and in Scots I feel here a strong note of pathos: sympathy focuses on the old man appealing to his imaginary audience: 'De grâce, si l'on sait des nouvelles de mon voleur, je supplie que l'on m'en dise' which is not quite matched by the thin Scots: '. . . if ye've ony information that'll lead to his arrest, I plead wi ye to tell me.' But more graphic touches follow in the Scots version: 'He's joukit in amang aa the fowk. They're aa peeran at me and beginnan to lauch.'

The fantastic story that unravels in the Fifth Act is of the stuff of romance shaped by the conventions of classical comedy. One is reminded of *The Comedy of Errors*, where Shakespeare, following Plautus, places the setting in the Eastern Mediterranean—Syracuse, Epidamnum, Corinth—and where old Egeon turns out to be the father of the separated twins. In Molière the tale of family separation through shipwreck is placed in and between Naples and Genoa; and the old man Anselme turns out to be the great 'dom Thomas d'Alburcy'. In Kemp the shipwreck is placed on the North Sea coast at St Abb's south of the Firth of Forth; and the old man Cramond turns out to be the MacRory o MacRory. In accordance with classical pattern, recognition scenes shape the ending of the play. The first comes when Mirren and Hector are revealed to be sister and brother separated by the wreck but now miraculously re-united:

HECTOR   . . . The son and an auld servant were rescued by a ship frae Leith. The
   Captain . . . brocht me up as his ain. For lang I thocht my faither deid in
   France. . . .
MIRREN   . . . Hector, I can finish your story! By what you've said I see that you're my
   ain brither. . . .
HECTOR   You, my sister!

The second recognition comes when Cramond reveals his true identity:

MIRREN   . . . It was mony a year afore my mither . . . could come back to Auld
   Reekie, whaur it was gien out that the MacRory was deid.
CRAMOND   Oh, heaven . . . the age o miracles is no at an end! Come to my airms,
   my twa bairns. Come and greet your ain faither! . . . I am the MacRory o
   MacRory! For saxteen years I have lived in France, thinkan my wife and bairns
   were at the bottom o the cauld North Sea.

Thus old-world Scots and familiar Scottish settings are tailored to fit the traditional material out of which great dramatists have fashioned their plays.

At the end of the play the focus concentrates on the old man as miser, gloating over the return of his 'sax thousand guineas'. Molière's laconic concluding line—'Et moi, voir ma chère cassette'—Robert Kemp expands into a final flourish of avarice: 'And me, I'll see my beloved, my darling strong-box again! My treasure, my guineas, my hert's delight!'

Robert Kemp was the author of a number of other successful plays that graced the Scottish stage in the mid-century; but for me the two adaptations from Molière[8] are of prime importance linguistically, for in them he uses a rich and dynamic Scots: traditional, at times strongly literary, but always firmly based on the rhythms of the spoken language, and vividly illustrating the links between French and the Lowland tongue. Frequently during performances and

study of the texts I have heard echoes from the speech of my Fife mother and
grandparents to whom Scots was the natural mother-tongue.

Alexander Reid[9] *The Lass wi the Muckle Mou   The Warld's Wonder*

Alexander Reid's 'Scots Comedy', *The Lass wi the Muckle Mou*, was first performed by the East Lothian Repertory Company at Dunbar, 24 October 1950,
and by the Glasgow Citizens' Theatre at the Gaiety Theatre, Ayr, 20 November
of the same year. It is based on two Border themes, the one from the reiving
history of the Murray and Scott families and the other from the legendary story
of Thomas of Ercildoune, Thomas the Rhymer, who flourished circa 1220–97.
The first tells the story of the love of Meg Murray, bonnie enough save for a big
mouth, for Willie Scott who was made prisoner and sentenced to be hanged for
raiding the Murrays' castle at Elibank. The second theme is concerned with the
relationship between the semi-legendary figure Thomas Learmont and the
Queen of Elfland, who spirited him away but released him after seven years to
re-visit the earth.

The play opens with a prologue in a fairy or supernatural frame. Thomas has
been accompanied not merely to the Borders but to the borderland between
Elfland and the real world by the Lady in Green, the Queen of Elfland herself.
Alexander Reid here strikes an opening poetic note that contrasts the mystery of
Elfland with the reality of the earth in all its variety of smells, and that also
sounds the reiving motif:

> THE LADY IN GREEN   . . . Thomas . . . I'll come nae further wi ye. . . . There's a
> snell wind blaws aboot thae crossways o the warlds that's ill tae thole.
> THOMAS   . . . I'd forgot what a grand smell the earth had to it. . . . There's grass
> in't, and coos, and middenstink, and peat reek. . . .
> THE LADY IN GREEN   There's kirkyaird moul, Thomas. . . . And the soor stink o the
> reivers' corpses on the Gallow Hill. . . .

There is a neat transition from this prologue—with its hint that Thomas may
find 'the makkins o a story here at the Murrays''—to the actual Ballad of True
Thomas which is acted out as a farewell flashback by the Queen and Thomas.

In the second scene we are firmly back on earth—in the Hall of Elibank
Castle where the Laird Sir Gideon Murray is sitting nursing a cold with his feet
in a tub. The language here admirably matches the realism of the situation.
This Mid Scots of Alexander Reid's is no literary pastiche: it has the genuine
'sough' appropriate to a Scottish domestic scene:

> SIR G.   Grizel, Grizel!
> GRIZEL   Noo, what's the maitter wi ye?
> SIR G.   There's mair heat in a deid puddock than in this watter! Ye micht pit a drap
> mair in, Grizel.

GRIZEL   Could ye no help yersel, Gideon? Ye ken I'm busy.
SIR G.   D'ye want me tae get my daith walkin aboot on a stane flair in my bare feet?

Meg herself is unobtrusively introduced as a sympathetic daughter 'whose face is spoiled by an even larger mouth than her mother's'. The focus of the drama however remains on the figure of Sir Gideon, sick and querulous, obsessed with the premonition that he is about to die. When Wattie enters to tell of the reappearance as if from the dead of Thomas the Rhymer after seven years' absence, legend and realism are fused together in a passage of dialogue that illustrates the author's sense of comedy and the colloquial ease with which he uses Scots:

WATTIE   Ay, Thomas. Dae ye no mind? Ye were drooned seeven years syne. . . .
THOMAS   . . . They didna find me, did they?
SIR G.   Na, that's true eneuch. . . . Gin ye're no deid, whaur hae ye been aw this time?
THOMAS   I've been . . . abroad, Sir Gideon. In foreign pairts.
SIR G.   England?
THOMAS   Na, no just as foreign as that. As a maitter o fact, I've been in Elfland.

The legendary figure of Thomas turns out to be, if anything, just too involved in the material things of life: he's 'ragin wi hunger' and he wonders why Meg is 'no wed yet' at twenty-two. This gives the playwright a chance to highlight the theme, and this he does with a sure sense of dramatic timing:

SIR G.   It's her mou, Thomas. I dinna ken whether ye noticed, but her mou's on the muckle side.

The nostalgia for the brave days of reiving and fighting (with references to 'the wild rose bloomin', 'the taste tae a bannock', 'the licht on the face o a quean') is set alongside the reality of present-day life at its most dreich. This mediaeval 'ubi sunt' lament for things past is part of the scheme of the play to emphasise that since Thomas has been away life has become dull and insipid— 'nae world for a poet'. It is at this point that romance re-asserts itself. When Drucken Rab enters with the exciting news that the Scotts are planning a raid on the Murrays, the first for eight years, Sir Gideon is transformed from invalid to warrior, galvanised by the prospect of a fight with the Scotts, and impatient at Meg's clumsy attempt to help him buckle on his sword: 'No that side, Meg. Guid God! D'ye no ken hoo tae belt on a sword yet?'

At the beginning of Act Two, as offstage noises represent the fight between the Murrays and the Scotts, Thomas is inspired to begin his ballad which he does in true conventional style:

> It fell aboot the Lammas tide
> When the gress grows lang and lank.
> The Harden Scotts they swore an oath
> That they'd reive Elibank.

It all works according to traditional pattern—the triumph of the Murrays and the taking of a prisoner; but Willie Scott's exit speech before he is taken to the dungeon has a fine Scots rhetoric and realism about it:

> Ye're gey haigh and flauchtersome and ye think ye can pit me doon, but ye can tak my word for it that gin I wasna sae shoogly on ma legs and peely-wally in the airms I would tak on the hale clanjamphrey o ye here and noo. . . .

The dungeon scene exploits the classic eavesdropping scene of comedy. Meg, passing herself off as a serving lassie, comes in with food and drink for Willie, conducting a kind of love scene by proxy. She is followed by Thomas who tries to persuade Willie to go through with the hanging. First Meg has to go into hiding in the straw to avoid Thomas, then Thomas to avoid Gideon. The unfolding intrigue brings out the contrast between the shifty meanness of the Laird and the subtlety and generosity of his lady. Grizel discusses the marriage plan from Meg's viewpoint as if not all that attractive to her; and in a masterly off-hand exit speech, she baits the hook with a more promising tocher than her husband had offered: 'The west meadow forsooth! She'll hae the east meadow, Willie. Ay, and the Greenacre grund ayont the knowe alang wi it.' The twist in the comedy of situation comes at the end, as Thomas emerges from the straw and struggles to drag out the 'lassie':

THOMAS   By auld Blin Harry, it's Meg Murray!

The final scene is a stock one depicting preparations for a public hanging that does not take place. A rise to drama comes with Willie's entry and news that he has decided 'tae mairry Meg', provided she brings 'a guid tocher'. This again proves the point at which negotiations break down, and the seesaw of the comedy of bargaining is resumed. Gideon finally refuses Willie's mounting demands: 'Stop, I've heard eneuch. Wattie, get up there and pit the rope aboot him.' Now comes the spectacular comic-dramatic threat of a double hanging: Meg appears alongside Willie on the parapet with a rope round her neck attached to a turret above; and it is against this background that the bargaining for a guid tocher builds up to its climax:

MEG   Dae we get the wee black bull or dae we loup?
SIR G.   Ye wadna daur.
MEG   I'm a desperate wumman, faither. Gin I canna live wi Willie, I'll no live athoot him.

This climax is swiftly followed by another—the arrival of the Scotts to rescue Willie. Eventually Meg does loup—into the arms of Willie; and a mock farewell is smartly annulled by Willie's insistence on the match: the wedding instead of the hanging.

The final scene slides back into its Queen of Elfland frame: Thomas declares himself 'dune wi ballads' and 'aff tae Elfland'. After the moment of doubt and the touch of mockery on the theme of the unsuccessful ballad, these oddly assorted legendary lovers go off, fairy and mortal, with a final stressing of the leitmotiv—'This is nae warld for a poet.'

The Warld's Wonder was presented at the Gateway in the 1958–9 season; but it had its premiere a few years earlier by the Glasgow Citizens' at the Royal Princess's Theatre, Glasgow, on 11 May 1953. It has as its primary theme the love of a shepherd laddie for his lass—Jock for his Jeannie, a love threatened by a forced marriage to the old Laird of Clartydykes. In this plot there are overtones of Molière situations; but the idea of a young woman feigning death to avoid an unwanted marriage, and, indeed, the opening situation itself—lover below his mistress's window—these are clearly of the prototype Romeo and Juliet plot going back to the conventions of classical drama. The secondary but by no means subsidiary theme—it is more of an enveloping theme—is that of the all-puissant Michael Scott, the Scottish 'wondrous wizard' who flourished between 1175 and 1230. He was famous as an astrologer, as a translator of Aristotle from Arabic versions, and as a magician: Dante refers to him in the *Inferno*. More important for this present study is his place in Border folklore. In *The Lay of the Last Minstrel*, II. xiii, the Monk tells of the wonders of the Wizard and can remember his '. . . words that cleft Eildon hills in three, And bridled the Tweed with a curb of stone'.

In the opening nocturnal scene ('Twal o the clock and gey nippy for Merch'), in which the idyllic love between Jock and Jeannie is set alongside the scheming of the Provost and his wife Lizzie planning to marry Jeannie to the old Laird, the Scots varies in style from the simple prose of the lovers—'Wha sin the warld began ever lou'd like us, Jock?'—to the more formal style in the blank verse of the Provost:

> I've telt ye afore, Jock . . .
> Gin ye set as much as a fit in the bounds o Dubbity
> Twixt noo and the hoor I've fixed for oor Jeannie's weddin
> I'll hae ye jiled for breechin the peace. . . .

Blank verse is used also to heighten the mystic or supernatural note. The Provost, in warning Jeannie she might become moonstruck, gives her the idea for her masquerade, and anticipates the flight at the end of the play:

> Aye, munestruck or waur—bespelled by some witch or warlock
> Besoming eastwards for the Law o Berwick.

The second theme and the dominating figure of the play are introduced in the second scene, in which, after the excited crowd have moved off to 'see the warlock', the Wizard himself and Lazarus the young man of inquiring mind are left alone to discuss the masquerading of the Faus Scott. Later, from the Bailie's proclamation, we learn of Jeannie's masquerade offstage: the Provost's dochter has been bespelled:

> Cast by enchauntment in a waukin dwam
> On her weddin morn.

The scene in which the two Scotts vie with each other in tricks of magic and cursing is essentially theatrical in tone; but it is rich and resonant in linguistic effects. For example, it uses a kind of intoned lyricism to accompany the magical changes of season:

> By a reid rose bud and a white rose flouerin!
> By twa fond lovers in a hedge-neuk coo'erin!

And in the cursing sequence it brings Latin and Scots into comic juxtaposition. An additional touch of comedy comes from the contrast of Scottish accents, the True Scott using the genuine one, the Faus Scott putting on Kelvinside: 'Kaindly alloo me tae choose ma ain weapons. . . .'

The heart of the play lies in the two scenes of the second act. Scott is seen at work as a magician in a room of the Provost's house where the important prop is the magic mirror in the back wall used for enacting supernatural episodes conjured up by the Wizard. In his opening dialogue with his apprentice he satirises dogmas and dominies: 'The dominie! The dominie! The deil hae the dominie! Aw the dominie kens is what the ither dominie telt him!' With the entry of the scheming quartet—Provost, wife, Laird, and Bellman—leading in Jeannie in a dwam, the play opens out and then focuses on two figures—the Wizard stooping over his patient Jeannie on the couch. The combination of Scots and the mumbo-jumbo of magician's jargon gives a resonance to the blank verse here:

> Afore I mak pronouncement on the case
> I mun hae time tae look mair fully intilt,
> Complete her horoscope, and hae a look
> At her basic turba and the centrum naturae. . . .

Jeannie's revelations of the villainy of the Provost develop a satire on small-town corruption; and we notice a mixture here of the literary and the colloquial in the Scots blank verse:

> he and the Bellman-Bailie
> Hae dipped sae deep in the Dubbity Toon kist
> They've scraped the fit clean clear o the tint o siller,
> And noo they're feard, gin I wed wi an honest man,
> The sorry tale of their reivin will come oot.

The play then returns to its central love theme as first Jeannie rhapsodises on Jock, and then Jock, conjured out of the magic mirror and seen tending his sheep on the hill, rhapsodises on Jeannie. The Scots verse here used by Jock is in formal eighteenth-century lyrical style:

> Oh, were I rich as Croesus was,
> Oh, then I'd deck ye fair, lass!
> Wi a silken goon and a gowden chain,
> And pearls tae hing in your hair, lass.

The second scene of Act Two reproduces the tableau of the first: the Provost and his party group round the central figures—Scott presiding at the table, book in hand, and Jeannie lying in bed. In this complicated scene the brisk pace comes from the handling of the chorus figures. Each of the schemers is made to repeat key words such as 'amor' and 'mairrage' and echo bogus phrases such as 'soothe doon the magus' and 'conserve the unity'. Alexander Reid's Scots is put to the test here to demonstrate its versatility in expressing pseudo-medical terms, indicating the melodrama of the deception and planned murder, and finally presenting the broad comedy of the marriage ceremony.

It is a striking feature of the epitasis of the play that the initiative should pass from Michael Scott the Wizard to Jock the Herd. When the Provost attempts to arrest Jock for 'sic crimes agin the common weal' and the plotters are only partially and temporarily immobilised by the Wizard (whose wand is having battery trouble) it is Jock, inspired by the magician, who rises to the occasion and becomes the hero of the hour, having been reminded of his noble ancestry:

> In my blood noo yon Caesar and Alexander,
> The noble Lancelot, King Arthur, the great Achilles,
> Hector and Hannibal and the Hebrew Joshua
> Are aw awauk! They shout in ma inner lug:
> Arise, Sir Jock!

The Finale is set on an old sailing boat 'in the deeps of the sky' in an atmosphere of abstraction, eternity, and space travel, with the focus back on the magician. 'Whauraboots are we noo, Maister?' asks Lazarus; and Michael answers: 'Haufwyes atwixt Fiddler's Green and the Throne o God'. As in the bow of the ship, Jock and Jeannie play an eternal love scene, Lazarus, still the young man of inquiring mind, asks the Wizard the ultimate question: 'Wha are ye?', leading up to the most stimulating speech in the play. Michael, admitting to 'dizzens and dizzens o names', traces the travels of the prototype scholar-wizard all over from Tweeddale as Merlin, to German lands as Faustus, to Bactria as Zoroaster, and to Black Spain where he was burnt by the Holy Inquisition—

> Echt separate times! Or was it nine? Aw weel,
> It maks sma difference. I aye rose again
> Up frae the ashes like the Phoenix bird. I hae been
> Complexioned every colour the skin can turn—
> Black, white, and saffron, broon and heich Indian rid,
> And aw the shades atween, and the combinations;
> Been doctor, barber, alchemist, hermit, friar;
> Transmuted nettles and brewed true-love potions,
> Invented a magic wheel, and a brazen heid
> That answered questions. Practised near aw professions
> Except the law, whilk I could never abide.

At the end Michael takes his most daring step. He changes course, leaving earth for eternity and jettisoning the charts. The Scholar-Wizard is setting off on the ultimate voyage of discovery and experiment:

> I've set a course ayont the last kent stars.
> Gin we win through, we'll burst the bands o space
> And beach the morn upon infinity. . . .

Of the two plays *The Lass* contains the finer and more human portraits and uses the freer and more idiomatic conversational Scots. *The Wonder* is more remarkable for its intellectual and linguistic scope. It is more experimental in its use of language, and is enriched by that exhilarating conclusion. These two plays in their original Scottish versions are unobtainable in print; and, although they have been translated into other languages and often staged abroad, they are now seldom performed by professional companies here. Who amongst publishers and directors of theatre companies will be daring enough to revive them? Is there a Doctor Michael Scott in the house?

CONCLUDING COMMENTARY

These three playwrights, in the plays dealt with, demonstrate in their different ways how far and how effectively Lowland Scots can be used as a linguistic medium for the stage. It is often asserted that we have had no developing Scots prose in recent times; and indeed it is true that generally, although we may think in Scots still, we write in English for most if not all purposes. On the other hand, the great revival of Scottish poetry in Scots in the twentieth century has been rightly acclaimed; and it is widely accepted that Scots is more than ever an effective medium for verse. Is it possible, however, that we have, without being aware of it—rather like Monsieur Jourdain—been developing and using a Scottish prose in our drama of the mid period of the twentieth century?

Robert McLellan in both of the historical comedies I have analysed, Robert Kemp in his adaptations from Molière, and Alexander Reid in most of *The Lass* and in parts of *The Wonder* experiment with a Scots prose in a variety of styles and for different purposes. All three are obviously successful in using the comic colloquial form; but it seems to me they have some success in using it for other purposes too. Robert McLellan shows how it can be used in political and religious argument and debate. Robert Kemp uses it as a medium for translating the works of a seventeenth-century French playwright who is a master in creating dialogue for dramatic situations and comic characterisations, and in expressing satirical comments on society. Alexander Reid shows how it can be exploited in naturalistic domestic situations and in artificial intrigues; and he experiments with it as a vehicle for the supernatural, the fantastical, and the imaginative. All three writers in varying degrees explore the serious as well as the purely comic possibilities of the language.

Apart from all this, however, what can we say about the appeal of Lowland Scots in the theatre? There has never been any doubt about its appeal and tremendous success in the revival of Sir David Lyndsay's *The Three Estates* for the Edinburgh International Festival in the late nineteen-forties—in a version by Robert Kemp. We are rightly concerned, however, about its appeal in more recent years. What of the viability of Lowland Scots in the Scottish theatre of the nineteen-eighties? Opinions will continue to vary on this issue; but I believe it highly significant that when two of the plays dealt with in this survey—Robert Kemp's *Let Wives Tak Tent* and Robert McLellan's *Jamie the Saxt*—were revived by the Scottish Theatre Company as recently as Spring 1981 and Spring 1982 respectively, there was a distinctly discernible stirring of interest in essentially Scottish theatre, and, particularly in the case of the *Jamie the Saxt* production, a scoring of a box-office success. It is also significant that when *The Lass wi the Muckle Mou* was revived fairly recently by a leading Edinburgh amateur company, it again received warm support and acclaim.

It was good to hear recently that the Scottish theatre, the Scottish Arts Council, and Scottish publishing firms have been encouraging the production and publication of new plays by contemporary writers. This is a healthy sign; but, we should remind ourselves, theatre and education cannot be concerned exclusively with the contemporary: earlier classic works should be available in revival and in print. Four out of the six plays here dealt with are unobtainable in print; and all six have been neglected over long periods by the professional theatre in Scotland. Visitors, ordinary Scots folk themselves, students in school and universities, aye and dominies and sic like, would be the better of having a chance to read and hear the Lowland Scots tongue as used by these three—and other—mid century playwrights. After all, in addition to having a flair for expressing the comic, Scots does reflect our different traditions, ethos, way of living and speaking—as well as having a treasure-kist of 'rare lexical items', as our friends from the world of linguistics might say.

NOTES

1 See *The Twelve Seasons of The Edinburgh Gateway Company 1953-1965*, (The St Giles Press, Edinburgh, 1965)

2 See *Doctors Devils Saints and Sinners*, (The Ramsay Head Press, Edinburgh, 1980), my critical study of the Major Plays of Bridie, particularly pp. 140-5.

3 See *Travelling Hopefully* (The Story of Molly Urquhart), Helen Murdoch, (Paul Harris Publishing, Edinburgh, 1981)

4 Pitlochry Festival Theatre under Dr Kenneth Ireland is one of the honourable exceptions. At least one Scottish play is featured on the programme each season. One can only wish that more worthwhile plays from the Scottish classic repertoire could be presented more frequently at this lovely new theatre in the heart of Scotland.

5   If there had been space, I should like to have dealt with other works which illustrate
     the effectiveness of Scots on the stage such as *The Wallace, Voyage Ashore,
     Torwatletie, The Friars of Berwick, Baptie's Lass.*

6   The texts used are those printed in The Scottish Library Edition—*Collected Plays,
     Volume 1, Robert McLellan* (Introduction by Alexander Scott), (John Calder/
     Riverrun Press, 1981).

7   I am greatly indebted to Mrs Kemp, widow of the author, and to her sons Mr
     Arnold Kemp and Mr David Kemp, for their kindness in letting me have access to
     typescript copies of these two plays.

8   My quotations from Molière are from *Oeuvres Complètes,* (Aux Editions du Seuil,
     Paris, 1962).

9   Alexander Reid died on 30 June 1982, as this essay was being completed. As I
     worked on his plays, Alex's personality was vividly in front of me. His death is a
     great loss to us all. I am most grateful to Mrs Reid for letting me have on loan
     typescript copies of the plays.

TEN

Glasgow Speech in Recent Scottish Literature

Edwin Morgan

The acceptable emergence of Glasgow speech, both as an object of linguistic study and as a medium for serious writing, is recent and still has much headway to make, but one can say today with some confidence that the long-ingrained attitudes—linguistic, social, aesthetic—which hindered that emergence have lost the almost automatic respectability they once enjoyed. In the 50-page introduction to the first volume of *The Scottish National Dictionary*, virtually nothing is said about the language of Glasgow. After a brief reference to the 'glottal catch', which the editor notes with some irritation ('not by natural development') has spread to other parts of Scotland, the speech of this large conurbation containing half the population of the country is dismissed in one sentence: 'Owing to the influx of Irish and foreign immigrants in the industrial area near Glasgow the dialect has become hopelessly corrupt.' That was written many years ago, and William Grant's refusal to come to grips with the unsavoury and amorphous phenomenon of Glasgow must seem today to be not only improperly moralistic but strangely incurious. But moralising or sceptical attitudes towards Glasgow dialect evidently take much dislodging. In 1974, in an article quoting favourably from Glaswegian prose by Alan Spence and George Friel, J Derrick McClure makes the more general point that what must in the end limit such writers is 'the impoverished and bastardised Scots spoken in present-day Glasgow'.[1] Strong words! Yet surely all language is, if one wants to use the term, bastardised (and that word, half French and half Greek, is a good example of the process); and it is the rural dialects of Scotland which are impoverished, not the thriving and inventive urban speech of Glasgow. McClure's underlying argument is, however, one that would need careful consideration, since his case is that naturalistic recorders of local speech like Friel and Spence cannot draw upon literary, traditional, non-local forms of Scots such as allow (say) Fionn Mac Colla in his prose to 'exploit the full expressive potential of the Scots language'. Obviously this is a possible view, yet one cannot help thinking that it is not entirely divorced from those pro

195

rural, anti-urban feelings which have found it so hard to accept the fact that whatever 'Scotland' or 'Scottish tradition' is, it must *include* Glasgow, it cannot cast it out or refuse to come to terms with it or to see its 'case'. Even if we accept the arguments put forward for a modern generalised literary Scots, as against a naturalistic locally-based Scots, such a Scots ought to include a significant admixture of Glaswegian forms and idioms if it is to be true to the linguistic realities of the country.

Reluctance to confer status on urban Scots has in the past excused itself mainly on the ground that slang rather than dialect is involved. That this belief will not pass muster, despite the fact that Glasgow like every large city uses much slang, was argued persuasively by Alexandra J L Agutter and Leslie N Cowan in their article on 'Changes in the Vocabulary of Lowland Scots Dialects'.[2] But a dislike or fear of slanginess or uncouthness has undoubtedly been an inhibiting factor on writers as well as educators in the first half of the century. J J Bell, author of *Wee Macgreegor* and many similar couthy and popular books which sold very widely in the Glasgow area (and elsewhere), wrote in his autobiography, *I Remember* (1932), about the two grandmothers he recalled from the 1870s:

> Of fair education, not slipshod in her grammar, she used the vernacular uncompromisingly—and that at a period when a great many Glasgow people were coming to regard the vernacular as 'not very nice'. At the same time, she was down on slang, such as it was in those days . . . Perhaps she was faithful to the old tongue because she had originally come from Paisley. I can remember that her sister used it, but that none of her nephews and nieces did so. She was the only person who made it really familiar to me. My other grandmother might, in a moment of freedom, have uttered the word 'bairns', but she would surely have swooned at hearing the word 'weans' issue from her own lips. Strangely enough, though listening to it daily, I echoed very little of her Lowland Scots; but, more than twenty years later, when attempting the first of a series of Glasgow sketches, the makings ultimately of a certain little book, I looked into my memory and found the old words and phrases I needed. (pp. 74–5)

Bell, in fact, made little distinction between 'Glaswegian' and 'Lowland Scots'; and his fictional dialogue, while liberally sprinkled with Glaswegian features, is an amalgam owing much to the homely humours of late nineteenth-century Kailyard. In his introduction to the New Library Edition of *Wee Macgreegor* (1933) Bell wrote:

> I am well aware that I have been suspected of eavesdropping on tramway cars and elsewhere, and of furtively lurking in close-mouths, and in sundry other places, in order to gain my knowledge, such as it is, of the Glasgow, or Lowland dialect; but the truth is that, just as I have never deliberately 'studied' a fellow-creature, I had never made any effort to 'learn' the speech of the people of the period. While I was familiar with the older men in my father's factory, who used the vernacular as a matter of course, I feel certain that I acquired little or nothing there. Indeed, I cannot

doubt that from the lips of my paternal grandmother, a lady of the old school, who died when I was seven, fell all the quaint words and phrases—many of them embodied in nursery rhymes—into my memory, there to lie quiet till the years should bring a use for them. (p. 8)

Ironically, at the same time as J J Bell was writing this introduction, Alexander McArthur in Glasgow's Gorbals was putting the finishing touches to his first draft of *No Mean City*, the book eventually published in a collaborative version with the London journalist H Kingsley Long in 1935, and rich in the bad language which Bell (and Bell's grandmother if she had known about it) would never have countenanced. *No Mean City*, crude and melodramatic though it was, had a certain archetypal power about it, reminiscent of effects in Jack London and Frank Norris, which made it not really surprising that it should have sold millions of copies and should seldom be out of print for long, even today. It was also a landmark in the wide currency it gave to Glasgow dialect, even though its London publishers, with an eye on their English readers, put those always irritating, non-accepting inverted commas round words like 'buroo', 'rammy', 'model', 'single-end', 'flyman', 'hairy', and 'sherricking'.

But any dialect breakthrough, in prose fiction, brings problems, and not only those of comprehension. The case against the use of dialect was put succinctly by Allan Massie, in a review of Iain Crichton Smith's novel *A Field Full of Folk* (*The Scotsman*, 8 May 1982), where he praised the dignity and seriousness the book gained by being resolutely non-regional. 'His characters are not insulted by dialect or by phonetic transcription of their speech.' This is clearly a dig (as we shall see) at other recent Scottish novels; but what of the general point? Are the servants in *Wuthering Heights*, the rustics in Hardy, the miners in Lawrence, the farmers in Lewis Grassic Gibbon, the Cockneys and Irishmen in Kipling, the Southerners in Faulkner, all to be regarded as 'insulted by dialect'? The answer is surely that given by Mark Twain in his prefatory note to a great dialectal story, *The Adventures of Huckleberry Finn*: 'In this book a number of dialects are used, to wit: the Missouri negro dialect; the ordinary 'Pike-County' dialect; and four modified varieties of this last. The shadings have not been done in a haphazard fashion, or by guess-work; but painstakingly, and with the trustworthy guidance and support of personal familiarity with these several forms of speech.' In other words, a loving particularity, not a putdown or a relegation. Nevertheless, a problem remains. It is hard to envisage a *Wuthering Heights* written *entirely* in Yorkshire dialect. Is this a snobbish or merely a realistic scepticism? It is realistic in the sense that a novel by its nature is interested in social gradations and distinctions, and that these, because of the nature of educational systems, often involve striking differences of speech. A dialect which was used into the highest reaches of education would in fact become a language, and would then itself begin to split into new dialects.

In Glasgow novels and short stories one main difficulty has been how to avoid too offputting a disjunction between realistic Glaswegian dialogue and a heavy authorial English in the narrative. Edward Gaitens' *Dance of the Apprentices* (1948) strikes a good balance but in a sense does acknowledge the existence of the problem, as the young shipyard apprentice, Eddy Macdonnel, grows up a great reader—of Dickens and Keats, Swinburne and Wells, pamphlets on socialism, anarchism, and pacifism—and not only loses much of his local language but is given less and less dialogue as the novel progresses; so that at the end we watch him, in prison as a conscientious objector during the First World War, entirely through the language of the author who purports to describe his thoughts, and beyond an occasional 'ach' or 'och' these thoughts are in pure English:

> Thank God the long day was almost over. As he walked he avoided looking at the door. If he remembered not to look at it he might not dream of it to-night. Would he sleep till morning? Yes. His nerves had been tranquil to-day and he had thought happily for a long time. Perhaps the draught the doctor had given him had steadied him. (p. 274)

Self-education—political awakening—deglaswegianisation—that is a well-known and often-delineated process. As a father in *Dance of the Apprentices* says of his schoolboy son: 'He's goat tae stick tae his English.' The Glasgow (and Glasgow-Irish) dialogue in Gaitens is lively and adequate, but it is not at the centre of the author's interest, and he shows no sense that anything might be lost if education or upward mobility in society should dilute or destroy the native speech.

In a similar sort of *Bildungsroman* (though set at a later time), *The Dear Green Place* (1966), Archie Hind uses the failure of his working-class hero to fulfil his ambitions as a novelist as an opportunity for expressing more directly negative views of Glasgow speech. Mat Craig probes the reasons for his failure:

> Was it in the language he spoke, the gutter patois into which his tongue fell naturally when he was moved by a strong feeling? This gutter patois which had been cast by a mode of life devoid of all hope or tenderness. This self-protective, fobbing off language which was not made to range, or explore, or express; a language cast for sneers and abuse and aggression; a language cast out of the absence of possibility; a language cast out of a certain set of feelings—from poverties, dust, drunkenness, tenements, endurance, hard physical labour; a reductive, cowardly, timid, snivelling language cast out of jeers and violence and diffidence; a language of vulgar keelie scepticism. (p. 226)

This angry English, if we believe Hind as the author, represents the actual thoughts passing through Mat's mind as he walks about the city—'collecting his thoughts', 'taking inventory of himself', 'ticking it all off in his mind'. The language is meant not to be authorial, but Mat's own. And this is not at all impossible, given the self-educating process he has undergone. Yet Hind is careful to show the persisting substratum, two pages later, when Mat suddenly and unintentionally verbalises his daydreaming in actual speech, his Glaswegian self addressing his anglified self:

> A voice, a shrugging Glesca keelie voice said to him, 'Ye're nut on, laddie. Ye're on tae nothin'.' Mat looked around the empty ferry, but still the voice spoke. 'Ye're nut quoted. A gutless wonder like you, that hasn't got the gumption of a louse.' (p. 228)

These deeply divided feelings about local speech do not prevent Hind from writing a moving and vivid novel, but they do mean that Glaswegian is not positively exploited for its creative potential, and this is where more recent fiction-writers have taken a new course. The seventies was the decade when Glaswegian began to fight back, in fiction, drama, and poetry. The 'gutter patois' of Archie Hind's soured hero became both an area of experiment and a badge of pride. Though certainly not devoid of polemic, this movement has by no means always wanted to show an aggressive face, but it has wanted to claim that if you want to use urban dialect it is first of all necessary to *listen*, and in doing so, to find distinctions and subtleties which the usual (and sometimes mythical) stereotypes writers have drawn on in the past have blunted or overlaid or simply missed. Emphasis on what is actually spoken, rather than on what legend or popular belief or the music-hall may in part have substituted for it, leads to thoughts about spelling, about that 'phonetic transcription of speech' which Allan Massie, in the passage quoted above, congratulated Iain Crichton Smith on having eschewed. The short stories of Alan Spence, James Kelman, and Alex Hamilton have addressed themselves to this controversial issue.

The stories in Spence's *Its Colours They are Fine* (1977) are blessed with very freshly and nicely observed dialogue and an orthography that few would regard as excessive.

> He sipped at it, fingering the blackened, brittle toast. He pushed the plate aside and started to retreat.
> 'Ah canny face the burnt offerin hen.'
> 'Ye need somethin in yer stomach.'
> 'Aye, maybe efter. Ah'm no feeling too good.'
> 'Aye, well hell mend ye, that's aw ah kin say.'
> 'Noo don't start! Ye gave me enough shirrikin last night. Bloody dog's abuse.'
> 'And no bloody wonder!' she said. 'God forgive me.' (Slipped in like punctuation · as she put down a plate so she could cross herself.)
> 'Ach be reasonable Mary. Ah mean it wis the boay's last night a freedom before e pits is heid 'n the auld noose.' He yanked an imaginary rope above his head and jerked his neck to the side. But that brought back the nausea, so he sat down before going on.
> 'We hid tae gie um a wee bit send aff, ye know whit ah mean.'
> 'Ah know whit ye mean awright, an ah know wherr ah'd send the perry yiz! Noo get ootma road. An will ye go an . . . DO something ABOUT yerself!' ('The Rain Dance', p. 115)

In that extract, the new and pleasing accuracy appears in words like *shirrikin*, which indicates the normal pronunciation (not the one given in SND); *kin* (not in SND, either in itself or under *can*, though it is the regular Glasgow pronunciation); *boay* (not in SND, either in itself or under *boy*, though again it is the standard and distinctive Glasgow pronunciation); and *perry yiz* khich looks the most outlandish of the lot but is in fact a good transcription of perfectly ordinary usage.

In a second extract, it may be noted that the language is more Glaswegian than it seems, since the ostensibly English words *team*, *mental*, and *brilliant* all have to be translated or decoded into the lyrical-sinister specifics they have in the city's teenage subculture—specifics which the context of the whole story makes reasonably clear.

> Through the doorway the crowds were beginning to spill out. Shuggie's eyes were fixed, watching for the two boys.
> 'Shouldnae be long noo,' he said.
> 'This should be good,' said Eddie. 'Didye see that wee guy's face when ah says we wur the Govan Team! Jist about shat is sel. That wis the best laugh. Fuckin tremendous!'
> Shuggie laughed and reached into his pocket, feeling the steel comb with the long pointed handle.
> 'Mental!' he said.
> 'Brilliant!' said Rab. ('Brilliant', p. 109)

James Kelman's stories are set in London, Manchester, and Jersey, as well as in Glasgow, and most of them are in English, often (as he says) 'with this Glasgow accent'; but two are of special interest on the present occasion as being written wholly in Glaswegian. 'Nice to be Nice' (in his volume of short stories *An Old Pub near the Angel*, 1973) is a first-person narrative by a Glasgow speaker, a device which usefully solves the problems often raised when local dialogue and English narrative are juxtaposed, though obviously courting the limitations imposed by the articulacy and interestingness of the speaker. In this story the narrator is a humorous, shrewd, good-hearted middle-aged man whose wife left him years ago because of his horse-betting. He describes himself as a better listener than talker, which, by an acceptable paradox, implies that he would also be one who would keep his talking for his writing. He lives in a room and kitchen, but is willing to share:

> Anywey it wis jist young Tony who'd firgoat his key, wi that wee mate a his in a perr a burds. Christ whit dae ye dae? Invite thim in? Well A did—nice tae be nice—in anywey thir aw right they two; sipposed tae be a perr a terraways bit A ey fun Tony aw right in his mate's his mate. The young yins ir aw right if ye lea thim alane. A've eywis maintained that. Gie thim a chance fir fuck sake! So A made thim it hame although it meant me hivvin tae sit oan a widdin cherr kis A selt the couch a couple a months ago kis ay that auld cunt Erchie in his troubles. They four hid perred aff in wir sittin oan the ermcherrs. They hid brung a cerry-oot wae thim so A goat the

glesses oot in it turned oot no a bad wee night, jist chattin away aboot politics in the hoarses in that. A quite enjoyed it although mine you A wis listenin merr thin A wis talkin bit that's no unusual. Wan i the birds didny say much either in A didny blame her kis she knew me although she didny let oan.

See A used tae work beside her man—aye in she's nae chicken, bit—nice tae be nice—she isny a bad lookin lassie in A didny let oan either. (p. 94)

Although one might not always agree with the spelling—*cerry-oot* would be safer as *kerry-oot* even if this disguises the verb—there is a continuous appeal to the ear to recognise the truth of signalled distinctions, as for example in *that wee mate a his, kis ay that auld cunt Erchie*, and *Wan i the burds*, where *a, ay,* and *i* all represent English 'of', but with correct contextual variations. Some would say that way madness lies; readers must be allowed to make their own mental variants of unstressed words whose spelling is known to be only conventional in any case. Perhaps. But there is clearly a value in calling attention to the realities of a speech that has never yet been fully described.

In Kelman's other story, 'The Hon' (in *Short Tales from the Night Shift*, 1978), he goes a step farther and uses Glasgow dialect for a straight third-person narrative. The language suits the black humour, which unrolls jerkily like an underground cartoon:

Auld Shug gits oot iv bed. Turns aff the alarm cloak. Gis straight ben the toilit. Sits doon in that oan the lavatri pan. Wee bit iv time gis by. Shug sittin ther, yonin. This Hon. Up it comes oot fri the waste pipe. Stretchis right up. Grabs him by the bolls.

Jesis Christ shouts the Shug filla.

The Hon gis slack in a coupla minits. Up jumps Shug. Straight ben the kitchin hodin onti the pyjama troosirs in that jist aboot collapsin inti his cher.

Fuck it he says Am no gon. (no page number)

The publisher's blurb to Alex Hamilton's *Gallus, did you say? and other stories* (1982) makes the claim that this collection is 'a landmark in publishing history, representing as it does the first conscious decision to reproduce in extended written prose the sounds of Glasgow English, as faithfully as non-phonetic transcription will allow'. The dubious term 'Glasgow English' makes it hard to know exactly what the claim is, since in fact only two of the stories use Glaswegian throughout, for both narrative and dialogue. The dialogue in all the stories, however, does go nearer than that of other fiction writers to 'faithful non-phonetic transcription'. Its strangeness on the page is immediately reduced if one reads the stories aloud, when the frequent Creole-like *zan* and *zim* and *ziv* and *zoaffice* sort themselves out in the flux. The most interesting technique occurs in 'Moonlighting', a cautionary tale about an unfortunate wealthy couple in Newton Mearns, recounted by a broad-speaking Glaswegian who retails it as he heard it from his presumably equally broad-speaking brother, a handyman working at the detached two-car home. Nice ironies are obtained by reporting the Newton Mearns couple's dialogue as the reporter would himself speak it; high marital comedy with an extra dimension. A car has vanished:

'Aw naw!' e ixplodes. 'Whitdji mean, *sno sittin therr eni merr*! A motir hisnae goat leg zan feet a it sain thitit kin jiss get up n tay ka walk tae itsel whinivir it feels lik a wee daunir doon thi toon! Yi lee vit wherr yi lee vit; yi pit oan thi haunbrake; yi loack thi door—n when yi cum back it's sittin jiss wherr yi walk taway fae it. UmAh right urumAh no right, ih? UmAh right urumAh wrang?' (p. 23)

Without drawing extravagant conclusions, one can perhaps find from such examples how dialect prose fiction is edging its way into new territory, and at the same time is consolidating its own ground by giving—what had never been given before—a truthful account of the spoken tongue. In this, it stands halfway between drama and poetry. In drama, there is in one sense no problem, since a play is all voices and no narrator, so that the most extreme naturalism, however odd it might seem if the play is printed, will be perfectly acceptable on the stage. In poetry, there is for an entirely different reason, and again only in one sense, no problem, in that the 'voice' of a poem, whatever the poet's own voice or accent or dialect may be, is something in itself, re-created through form and structure away from whatever naturalism the poet has started with. Both poet and dramatist, for opposite reasons, are more free than the writer of prose fiction. It would appear therefore that 'more can be done with' local dialect in plays and poems, and especially, because of their natural complexity, in poems. What would be too easy would be to assume that no problems are involved—whether problems of communication or problems of limitations of creative potential.

Since the 1940s, and more particularly since 1970, plays in Glasgow dialect and usually with a Glasgow setting have regularly appeared, proved popular, and built up a tradition. Because of the language, the tradition has been mainly realist and working-class, and often political; strong on humour and pathos, on veracity, on the pleasures of recognition, less strong on imagination, on shock, on analogies and vistas. The succession of plays that would include Ena Lamont Stewart's *Men Should Weep* (1947), George Munro's *Gold in his Boots* (1947), Roddy McMillan's *All in Good Faith* (1954) and *The Bevellers* (1973), Bill Bryden's *Willie Rough* (1972), Hector MacMillan's *The Sash* (1974), Tom McGrath's *The Hard Man* (1977), and John Byrne's trilogy *The Slab Boys* (1978), *The Loveliest Night of the Year* (1979; later re-titled *Cuttin' a Rug*), and *Still Life* (1982), has made a powerful impact, and has employed a wide range of themes: war, politics, unemployment, crime, football, religion, work. Linguistically, of course, there is less to be learned from the printed text of a play than from that of a poem or novel. A play text is a script for performance, and the language indicated by the playwright is filled out and may indeed be transformed by actors and director. Because of the assumption that authentic accents will be available, playwrights have not been so consciously concerned as their recent fellow-writers in fiction and poetry to sharpen orthography. The language in *All in Good Faith* is just as convincing as that in *The Hard Man*, except for greater realism in the use of swear-words in the later play, and one or two more indicative spellings like *loat* for *lot, stoap* for *stop,* and *wahnt* for *want.* What most of the plays do particularly well is to modulate between more-Scottish and more-English according to dramatic occasion and emotion, in ways that actors can manage and the silent reader of a novel cannot. In *The Bevellers,* which deals with the initiation of a new apprentice in the bevelling shop of a Glasgow glass-works, there is a well-marked difference between the wildly racy and inventive fury of Rouger, caught in the act with a girl, and speaking as if he had been brought up on centuries of flytings and Gavin Douglas's 'fowth of langage'—

> Ya knee-crept, Jesus-crept, swatchin little fucker, ah'll cut the bliddy scrotum aff ye! Ah'll knacker an' gut ye, ah'll eviscerate ye! Ya hure-spun, bastrified, conscrapulated young prick, ah'll do twenty year fur mincin you. Ye hear me? Ah'll rip ye fae the gullet tae the groin, ah'll incinerate ye! . . . Another minute, ah wid have scored where he's never scored, an' you shankered it, ya parish-eyed, perishin bastart. (pp. 50-1)

—and the quiet, level reminiscence of Bob as he talks to the apprentice and thereby brings the work theme of the play into clear focus—

> You might think this is a rough trade and rough folk in it. But that's jist because we havenae broke away fae the oul' days—no a'thegither anyway. Ye cannae wipe oot years o' hard men an' hard graft jist because the machinery changes a wee bit. No that it's a' that different, mind you. The wheels are a wee bit different here an' there, like the carborundum stone. That used to be the ould mill wi the hopper feeder and a sand-drip. That's when boys younger than you really grafted. Cairryin pailfuls o saun an' sievin it in the trough beside the mill. They still use them in wan or two places yet, an' if somethin' had tae go wrang at Peter's end we might have tae use it yet, but it's no likely. As ah said, there wis a lot o Irishmen in this game at wan time. The Rouger's oul' man wis a beveller. You think he's twistit. Ye want tae have seen his oul' man. They worked on piece work, each man seein his job through fae start tae finish, an' they had tae shift. The Rouger's father wis a beaster. He'd collect his ain wages at the end o the week an' take the Rouger's tae. That wis the last they'd see o him tae the pubs shut on Setterday night. They were lucky if he had enough left tae get them pigs' feet fur the rest o the week. (p. 34)

The Hard Man uses a different kind of contrast, which works much better in the theatre than the printed text would lead us to believe. Tom McGrath, writing in collaboration with Jimmy Boyle whose life-story is the basic material of the play, uses a full, broad Glaswegian for the quick succession of scenes presenting the early years of the hardman and his acquaintances, but intersperses these with solo passages directly addressed by Johnny Byrne (= Jimmy Boyle) to the audience; and these speeches, coming from the older Byrne who has done much reading and educated himself, are (as printed) virtually in English. The seeming artificiality of the disjunction disappears in the theatre, where a strong Glasgow voice or accent in the actor transforms the 'English' passages and readily effects continuity.

How far we should be happy with the large gap that may exist between printed and performed texts is another matter, though it is difficult to see what can be done about it. When John Byrne's 'Slab Boys' trilogy was produced at the Traverse Theatre in Edinburgh in 1982, Simon Berry gave it an enthusiastic review in the *Times Literary Supplement* (23 July 1982) and noted that its 'particular joy' was its 'authentic use of West of Scotland patois'. Put on at the Royal Court Theatre in London later in the year, the trilogy drew an equally sympathetic response from the London critics, with comments on the language ranging from 'the Glaswegian accents are intense' (Victoria Radin) through 'it takes a little time to tune into the dialect' (Robert Hewison) to 'though the language is Glaswegian it is never as impenetrable as legend holds' (Ned Chaillet). However, one could read the printed text of the three plays (published by Salamander Press, Edinburgh, 1982) and be only very intermittently aware that the characters are speaking Glaswegian or West of Scotland patois. This seems a pity, even if the aim is a wider readership. Texts of plays tend to establish themselves, and the result might be with plays of this kind that homogenised and emasculated versions could emerge, as more suited to very English or very American markets. The disgraceful dubbing of the Glasgow voices in the film *Gregory's Girl,* for American export, is a warning.

In the use of Glasgow dialect in fiction or drama, it is difficult to pick out one name as being central to the development; in poetry, such a name does at once offer itself: Tom Leonard. At the beginning of the 1960s, the present writer began using Glasgow speech in a few poems like 'Glasgow Green' and 'Good Friday', but with only a sketchy indication of pronunciation through spelling; the full Glasgow characteristics were meant to be supplied by the reader, preferably reading aloud. The main purpose was to suggest that, as in 'Glasgow Green', the local speech could be employed in poetry in a serious context far removed from the usual music-hall associations. Later, I tried extending this through a range of different Glasgow voices in 'Stobhill' (1971), again with the intention that the poetry, though printed in a book, should also be read aloud, and this time with the spelling brought nearer to pronunciation. Tom Leonard brought out his *Six Glasgow Poems* in 1969, and went on to publish actively and variously during the 1970s. Other poets joined in—Stephen Mulrine, Tom McGrath, Alan Spence, David Neilson—until there was something that in hindsight might be called a movement, although at the time it was ill-defined. The book *Three Glasgow Writers* (1976), which contains prose by Alex Hamilton and James Kelman, and poetry and prose by Tom Leonard, shows the wider links of a 'Glasgow school' which is not confined to poetry.

It is a not unexpected feature of such movements, when a language or dialect is being looked at afresh or given a push in a new direction, that poets will make translations as a test or challenge, to see what the language can do. Alan Spence's versions of haiku by the Japanese poet Issa (1763–1827), included in his book *Glasgow Zen* (1981), are affectionate reworkings from a poet who himself liked 'voice' and dialect:

> wid ye lookit
> the state ae it—
> me in ma new jaicket!

or

> the full moon shinin
> on this buncha heidbangers
> (me included)

Very different are the rude and reductive versions of Catullus by David Neilson (*XII from Catullus*, 1982), where the Latin poet's persona of 'a drunken, impoverished and acid commentator' interested in the 'rather déclassé activities' of his friends (as the translator's prefatory note describes it—though there is more to Catullus than that) finds no barriers in Glasgow demotic. The translations are very free, pared-down, laconic (the *oculos . . . oculis . . . oculis . . . oculis* of No. 82 become a single *contak lensis*), but comparison with the originals generally shows that points survive, if tone does not—and who can be sure what tone a Catullus poem had for his contemporaries? The more satirical modes work better than the lyrical; but the experiment was well worth doing. Here is No. 83, 'To Lesbia's Husband' ('Lesbia mi praesente viro mala plurima dicit'):

> Gaun ye clown
> ye canny see
> through Lesbia furiver
> cursin me

> Roar an laff

> it's nothin new
> thit you'd be better aff
> if she effed at you.

The remarkable work of Tom Leonard opens up a new range of possibilities. His Glasgow-language poems, though usually quite short, bring together in highly concentrated form a number of separate interests: 'voice' and sound and the transcription of sound; sociolinguistic and political concern; poetic structure, and especially line-structure; and comedy, from the playful to the ferocious. What he does *not* want, the journalistic and vaudeville stereotyping which in the past has made it so hard for seriously intended writing to emerge in Glasgow, was very clearly spelt out in a cobra-like review of Albert Mackie's pawky vade-mecum *Talking Glasgow* (1978):

It's another of those 'warm-hearted' linguistic racist affairs, where all of 'us' good
middle-class or ex-working-class folk can sit back and have a good laugh at how 'they'
working-class Glaswegians talk. . . . Not a 'fuck' or a 'cunt' will disturb the pleasant
time to be had by the reader. . . . As is usually the case with this sort of production,
not listening accurately is the necessary precondition for perpetuating the various cosy
myths. . . . But if you don't treat language seriously, you don't treat people
seriously. . . . Nowhere will real linguistic aggression or anger show alongside the of-
course-always-bowdlerized 'humour'; the natives here are not even allowed the
luxury of getting restless. There are very serious linguistic political points to be
discussed here in relation to speech registers as a barometer of economic and political
power in Britain, but it would be a waste of time discussing them in relation to this
book. (*Aquarius*, no. 12, 1980, p. 124).

'If you don't treat language seriously, you don't treat people seriously.' The
consequences, for a writer brought up speaking broad Glaswegian , are formidable. The young apprentice in Roddy McMillan's play, *The Bevellers*, had been
good at English at school and had written good essays. 'Might no talk it very
good, but ah was a'right when it came tae writin it doon' (p. 35). The comedy,
or tragedy, depending on how you look at it, is that young Norrie can write but
not speak English, and can speak but not write Glaswegian. He will probably
never speak English, since he is not bookish or ambitious, and he has been
thoroughly brainwashed into believing that it would be wrong to write
Glaswegian, so he never will write it. It was not McMillan's concern to develop
this point, but if Leonard had written the play it would have become a main
theme. In his highly amusing but also very perceptive prose monologue,
'Honest' (in *Three Glasgow Writers*), Leonard presents the classic triple search
of a young Glasgow writer for theme, language, and audience. The speaker toys
with the idea of writing a story about a fisherman, and decides that with a bit of
research and hard thinking he could manage it, but urban scepticism breaks in.
The fisherman's life is not really very interesting: 'kinni no day sumhm else
wayiz time?'. As for writing about it: 'can *a* no day sumhm else wi ma time?'
And reading about it: 'huv *they* got nuthn behtr ti day wi their time?' As for
language, is this not shifting sand?—

But ifyi write down 'doon' wan minute, nwrite doon 'down' thi nixt, people say yir
beein inconsistent. But ifyi sayti sumdy, 'Whaira yi afti?' nthey say, 'Whut?' nyou
say, 'Where are you off to?' they don't say, 'That's no whutyi said thi furst time.'
They'll probably say sumhm like, 'Doon thi road!' anif you say, 'What?' they usually
say, 'Down the road!' the second time—though no always. Course, they never *really*
say, 'Doon thi road!' or 'Down the road!' at all. Least, they never say it the way it's
spelt. Coz it *izny* spelt, when they say it, is it? (p. 47).

But after an abstract discussion on the difficulty of getting others to take your
writing seriously, the monologue quickly shifts gear and ends with an anecdote
of almost surreal defiance:

'Ahma writur, your only a wurkur,' a said, to thi plumbir.
'Fux sake Joe stick wan on that kunt,' said the apprentice.
'Ball an cocks,' said the plumber, 'Ball an cocks. A firgot ma grammur.'
'Gerrihtuppyi,' a said, to thi apprentice.
'Lissn pal yoor tea'll be up na minit,' said the plumber.
'Couldny fuckin write a bookie's line ya basturdn illiturate,' a said, ti the
plumber.
'Right. Ootside,' said the plumber. 'Mawn. Ootside.'
Sorry. That comes later. (p. 49)

Any answer to this agon between the writer and the worker, between the
highly literate but regarded-as-illiterate Glaswegian monologist and the
illiterate plumber whose language is not rejected but given status by the act of
writing, 'comes later'. Leonard's poetry enjoys every kind of dramatic contest
and contrast between different voices, accents, registers, social classes,
philosophies. One man after assuring him that 'thi langwij a thi guhtr' is all
right for funny stuff but no use for emotional or intellectual matters falls down
an empty lift-shaft; another speaker argues with him in favour of electronics
instead of the parochialities of 'bunnit husslin'; a linguist who regrets she has
'lost her accent' is mocked and asked if she would really 'swear tay swerr'; a glib
'liaison co-ordinator' is attacked for having no real experience of
unemployment, alcoholism, or 'hoossyz fawnty bits'; a series of characters like
figures in a medieval morality-poem try to tell him that his language is
'disgraceful', and the charge, while not denied, is defied: 'all living language is
sacred.' This emphasis on 'living language', however comedic the means may
be which are used to talk about it, is important to Leonard because it is related
to the realities of power in society, to what we believe or are persuaded to
believe is true, and the defence of his concern with what people actually say, as
opposed to what they are taught to say, or what they hear others say, or even
what they think they themselves are saying, is that to sweep speech under the
carpet is to academise, and indeed tarmacadamise, systems of stasis and control
that are perpetually in need of re-examination. Not surprisingly in such a
slippery subject, irony is one of his favourite weapons, and Glaswegian finds
one of its happiest expressions in the transvestite linguistics of 'Unrelated
Incidents—3', which is also highly thought-provoking about the matters just
discussed:

> this is thi
> six a clock
> news thi
> man said n
> thi reason
> a talk wia
> BBC accent
> iz coz yi

widny wahnt
mi ti talk
aboot thi
trooth wia
voice lik
wanna yoo
scruff. if
a toktaboot
thi trooth
lik wanna yoo
scruff yi
widny thingk
it wuz troo.
jist wanna yoo
scruff tokn.
thirza right
way ti spell
ana right way
ti tok it. this
is me tokn yir
right way a
spellin. this
is ma trooth.
yooz doant no
thi trooth
yirsellz cawz
yi canny talk
right. this is
the six a clock
nyooz. belt up.
(*Three Glasgow Writers*, p. 36)

NOTES

1   'Modern Scots Prose Writing', in *The Scots Language in Education*, Association for
    Scottish Literary Studies Occasional Papers no. 3, p. 62.
2   'Changes in the Vocabulary of Lowland Scots Dialects', in *Scottish Literary Journal*,
    Supplement no. 14, (Summer 1981), p. 54.

ELEVEN

An Onomastic Vernacular in Scottish Literature

W F H Nicolaisen

That each work of literature has its own onomasticon, its own appropriate, peculiar and structured nomenclature of both persons and places which only functions within the covers in which it is contained, is an assumption which few might be prepared to contradict. That this assumption applies to both fictive and non-fictive names is perhaps less obvious, but is nevertheless substantiated without great difficulty when one considers that the 'Glasgows' of Scott's *Rob Roy*, of McArthur and Long's *No Mean City*, of Chaim Bermant's *The Second Mrs. Whitberg*, of Robin Jenkins' *A Would-Be Saint*, of George Blake's *The Shipbuilders* and of William McIlvanney's *Laidlaw* are, in spite of the identity of name, very different 'Glasgows'. Although there is some potential semantic overlap, the name *Glasgow* has, in fact, very different contents in each of these novels, as well as in all those other works of fiction in which it is said to be the 'setting'—has essentially different onomastic meaning. The name *Glasgow*, in these literary contexts, is as fictitious in its reality as, let us say, *Fairport, Kennaquhair, Kinraddie, Barbie, Dalmailing,* the two *Toddays, Crask,* or *Auchengillan* are real in their fictitiousness. Its function as a device to ensure the possibility of identifying reference in each novel, or set of novels, is the same as that of any other name, while its apparent identity with a place of the same name in the actual world outside the literary works in question is, despite the author's intentional allusions and deliberate hints, in the long run illusory. As Lewis Grassic Gibbon says of his *Duncairn*: 'Unfortunately, several English journals . . . described my imaginary city as Dundee, two Scottish sheets identified it with Aberdeen, and at least one American newspaper went considerably astray and stated that it was Edinburgh—faintly disguised. Instead, it is merely the city which the inhabitants of the Mearns (not foreseeing my requirements in completing my trilogy) have hitherto failed to build.'[1] Similarly, the imaginary cities of Glasgow are cities which the inhabitants of Clydeside have so far 'failed to build', and which, since they cannot be Scott's, McArthur's, Bermant's, Jenkins', Blake's, McIlvanney's, and a dozen other 'Glasgows' at the same time, never will be built.

209

Despite their semantic emptiness until provided with contents by the author, literary names, both of persons and of places, are, however, often not without deliberately evoked associations and suggestive linguistic embeddedness. In their contrived imitation, intensification or persiflage of the names of the relevant actual world which they reflect, they, of necessity and by design, carry with them associative burdens which they cannot, or ought not to, shed; in their selective inclusion and application they form nomenclatures with much tighter structures and much more exposed juxtapositions than their non-literary counterparts. They contain philosophies and perceptions, convictions and accusations, worship and ridicule, authorial comment and cultural teasing; above all, they attempt to convey trustworthy authenticity, even when remodelled to elicit a smile or outright laughter. As an integral and interrelated onomasticon they are the net thrown by the writer over a chaotic world, that it might be tamed and given order according to his designs. They structure what is amorphous and they locate—spatially, temporally, societally—what otherwise would have had no location. They guide and give direction, they define and they suggest, they encourage respect or invite contempt.

As far as that systemic subset of names which refers to places, the toponymicon, is concerned, its primary literary function is obviously the creation of a believable topography. However, as required by the very selectivity of the employment of names in a literary context, the number of names mentioned is almost always comparatively small; and, what is more important, predominantly tied to human events and constellations, thus creating not only sparse patterns but also a social, as much as a spatial, topography.[2] Every name counts in the literary landscape, and the names to be included in that landscape therefore have to be carefully chosen. They have to be appropriate as well as acceptable, and they must be capable of serving as foregrounding devices and symbols, frequently as verbal icons,[3] in a wide variety of ways: a task which no name in the non-literary landscape ever has to, indeed could, perform with the same degree of condensed multiplicity.

In a sense, names thus become the onomastic dialect of a book, expressing as total inventories an author's general views on naming and on the use of names and, individually or in clusters, narrower linguistic concerns. Names, after all, usually start out as words, and therefore share with them certain morphological and other lexical characteristics. As far as their linguistic properties are concerned they provide a discerning author with the opportunity to employ them as markers of linguistic distinctions and stratifications, and in extension to suggest related extra-linguistic matters, such as the indication of social status or the signalling of behavioural responses in a particular cultural register.

Certainly, not every author consciously seizes this opportunity. The question is nevertheless worth asking whether, or to what extent, the theoretical concept of an onomastic 'vernacular', paralleling or closely linked with linguistic vernacular elements, though opposed to the literary and educated language standards of the day, can be isolated within the onomastic inventories of particular works of fiction. While such a question and the answers it elicits are potentially just as capable of shedding light on the basic theme examined in this volume of essays as the contributions more directly and more conservatively concerned with the non-onomastic use of dialect in literature, it is nevertheless worth noting that the results achieved by the investigation of names in general, and of aspects of literary onomastics in particular, should never be expected to be as wide-ranging as, or merely supportive of, those arrived at through those other approaches. If the study of names were aimed at no more than the secondary, though perhaps idiosyncratic, confirmation of findings obtained by other means, it would be playful at best and superfluous at worst. In other words, an onomastic, and specifically a toponymic, vernacular cannot be expected to be merely the same as its linguistic counterpart; nor should onomastic strategies applied to a literary text be expected to yield merely linguistic insights. Otherwise such expectations might easily be defeated while the peculiar manner in which names in literature tend to operate as a text within a text[4] is overlooked.

In Scotland there is, as in the quest for so much other information pertinent to the nature and function of literature, no more tempting testing ground than that extensive corpus of fiction, the Waverley Novels, especially those which have a Scottish setting and address themselves to Scottish concerns. At least initially, an enquiry of the kind we envisage might profitably try to determine whether there is an onomastic equivalent to what David Murison has called 'The Two Languages in Scott':

> . . . in the first half-dozen at least [of the Waverley Novels] Scott has two languages, English for the narration and background description, and Scots for the dialogue of those who are natives of Scotland and belong in general to the lower social classes; . . .[5]

Exploring these same six novels—*Waverley, Guy Mannering, The Antiquary, The Black Dwarf, Old Mortality, Rob Roy*—as our main text, but augmenting it from certain later novels with a Scottish setting, we have, indeed, no difficulty in detecting names which are ascribable to either an English or a Scots onomastic register. The former category would contain such names as Mr Morton, the Hazlewoods of Hazlewood, Viscount Archerfield, Monkbarns, Sir Arthur Wardour, Isabel Vere, Young Earnscliff, Lucy and Nancy Ildeston, Ravenswood, Sir Frederick Langley, Mauley-Hall, Polverton, Lord Evandale, Milnwood, and others; not included in this list are, of course, names of Englishmen in Scotland like Waverley, Mannering, or Staunton. To the latter category, immediately recognisable as much more extensive, would belong such personal names as Maister Goukthrapple, Ebenezer Cruickshanks, John Mucklewrath, Gibby Gaethroughwi't, Sandy Goldie, Jamie Howie, Duncan Robb, Lawrie Lowther, Edie Ochiltree, Saunders Mucklebackit,

Tammie Norie, Steenie Wilks, Mrs Heukbane, Provost Mucklewhame, Jingling
Jock, Lang Linker, Jock Wabster, Connie Elshie, and Cuddie Headrigg; such
place names as Shinnyheugh, Stagshawbank, Corse-Cleugh, Derncleugh, 'The
Gauger's Loup', Heavieside-brae, Charlieshope, the Heuch, Staneshiebank,
Willie's Brae, Hazleshaws-burn, Touthop-rigg, the Limestone-rigg, the
Shellicoat-stane, the Lang-hirst, Windyknowe, Hailziecroft, the Crooked
Dykes, Gibbbie's Knowe, the Brierybank, the Craigburnfoot, Kittlebrig, the
Wellbrae-head, Mucklestane-Moor, the Stenhouse, the Shaws, Haggisha, the
Howff, Haggie-holm, Mucklewhame, Nethersheils, the Deil's Loaning, the
Netherwoodhaugh, Dobs-linn, Creehope-linn, and the Brigg-end; and such
combinations of personal and place names as Tam o' Todshaw, Will o' the Flat,
Hobbie o' Sorbietrees, John o' the Girnell, Francis o' Fowlsheugh, Hobbie of
the Heugh-foot, Simon of Hackburn, Tam o' Whittram, Dick of the Dingle,
and Jock o' the Todholes. Even a mere inventory of names of this kind and
their categories, therefore, leaves little doubt as to the onomastic division which
exists in these novels or the strong, potential foregrounding powers inherent in
it.

Especially striking in this respect is the numerical preponderance of names in
the Scots register over those in the English mode. This is surprising in novels in
which members of the upper classes and the places in which they reside play
such an important part. The seeming contradiction is resolved when one
realises that the aristocracy and its lands are also seen and presented in terms of
the Scots register, such as the Laird o' Kittlegab, Sir Thomas Kittlecourt, Sir
Gilbert Grizzlecleugh, the Lairds of Cringlecut, Haltweary, and Halfstarvet, Sir
Thomas Kittleloof, the Lairds o' Dunder, Broken-girth-flow, Smackawa,
Lickitup, Langcale, Girdingburst, Dumbiedikes, Cuffabout, Loup-the-dike,
and Lickpelf, or the parishes of Gatherem, Dreepdaily, and Skreigh-me-dead,
and the Kirk o' Kilmagirdle.

The last of these not only epitomises the predominantly humorous, or
perhaps rather scurrilous, selection and re-arrangement of names for which
close parallels exist on the actual Scottish map,[6] but also the teasingly and
maybe even condescendingly offered reinterpretation of Gaelic place names in
terms of Scottish English, for which there are many other examples:
Killancureit, Bumperquaigh, Balmawhapple, Tipperhewit, Pickletillim, Inchgrabbit, Kailychat, Letter Scriven, Hochmagirdle, Glenamuck, Kippletringan,
Balruddery, Drumshouroch, Tamlowrie, Kinprunes, Glenstirym, Benarbuck
and, best known of all, Tillietudlem.[7] Most of these intentionally amusing, but
just as deliberately distorting, Scotticisations of purported Gaelic names are
again associated with the landed gentry, its possessions and titles. While in
some of these compound names (Killancureit, Bumperquaigh, Pickletillim,
Inchgrabbit, etc.) the intended humour is expressed in the semantic allusions
of either the generic or the specific (or both), others (Kippletringan,
Balruddery, Tillietudlem) are simply meant to amuse through their sounds,

making fun of Gaelic while being funny in Scots. In all instances, the names in question contain Gaelic elements which in the Scotticised form given do appear on the Scottish map. For readers familiar with these, Scott's names are therefore comic exaggeration rather than humorous invention, and consequently lose much of their apparent unbelievability. Their impact is probably due much more to their cumulative effect than their individual re-interpretative capriciousness.

What emerges therefore—and this should be no surprise in novels said to have originated in a town called Gandercleugh on the river Gander, with Gusedub and Goslin-brae nearby—is a vernacular onomasticon, and especially topo-nymicon, which easily matches in extent and variation the linguistic vernacular spoken by those people who live in places bearing such names or who have dealings with persons who are associated with such places. The place nomen-clature in question, with its implications of social status or linguistic adherence, seems in these novels to represent a second landscape, in addition to the official one which is indicated by place names existing in the actual world (Edinburgh, Glasgow, Dundee, Queensferry, Dumfries, Aberbrothock, Galloway, Mar, Solway, Kirkcaldy, Pittenweem, the Salisbury Crags) and by those in the English register. The contrast is therefore not between actuality and fiction but rather between standard and vernacular, and it is in this vernacular landscape, with its Windyknowes, Briggends and Tillietudlems, that some of Scott's most persuasive and most appealing characters move and have their being—Cuddie Headrigg and Dandie Dinmont, Edie Ochiltree and Connie Elshie, Meg Merrilies and Caleb Balderstone, and, of course, Jedediah Cleishbotham. Although second or secondary, it is a landscape that is, if anything, more vital, more full of human endeavours and emotions, more fraught with danger and more pregnant with promise, both humbler and more genuine, perhaps even more enduring, than the official landscape of the maps which it complements, enriches and vitalises. It is not a landscape which is separate from that seen through the eyes of those who speak English in its standard variety but rather one which in its very 'verna-cularity' structures the world out there differently and imposes on it different values and taxonomies. It is a landscape in which the behavioural peculiarities of the outsider, the cultural perplexities of the stranger, the threatening superiority of the priest, the lawyer and the schoolmaster, and the unpredictable quirkiness of lordly authority are reduced to safe ordinariness through silent laughter and a twinkle in the eye. It thrives on the recognition of its smaller, less imposing elements, the *heugh*, the *cleugh,* the *brae*, the *hope*, the *shaw*, the *rigg*, the *stane*, the *croft*, the *sheil*, and the *haugh*. It singles out the Wellbrae-*head*, the Brigg-*end*, and the Heugh-*foot* in its attention to locations that have micro-cosmic relationships. Its nomenclature is a net with finer meshes but made of a stronger yarn than that of standard usage. It is the landscape of a different kind of people for whose lives it is more than just setting, but rather limitation and opportunity, home and the world. It is the landscape of life.

It is also a landscape which, surviving Scott, has since been ever-present in Scottish fiction, and has been asserting on it its special characteristics and expectations. There may not be another writer who has created vernacular toponymies of the same dimensions and varieties; but the stamp is there for all to see, and the places are all the better remembered for it. John Galt's *Annals of the Parish*, following so soon after the Waverley Novels just discussed, acknowledges the official landscape by mentioning and utilising such places as Ayr, Lugton and Lugton Water, Kilmarnock, Eaglesham, Glasgow (with its Saltmarket and the Gorbals), and Port Glasgow, only to create within it its own topography with strong vernacular overtones—the parish of Dalmailing with the Braehill, the Loans, the Loanhead, the Douray Moor, the Gorbyholm, the Vennel, the Covenanters' Close, Gowanny, Annock, the Wheatrigs, the Witch-Linn, the neighbouring town of Irville, such other parishes as Swappington and Loupinton, and the new mill-town of Cayenneville— appropriately shortened locally to Canaille, in response to its strange intrusion upon the local onomastic dialect. There are, of course, also the Lairds of Yillcogie and Breadland. For a complete work of fiction this may seem a fairly small number of names compared with Scott; but then the *Annals* are, after all, so much more concerned with human actions and reactions than with the topographical environment in which these take place, a consideration which makes the number of place names much more impressive. *The Provost* adds to this array the royal burgh of Gudetown, with its Cross, Tolbooth, New-inns, Green, and Cross-well; and, while including Dalmailing and Braehill, also offers the Beerland estates, the Niggerbrae park, the Greenland, the Kilbeacon cotton mill (with Mr Shuttlethrift), the Gatherton Holme, Bodletonbrae, and Kirkbogle, as well as Lucknoo House as the toponymic stranger.

George Douglas Brown's *The House with the Green Shutters* has a more variegated environment for the town of Barbie which is its setting. Only a few miles away are Skeighan (and Skeighan Drone), Fleckie, Tenshillingland, Templandmuir, Poltandie, Fechars, Loranogie, Donnerton, Auchterwheeze, Brigabee, Irrendavie, the Mill o' Blink, and Milmannoch Hill; more closely associated with Barbie are the Braes of Barbie, Barbie Water, Barbie Valley, the Lintie's Burn and the Lintie's Linn, and within Barbie are Main Street, the Bend o' the Brae, the Weaver's Vennel, the Tinker's Wynd, the Cross, and the Brownie's Brae. This highly confined regional landscape widens into the actual world through such places as Edinburgh (Embro), Glasgow, Aberdeen, Kyle, Cumnock, Kincardine, the Nith, Carlisle and London, and offers a Barbie perspective of the Hebridean island of South Uist and its place names through a brief encounter with a Mr Alexander MacTavish of Benmacstronachan, near Auchnapeterhoolish: names which are obviously meant to confirm the throaty chuckle caused by the anglicised Gaelic name Auchterwheeze.

Galt's and Brown's toponymies are perhaps not so much foregrounding devices for a vernacular landscape embedded in the topography of the official map and partially overlapping with it, as fictive place nomenclatures surrounded by place names of the actual world, toponymic enclaves created to enable fictitious human beings to interact as if they were part of a wider world. The imaginary areas they cover are insets which might be placed anywhere or nowhere on the map of Ayrshire, as long as the real places mentioned are not part of them.

One might have thought that the regional place nomenclature of the Mearns —Mondynes, Dunnottar, Kinneff, Auchinblae, Stonehaven (Stanehive), Laurencekirk, Gourdon, Glenbervie, Drumlithie, Arbuthnott, Fordoun, the Howe, Forthie—would in itself have enough vernacular appropriateness to accommodate the lives of the Guthries, Chae Strachan, Long Rob of the Mill, the Reverend Gibbon, Mistress Munro, Sarah Sinclair, Ewan Tavendale, Alec Mutch, Sam Gourlay and their world, but Lewis Grassic Gibbon somehow finds room to nestle among them Kinraddie and Peesie's Knapp and Blawearie, as well as Cuddiestoun, Netherhill, Upperhill, and Bridgend, and later Segget, the Meiklebogs road, Culdyce, Dundon (Duncairn), Ecclesgriegs, Kirriebean, Paldy, Tangleha', and Doughty Park. Thus the toponymic authenticity of the display of actual Mearns names is given even greater force through the additional creation of a fictitious onomastic focus. There is a Kinraddie view of the world, as there are Gandercleugh, Dalmailing and Barbie perspectives, and it is not enough to live in Drumlithie or Auchinblae to be part of that secondary landscape that really matters in its shaping, honing, texturing influence on the lives of those ordinary men and women who are of the author's making. Naturally, Kinraddie and the place-names associated with it function as Mearns names, deriving their special Mearns characteristics from those actual place-names which surround them and entering convincingly the interrelated patterns of their onomastic field. The fictitious reality of Kinraddie is made possible through Laurencekirk, Glenbervie and the Howe, just as Laurencekirk, Glenbervie and the Howe are given substance, are legitimised, in *A Scots Quair* through their relationship with Kinraddie.

Though, on the whole, Gibbon's names are serious attempts at verisimilitude in the onomastic vernacular, some of them are not without a certain wryly subtle humour. *Blawearie* could presumably come from any of Scott's novels in its punning re-interpretation of what must have been originally a Gaelic compound; *Cuddiestoun* is both endearing and whimsical in its utilisation of a Scots specific; and *Ecclesgriegs* surreptitiously introduces a historical element through its quiet reference to the older name of St Cyrus. While such names might cause a quick, almost imperceptible smile, they are not likely to produce guffawing hilarity, even in their partial incongruity. The onomastic vernacular of *A Scots Quair* is too existential to be facilely risible.

Quite the opposite is true of that connected set of prose comedies with which Sir Compton Mackenzie delighted readers between the early forties and the late fifties—*The Monarch of the Glen* (1941), *Keep the Home Guard Turning*

(1943), *Whisky Galore* (1947), *Hunting the Fairies* (1949), *The Rival Monster* (1952), *Ben Nevis Goes East* (1954), and *Rockets Galore* (1957). Through clever manipulation of well-established Scottish toponymic patterns in the Highlands and Islands, Sir Compton produces onomastic buffoonery at its ridiculing best. The trick here is again the creation or restoration of lexical meaning in a Scots, or at least Scottish-English, register, through semantic insinuation or punning re-interpretation. Place names of purported Gaelic origin thus made to sound and look ludicrous in English are, for example: Glenbogle, Glenbristle, Drumcockie, Kilwhillie, Tummie, Cloy, Knocknacolly, Kenspeckle, Glenbore, Ben Cruet, Clacknaclock, Ben Goosey, Kincanny, Drumstickit, Loch Stuffie, Coolish, Traigh Swish, Knockdown, Loch Bob, Loch Skinny, Loch Dooin, Loch Stew, Skerrydoo, Ben Quilt, Tyntackit, Invercoddle, Pills, Ballyhoo, Ellen Whillie, Crackoyne, Dundreary, Bones, Ardmoney, Kiltod, Battledore, Pendicula (modelled on Benbecula), Drumbooey, Loch Luny. Their intended parody is heightened when they are presented in alliterative pairs or clusters, especially in the title of Donald MacDonald, twenty-third of Ben Nevis (itself a peak of parody)—'the Lord of Ben Nevis, Glenbogle, Glenbristle, Strathdiddle, Strathdun, Loch Hoch and Loch Hoo'. Laughter here is not only at the expense of the Gaelic-speaking Highlander but also of the monolingual English-speaking lairds like Ben Nevis himself or Hugh Cameron of Kilwhillie who have difficulty in pronouncing Gaelic place names (even on their own estates), as when Ben Nevis refers to *Achnacallach* as *Ackernercallick*, to *Traigh nam Marbh* as *Trynamarruf*, to *Tigh Dhà Chridheachan* as *Tiger Creaking*, and to [*Fàire?*] *Mhic 'ic Eachainn* as *Fairyvikickyacken*, or Kilwhillie calls *Uaimh na Laoigh—Oov na Loogh*.

Names of Norse origin do not fare any better when subjected to Sir Compton's treatment. Thus the two islands featuring centrally in several of the novels are appropriately called Great Todday and Little Todday (Whisky galore!) or *Todaidh Mór* and *Beag* in Gaelic; but there are also the neighbouring islands of Poppay and Pillay, again significantly linked through alliteration. For both of these, mock-etymologies are provided in derisory imitation of semi-learned, pedantic, wrangling, name-mongering antiquarianism:

> The origin of the name Pillay is in dispute. Some Gaelic topographers say it means 'the island of the winnowing,' others argue for a purely Norse derivation from a word cognate with pillow, but the majority agree that it means 'the island of the return' because so many people had tried to land there and failed.
>
> The origin of the name Poppay is in dispute, but most philologists now accept it as a variant of Pabbay—the Priest's Island. There is, however, a small but noisy minority which prefers to seek for the etymology of the name in *pìob*—Pipe Island—from a fancied resemblance to a piper of an isolated basaltic fragment rising from the sea just off the point of the northerly horn of Bagh nam Marbh. Certainly this rock is still known as *Am Pìobair*, but, as Mr. John Lorne Campbell of Canna has observed

sternly, 'there is no excuse for flouting every canon of etymology in order to gratify a taste for the facile picturesque. Poppay is clearly a piece of debased eighteenth-century topography for Pabbay, and indeed, on a rare map of Todaidh Mór and Todaidh Beag in my possession dated 1780, I find Pobbay. After the deliberate efforts of the S.P.C.K., financed from London, to extirpate Gaelic and Latin from the Islands and Wester Inverness through the latter half of the eighteenth century, it is a matter for grateful surprise that corrupt nomenclature like Poppay is not more frequent.[8]

How can one ever take oneself seriously again as a name scholar and purveyor of etymologies for Scottish place-names after such effective leg-pulling?

Other names similarly mangled round out the Norse stratum: Snorvig, Ben Sticla, Bobanish, Watasett, Ben Pucka, Ben Bustival, Obaig, Loch Sleeport, Nobost, Ard Snor, Ardvanish, Gibberdale, Fearvig. All of them are, especially in their generics, so convincingly close to their models that it is not always easy to refuse such tongue-in-cheek authenticity one's smiling acceptance.

Here, too, in both the pseudo-Gaelic and the pseudo-Norse place-nomenclature of these novels resides a secondary toponymically oriented landscape, expressed in an onomastic vernacular eminently suited to fore-ground the comic plots and the eccentric behaviour of outsiders and strangers in a world of Scottish values and expectations. Perhaps the name *Ballyhoo*—where Mrs Florence Urquhart-Unwin (Yu-Yu), President of the Ossianic Society of Boston, Mass., and her rival Mrs Linda Wolfingham, record their folk and fairy lore from a less than sober informant—is iconically the most central and the most explicit in this whole array, remorselessly focusing the irony of it all.

Naturally, there are other ways of illustrating in Scottish literature the existence of an 'onomastic vernacular', but the examples referred to should suffice to make the point. These examples have shown that, in a manner of speaking, there is not only one map of Scotland and certainly not just one place-nomenclature. In the works in question, the alternative maps take on their own peculiar shape not through a total denial of the recognised, 'official' maps of the country and an exclusion of their standard and standardised place-names, but by supplementing them. This supplementation, of course, also happens in the actual world outside literature, mostly through popular nicknames, minor names and dialect pronunciations which are never recorded by official map makers. There is a certain echo of these devices in literary works, too, including the ones examined in the foregoing. What this paper claims to have demonstrated, however, is that the vernacular landscape of Scottish literature consists of more than that because of the demands made by the greater structure and denser patterns expected in a literary work compared with the non-literary world.

It is symptomatic that all the works paraded, from Sir Walter Scott to Sir Compton Mackenzie, leave the framework of the official Scottish map including its toponymy intact, using the names mainly, although by no means solely, as reference co-ordinates. In the first six Waverley Novels, for example, the tally of non-fictive Scottish place-names mentioned is as follows: *Waverley*, 43; *Guy Mannering*, 21; *The Antiquary*, 24; *The Black Dwarf*, 8; *Old Mortality*, 20; and *Rob Roy*, 42. These figures do not include street names or names of other minor urban features. This is a severely restricted toponymicon mostly geared to the pinpointing of locations relevant to certain events or to the provision of historical depth, especially in connection with past battles. It does not contain many minor names of the kind which is so important on the vernacular map. It helps to produce a map which is clearly and intentionally geared to and controlled by Standard English: a very serious map.

The secondary, alternative, supplementary, vernacular map is linguistically conceived with Scots or Scottish English in mind. Whether through the intensive use of 'homely' generics referring to minor geographical features, through the enriching infiltration of a story-bound onomasticon, or through the re-interpretation of names of Gaelic or Norse origin, this map not only locates and connects; it is also meant to delight and to entertain, both through native wit and authorial clowning. It is probably not too outrageous to claim that, despite its fictive origins, the onomastic vernacular of this literary map, even in its chuckles, is close to, more in tune with, altogether more representative of the real Scotland.

NOTES

1   Lewis Grassic Gibbon, *A Scots Quair: Grey Granite*, (London, Jarrolds, 1946) (first published 1934), p. 4

2   See W F H Nicolaisen, 'The Toponymy of Literary Landscapes', *Literary Onomastics Studies* 6 (1979), pp. 75-104

3   W F H Nicolaisen, 'Names as Verbal Icons', *Names* 22 (1974), pp. 104-10

4   W F H Nicolaisen, 'Literary Names as Text: Personal Names in Sir Walter Scott's *Waverley*', *Nomina* 3 (1979), pp. 29-39

5   David Murison, 'The Two Languages in Scott', *Scott's Mind and Art:* Essays edited by A Norman Jeffares, (Edinburgh, Oliver and Boyd, 1969), p. 206

6   Cf. *Exmagirdle* and *Kilmahog*, both in Perthshire

7   This, of course, became a 'real' place name on the Scottish map when the passenger station near Craignethan Castle was opened on 1 December 1866, and named Tillietudlem in honour of Scott.

8   John Lorne Campbell of Canna is, of course, a real person and respected scholar who either agreed to enter into Sir Compton's etymological 'high jinks' or was fictionalised by the author for his purposes. Both quotations are from *The Rival Monster*.

INDEX